MW01125463

MY VERTICAL WORLD

MY VERTICAL WORLD

Climbing the 8000-metre peaks

JERZY KUKUCZKA

translated from the Polish by Andrew Wielochowski

The Mountaineers
Seattle

Published in the USA in 1992 by
The Mountaineers: Founded 1906 ". . . to explore, study, preserve
and enjoy the natural beauty of the outdoors . . ."
1011 SW Klickitat Way, Seattle WA 98134

Published simultaneously in Great Britain by
Hodder and Stoughton Ltd
Mill Road, Dunton Green, Sevenoaks, Kent TN13 2YA.

ISBN 0-89886-344-9 (USA)

Manufactured in Great Britain

CONTENTS

CONTENTS

'You are not second. You are great.'
Reinhold Messner

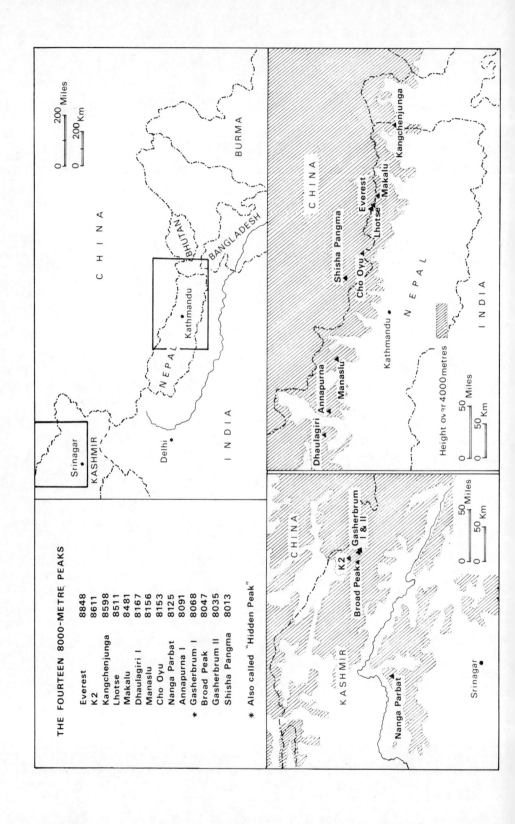

THE FOURTEEN 8000-METRE PEAKS

Everest	8848
K2	8611
Kangchenjunga	8598
Lhotse	8511
Makalu	8481
Dhaulagiri I	8167
Manaslu	8156
Cho Oyu	8153
Nanga Parbat	8125
Annapurna I	8091
* Gasherbrum I	8068
Broad Peak	8047
Gasherbrum II	8035
Shisha Pangma	8013

* Also called "Hidden Peak"

Author's Note

I touched rock for the first time on Saturday afternoon, 4th September in 1965. From that moment nothing else mattered, not even those trips to the Beskid Mountains to get away from our grey Silesian reality for some greenness and freedom, if only on Sundays. A friend drove me to the twenty-metre outcrops at Podlesic and there I saw that people could even move around on vertical walls. I touched the rock, pulled up on my arms and felt that not only can I hold on to the rock, but I can conquer it.

Thus I discovered my vertical world.

A year later, after a ten-day course, I stayed behind in the Tatra, because I felt this is it. I did an old classic route on Zamarła Turnia. Next year I returned with Piotr Skorupa to tackle the hardest route in the Tatra, the Left Pillar of Kazalnica. After four pitches we retreated because I broke my home-made hammer. As soon as possible we took an extra week's holiday and returned; thoughts of the Pillar gave us no peace. We climbed it, repeating in one and a half days what only the top few climbers in Poland had managed to achieve.

We were invited to a training camp which would place us on the road to the Dolomites and Alps. But it was not to be. Army call-up papers came as a major disaster in my life, dragging me away from what had become my be-all and end-all – mountains.

After our two years' national service finished we decided to try a winter ascent of the direct route on the Pulpit, so far an unsolved problem, despite several attempts, and considered to be the hardest problem in the Tatra. Half-way up on the second day of the ascent, my partner, Piotr Skorupa, fell to his death because of icy ropes. It was the first time I had encountered tragedy in the mountains, and the death of a friend. As I returned to Katowice and a painful meeting with his parents, his funeral, I asked myself is it worth continuing, is there any sense? Terrible indecision. The mountains called, but my common sense told me give it up. After three weeks I returned to the Tatra and make several first winter ascents which helped me shake off my doubts.

In 1971 I climbed the direct route on Torre Trieste with Janusz Skorek and Zbyszek Wach, then a new route on the Cima del Balcon.

Once I read about the Himalaya as if these mountains were beyond normal people, the stuff of dreams, but now impudent thoughts began flashing through my mind. Maybe one day I would find my way to those highest peaks.

During the Silesian expedition to Alaska I was brought to my knees by altitude sickness at just 4500 metres, and made it to the summit of the 6000-metre Mount McKinley by sheer willpower. On my way down I got frostbite, and returned home to go straight to hospital. My mountaineering career was thrown into doubt. I dropped out of the mainstream, joining holiday trips and student expeditions. I managed to get two new routes done with Wojtek Kurtyka on the North Face of the Petit Dru and on the Grandes Jorasses, but the road to the big mountains was closed. At last, in 1975, I got onto an expedition with the Gliwice Mountaineering Club to the Hindu Kush, a stone's throw from the Himalaya. Right from the start I was ill and I was not on the summit attempt on Kohe Tez. A day after reaching the summit, Marek Łukaszewski, Grzegorz Fligel and Janusz Skorek slipped and fell several hundred metres. They were badly hurt but alive and the expedition turned into a successful rescue operation. At the last moment I went up alone to the summit of the 7000-metre Kohe Tez by the normal route.

In 1977 my Katowice Mountain Club organised an expedition to the real Himalaya, to climb the East Pillar of Nanga Parbat. Arriving at the base of this 5000-metre wall, we wet ourselves. We set off up the normal Rakhiot Face route instead and just above 8000 metres were stopped by a rock barrier. We retreated in glorious autumn weather, walking through thin forests painted red and gold. I tried not to look behind me to where the sun was setting on the towering walls of the great mountain that I had not climbed. The view made me feel very sad. So little more had been needed to be able to stand on the summit.

I consoled myself with the thought that the Himalaya are, after all, for normal people, that one day I would return. I must return. I did return. Then I wrote this book. There is no answer in this book to the endless question about the point of expeditions to the Himalayan giants. I never found a need to explain this. I went to mountains and climbed them. That is all.

Jerzy Kukuczka

1

A Bit to the Right of the Highest Mountain in the World

Lhotse, North-West Face, 1979

'For what you propose there are, you know, big highly specialised companies. For example the Steelwork Reconditioning Contractors. Have you heard of them?'

The director had clearly set himself the target of not losing any of his majesty. It was 1978. On the office wall hung the national emblem, beside the bureau stood a spiny fern, in a glass bookcase were several volumes of Lenin. Through the window one could see a great, old chimney. It all concerned this chimney, but everything in that room was a carefully thought out game, in which there was no place for a single mistake. So we got up from the chairs on which we had sat down only minutes before.

'We understand. In which case we'll . . . Maybe another time.'

We made for the door. But the game went on, nothing was yet settled.

'Just wait, wait a moment. Let us chat a bit . . .'

The director knew that we knew that the giant Steelwork Reconditioning Contractors were capable of doing anything, even building a new furnace. They had plans for everything, and horrific price estimates to match. Only they never had the time for painting chimneys as a rule. So the director knew that, although his majesty would be eroded somewhat, he must not let us leave his office.

'I'm interested to know, gentlemen, how long it would take you?'

Through the window we could see the mighty, but already badly corroded, chimney. We looked and shook our heads, with long faces.

'About two weeks? We might be able to manage in one.'

'A week?' The director shifted around in his armchair, he was finding

I

it amusing. He was one up. 'A week, you know, is not enough time to put up the scaffolding.'

'We paint without scaffolding.'

'How?'

'On ropes.'

There was a moment's silence, which could decide everything. Various thoughts jostled around in the director's head. With good reason. In front of him were two, at a first glance cheeky, young men, and there outside that blasted chimney. For years it had been rusting. It should be reconditioned and painted once a year, at most every two years. Regulations. But who could do it? There was no one and, just his luck if some commission came along and picked on it. Or it could stand there a few more years and then simply fall apart. And then ... No, the director shuddered at the consequences. His look of concentration increased, then changed to one of cheerful interest.

'Coffee, tea?'

'Either, we don't want to trouble you.'

Then, if he was an important director of a big steelworks, he would press a button; if less important pick up a telephone; if just a manager of a very old works he would get up and call through the door, 'Bring two coffees, please,' adding, 'I have already had three coffees and attended several meetings, excuse me if I don't drink –' his hand gesturing towards his heart, his expression serious and afflicted. We must be made to realise the great responsibility that rested on him, the many matters brought to him alone, as if no one else existed in that great factory. But we knew better. The director was simply cracking.

We needed a million. That was the sum required for our expedition to the Himalaya. To Lhotse.

Recent inflation has made us only too well accustomed to seven-figure sums. But in those days it was big money. In 1978 a million złotys was two hundred average monthly wage packets. The stakes were high. Sometimes we only managed a quarter of a million for an eighty-metre chimney like this one. In other words we could cost-out our expedition to Lhotse as five such chimneys. Perhaps a bit more. There are club contributions to pay, incidental expenses, taxes, the cost of paint, which has to be 'acquired' or, if you like, 'organised'. Let's say six chimneys maximum! But for each such job we had to be contracted, hence our visit to the director.

'On ropes?'

We could see he was finding it hard to believe, but the phantom of the commission which could come any day and look for faults did not go away.

'We are climbers. We really can do it.'

'Hmmm. On ropes.' The director was still unable to imagine this, but at the same time knew, though he would not admit it in a month of Sundays, that we were heaven sent. From heaven straight down to that cursed, rusty chimney. He was now only fighting for his respect.

'You must realise that we are a state organisation. It is impossible for us to contract such a job to any Tom . . .' he bit his lip, 'what I mean is to private individuals.'

'This money is designated for the Youth Social Action Fund. Everything is carefully laid down in regulations, this is not the first time we . . .' If necessary we were able to quote the precise number of the regulation booklet, and even the article. We were well rehearsed.

'Okay, fine, fine. I will still have to consult the legal department. In which case, when could you start on this chimney?'

We had won. So had the director. But we had to attend many such meetings, often shorter and fruitless. It was hard to raise a million in those days.

Why Lhotse? There is a story here as well. In the 'seventies we still climbed most often in the Tatra, to get to the Alps was a major achievement. Then we discovered a chance of cheap trips to the Afghan Hindu Kush. For a relatively small sum we could climb 7000-metre peaks. Polish alpinists' appetites grew rapidly.

The late 'seventies saw the first Polish expeditions to the Himalaya – Kurczab's expedition to K2, Wanda Rutkiewicz to the Gasherbrums, the Wrocław club to Broad Peak. All these were just the beginning. 1977–9 saw an increase in the number of expeditions. The Polish Alpine Association (PZA) eventually obtained permission to climb Lhotse, at the same time as it was asking for other peaks. Success led to an embarrassing problem when news reached Warsaw that the Polish Alpine Association could also organise an attempt on the virgin summits of Kangchenjunga Central and South. Kangchenjunga is a more prestigious summit, so the main efforts were turned to this. But what about Lhotse? The Polish Alpine Association decided to give up this mountain. Maybe someone else in Poland would be willing and capable of mounting this expedition? Gliwice decided to take it on and this daring undertaking was to be led by Adam Bilczewski.

That is how it started. We climbed chimneys and thought of Lhotse. As to those chimneys, no one seemed surprised that to bolster the Youth Social Action Fund quite often forty-year-olds, sometimes with further degrees, could be seen climbing with great paint brushes and buckets of paint. Dreams of the Himalaya gave them wings, degrees and qualifications became unimportant. And this whole struggle for the chimney millions took place on late Saturday afternoons and Sundays, because we all had to work or study during the week. Some hung on the chimneys more, some less. The latter made up for this by working on organisational aspects, like travelling all over Poland in search of good down for sleeping bags and jackets. Once we had scraped together ninety per cent of the million złotys, small donations came from the WKKFiS (the Regional Committee for Physical Culture and Sport) and other institutions.

Dollars were another matter. In those days, with the help of the WKKFiS it was possible to obtain permission to exchange 150 dollars a head for such an expedition. These greenbacks went to a communal stocking and formed a foreign exchange expedition kitty. But no matter how much we skimped and saved, our stocking would not have taken us very far. It was here that we were saved by Robert Niklas who climbed with us in the Tatra, and was one of my first instructors. In 1970 he settled in West Germany. Now he was going with us and paying his share in hard currency. Thanks to him the stocking acquired some weight.

But let's give these financial issues a break. The Lhotse expedition of 1979 had a special meaning for me, since the invitation to take part was a signal that my past failures at high altitude had been put behind me. Adam Bilczewski and Janusz Baranek knew how poorly I had performed in Alaska when altitude sickness had struck me at only 5000 metres, but they had still remembered me.

None of us, in fact, had been really tested at great altitudes, though I had been to 7000 metres in the Hindu Kush, and once to 8000 metres on Nanga Parbat. Now in the large party of nineteen selected for the Lhotse expedition, a group of six to eight people were going to make up the main assault group. I felt that I was considered one of this élite. Lhotse, at 8511 metres the fourth highest summit in the world, could redeem me, particularly in front of those who had been with me in Alaska.

We flew to Bombay where our Star and Nysa trucks were already waiting, full of equipment, having come by sea. It was my first visit to India and the beginning of the monsoon season. It poured. We left the relatively decent airport, got a taxi and found ourselves in a quarter of the city where we could afford the hotels. Two dollars a night for dirty cubicles with a bed of boards and rats scurrying in the corridors. The rain poured, it was terribly humid and hot. I lay on the bed, which was marginally better than the dirt floor, in a semi-sleep disturbed by the drumming of rain on the windowsill. Was this how the great expeditions of famous travellers were conducted?

At each step we were warned not to eat anything here and not to drink the water. In fact nothing that is necessary for a European to survive was allowed. Coca-Cola and bottled lemonade were allowed, because they are sealed and free of amoebas. But Małgosia Kiełkowska, the expedition treasurer, defended the stocking with all the dollars like a lioness. Once, only once, did she give us all some money to buy one Coke. It was a day to remember. If one of us did have some foreign exchange hidden away, those ten or twenty dollars were treated as an untouchable treasure. They would be fingered, caressed, but invariably returned to the pocket. They would not be spent on trivia. This was Polish-style travel with all its associated pleasures.

Soon theory and Indian reality were in collision. Theory is all one has read about India, or heard from more experienced and well travelled friends. It does not take long to dispel the myth. India has to be discovered here, now, and afresh. I was told, for example, to bargain determinedly at each step, which ended up with one being so street-wise that one haggled where it was not required. I discovered very soon that though I was among completely different people, they were still people and worth talking to as individuals; that everything functioned, and not necessarily in the primitive way I had been indoctrinated to believe. As time went on I lost all trust in my European received wisdom about the East and made up my own mind about things.

After two days our luggage was out of customs and our journey north-east across India began. I'll never forget that journey. Wiesiek Lipiński and Andrzej Popowicz were our drivers. The great Star with its trailer, followed by the Nysa, blundered in a stream of taxis, bicycles and other trucks, trying to cope with different traffic codes. Codes? It was more a continuous battle of nerves, the strongest wins, the weakest must give way. Lunacy.

Everywhere one could almost feel the swarms of humanity. We could stop in empty fields, not a soul to be seen, but in three minutes we would be surrounded by a crowd of locals, looking at us, touching us; we were something new, something different. They were not aggressive, but persistent. They destroyed any concept of privacy one might have grown up with. If you ate, they stood and stared at your mess tin. They almost put their fingers in and licked them. It was a curiosity which wipes out the concept of individual existence. They were not begging. They didn't ask, just looked. If given something, they accepted silently.

This lasted two weeks. All the time it poured. We had nothing dry left, clothes were either clean wet or dirty wet. Nights were either in rat-infested 'hotels' on wooden beds, or in fields where one was immediately surrounded by Hindus, like a swarm of mosquitoes. You just had

5

to tell yourself over and over again that there was nobody there, don't worry, do your own thing. Otherwise you'd end up with a nervous breakdown. It is hard now to assess which was the greater trial, a night in a 'hotel', or a camp with the weight of a hundred eyes watching you all the time.

We reached Kathmandu and drove with great pomp into the grounds of the Polish Embassy. The minister plenipotentiary there was Andrzej Wawrzyniak (known in Poland as the founder of the Asia and Pacific Museum). He was friendly and helpful, partly perhaps because up to then not many Polish expeditions had reached Nepal. As years went by, four or five such expeditions started to arrive each season and gradually the goodwill and hospitality of the Embassy was, not surprisingly, eroded. Andrzej Wawrzyniak acted like a host and demanded to be treated as such, which meant his time was being taken up beyond reasonable limits as the expeditions multiplied.

We repacked the luggage, making up thirty to thirty-five-kilo loads, and leaving behind in the embassy anything we did not need, while Bilczewski and Kiełkowska rushed around government offices dealing with endless formalities. The walk-in took almost nineteen days, at first out of the Nepalese valleys over rice-covered hillsides. Then we gained height.

Like other expeditions, we made use of the services of a local agent. The Sherpa Co-operative guaranteed a sirdar and a cook, and said its aim was that every expedition should be comfortable (read: expensive). To this end it tried to bestow on us the maximum number of its own employees. We would sooner sacrifice this comfort completely, but after a lot of bargaining we agreed to five of their 'specialists', namely a cook, two assistants, a sirdar and a liaison officer who is the obligatory official representative of the Ministry of Tourism, and accompanies every expedition to make sure it keeps the rules.

We did not enjoy this success for long. At the very start the sirdar announced that he absolutely must have assistants, and the agency officials nodded in agreement.

'It will, of course, involve you in certain extra expenses, gentlemen, but you will then have all walk-in problems off your mind. You simply walk to base camp without lifting a finger,' they assured convincingly.

But a finger had to be lifted, on the very first day. The sirdar requested seven days' advance payment for the porters. He got it. We decided to enjoy the walk-in fully, making use of the freedom gained by entrusting our fate to such a professional.

We watched the way the porters worked as a unique insight into local traditions. But some things I could not understand, for example how

6

one porter walked along with his hands in his pockets, while another was bent under a double load. The one with the hands in his pockets was obviously a more superior being who subcontracted his work to others. Fascinating people. But after two days the procession came to a stop, and the fascinating people announced that they would go no further until they were paid. The magic was dispelled. We summoned the sirdar.

'Why did these people not get the money?'

'Because I have no more. I paid out everything.' He beat his chest.

'Yesterday you received money for a week's wages.'

'I did,' he agreed with unshakable calm.

So we picked up paper and a pencil and started calculating. 'It appears that you should still have 10,000 rupees.'

'But I don't.'

'How do you mean, you don't?'

'I don't know. I paid out everything.'

'Who to?'

'I paid my assistants.' Nothing could upset the sirdar.

'So they then should pay the porters.' We pressed our reluctant interlocutor.

'They should, but there is not enough.'

The conversation we saw was becoming hopeless. You couldn't talk to him. He had spent it and that was that. Ten thousand rupees is 1000 dollars, to a rich European expedition peanuts. But not to us. We had calculated our expenses so finely that the whole expedition could grind to a stop for want of a hundred rupees. We simply had no more foreign exchange. We were not an expedition from the West, whose members in such a situation could dig a hundred greenbacks out of their back pockets to add to the funds.

Visions of hours spent hanging on a chimney returned, and the 150 dollars stuffed into the 'stocking', so carefully guarded by Małgosia. How many Cokes would there be, cold ones, with condensation dribbling down the icy bottle, for 10,000 rupees? But we had to do something. For a start we kicked out the sirdar and his thieving staff and wrote to the agency, informing them what had happened and expecting a refund.

From that moment the whole mess fell into our hands. We paid a high price for our inexperience. The cooks for the day had to get up before dawn in order to cook something. Everyone had a defined role. One paid off porters who had finished their work, and hired new ones. If a load came apart, it had to be repacked. During the course of this there were always a few items that didn't fit, and had to be given to another porter. He would complain, as he reckoned he had enough already. Every day it was the same. But they were moving forward.

In this whole crazy turmoil of people and loads we had no help from our liaison officer. Apparently there are some who turn out to be real guardian angels to the expedition, and are really helpful. Our liaison officer did not belong to this category; he was simply a burden to us. Nothing concerned him, particularly the porters, whom he treated like dirt. He was from a higher caste, so he did not even talk to them. Nineteen days of this was for us a life-long lesson in Nepalese relationships.

An attempt to organisc the porters ourselves failed miserably. They had their own set ways of doing things which we simply did not understand. For example one of them would say, 'Tomorrow we have a rest day.'

'What rest day?' I could feel my blood pressure rise. 'A rest day cannot even be contemplated. We pay for work, not rest. We are carrying loads ourselves, we are in a hurry!'

'Don't worry,' the Nepali quietly waited until I had finished fuming. 'You have to change porters tomorrow anyway. We cannot go to the next village, otherwise we will get beaten up.'

Convinced that someone was trying to pull a fast one, we insisted. 'Forget it, we are not changing any porters. Get it out of your heads!'

But it turned out that indeed we did have to change porters, because such are local customs. A man from one village can't do the work which is the prerogative of the next village. The situation was serious, a big fight threatened the collapse of our expedition. It was important to bear in mind a hundred and one similar problems, but in particular to keep cool. It was not easy. When it almost came to a fight between the rather hot-headed Wiesiek and one of the porters, then a second and third, they all started running away and none of them wanted to carry anything.

On top of that it rained all the time. Non-stop. As a result, my tent which normally weighed seven kilos, after a night's downpour weighed twice that. My porter quite rightly protested. But it was impossible to lay out the sheet to dry, as it poured and poured. Leeches completed the picture; this endless watery world was paradise to them. Pushing our way through undergrowth and brushing past long grasses, we gathered them unknowingly. Painlessly, they burrowed themselves into us, only to be discovered at the campsite, clinging onto the least expected part of our bodies, lazy, full of our blood.

But even the most trying journeys come to an end. As we straggled into Namche Bazar a few days later, the weather improved. We were at 3400 metres, in a typical Sherpa town, inhabited by completely different people. Khumbu is the land of the Sherpas. Our troubles were behind

Lhotse, North-West Face, 4th October, 1979

us. It was as if we were in Podhale among the Tatra foothills.

Yaks now joined our procession to carry the loads and from that moment on our transport problems were effectively over. If one of these four-legged trucks brushed against a rock and his load fell off, we patiently repacked the load, and this was an event to be expected which did not upset us. Although we were climbing steeply, we were also able to rest for the first time.

At the beginning of September we finally arrived at the base camp area below Everest and Lhotse. After all the troubles travelling through the lower regions, sucked and bitten by leeches, I was finally in the place I had read and heard so much about, the place which I had for so long dreamt about and longed for.

Just a few days before us an International Everest expedition had arrived and pitched their tents in the same area. It was effectively organised by Germans, although there were Swiss and French members, and even our friend Ray Genet had joined it from Alaska. We found good sites, pitched our tents, and unloaded the plastic drums of equipment. Getting ourselves organised took three days at an altitude of 5400 metres. The initial need to force oneself to work made even the smallest of jobs into a nightmare. My head pounded, I felt nauseous, I would have liked simply to collapse under a boulder and give myself up to this

9

debilitating weakness. It was now that I discovered the best cure for altitude sickness is action, continuous physical effort. It forces your body to deeper breathing, quickening your blood, forcing you to adapt to the new conditions more quickly.

When at last everything had been sorted out and stored in its correct place, we could for the first time start looking seriously at the mountains around us. Our aim was an ascent of Lhotse, but all our eyes were drawn towards its northern neighbour towering above us, Everest. There are many more beautiful mountains, but it is that highest tag that makes one want to 'tick it off', with a desire that is akin to a physical need to possess it. Possessing the Highest would mean organising a whole new expedition. But we were there already . . . An idea was born. Maybe we could have a chat to the International group, maybe there was someone there who might just prefer to climb Lhotse instead of Everest? Then one of us could slip in, thanks to their permit, as it were through the back door onto Everest? Cautious overtures to this effect ground quickly to a halt. They were in no hurry. We decided to return to them after our summits had been climbed, once we knew how things worked out.

It is difficult to say which of these two giants is the harder mountain. Technically they are similar, but Everest is 337 metres higher, which is a lot at the altitudes involved.

Up to 7300 metres the route to both summits is the same. But we could already visualise the moment when some, because of their permits, would turn right, others left. Assuming we were up to this challenge, this would be the first Polish ascent of the fourth highest mountain, and also its fourth expedition ascent. But I couldn't stop myself wishing, instead of letting these patriotic ambitions satisfy me.

It did not even cross my mind that these thoughts, going through my upturned head, could be simply humbug. Here was I, the man who had collapsed on McKinley, had once climbed a seven-thousander in the Hindu Kush, but who was defeated at 8000 metres on Nanga Parbat, who was rumoured to be no use in high mountains, standing there now with his head in the air, turning up his nose at the thought of 'only' climbing Lhotse.

Impudence? No. I have something inside me that makes me have no interest in playing for low stakes. For me it is the high bid or nothing. That's what fires me.

Only one thing now upset my mood. That was that we were proposing to ascend Lhotse by the normal North-West Face route, so we would achieve nothing new. We pondered with Janusz Skorek and Andrzej Czok the possibility of going a bit further right to do a sort of West Face directissima. There was little enthusiasm for the suggestion. The opinion that won the day was that to do a variation, though technically much harder, is an artificially created difficulty. It would remain just a variation, a hundred metres to the left of which there is an easily accessible, straightforward couloir. Such thinking is fine in the Tatra but not worthy of the Himalaya.

It was during these deliberations at the feet of the world's highest mountains that another plan was born. We should try Lhotse without oxygen. Four of us decided to try this at first. Apart from Andrzej Czok and me, there was Zyga Heinrich and Janusz Skorek. Zyga soon gave up the idea, announcing it was simply too great a risk. It must be remembered that at this time people still thought that lack of oxygen could result in permanent brain damage. In our base camp we were told only half-jokingly, 'You'll see, you'll lose half your grey cells and become a moron.' This did create a psychological barrier, and no one dared laugh at Zyga's decision to back off.

Right up to our last night spent at Camp 4, which we had established after a month's efforts, the rest of us wanted to try for the summit without oxygen. Nobody said so directly. Everything was left open. What is more we all behaved as if we were to use oxygen. We carried up the breathing apparatus and cylinders to be stowed scrupulously in Camp 4 at 7800 metres. We went down to base camp before the final attempt, but they were up there, high, waiting for us.

At base we decided the first summit push would be by Janusz Skorek, Andrzej Czok, Zyga Heinrich and myself. Adam Bilczewski, our leader, had adopted a very democratic approach, knowing he had a well defined summit group and when the time came he gave us a completely free hand to make our plans.

We left base camp, reached Camp 4, and would leave for the summit in the morning. The time had come to make the decision.

'What about this oxygen?'

Andrzej Czok, determined from the start, did not surprise any of us. 'I am going without.'

'I'm taking no risks, I'm turning mine on now,' stated Skorek.

'Me, too,' Zyga said dryly.

I worked out a compromise. I picked up the full load of breathing apparatus and bottles, which together weighed about ten kilos, but I did not put on my mask.

'I'm taking it,' I said, 'but I won't use it. First I'll see if there is a difference between us in performance.'

I decided to stick with Andrzej for the first hour. I would soon see if those with oxygen were being carried along faster. I knew that there must be some difference in performance, because breathing oxygen-enriched air one can act far more efficiently. But I know myself, and feel able to monitor the state of my body in the mountains, sometimes by checking my own pulse. I therefore felt quite entitled to carry out this experiment.

Zyga and Janusz started off. After an hour I had only dropped back a short distance, hardly worth worrying about. The moment came for the decision.

'Blow this,' I said to Andrzej. 'I'm dumping this ballast.'

I left the bottle in the snow and moved on more easily.

After three hours the gap widened. We were an hour behind the other two. We had been above 8000 metres for a while now. The higher we went the bigger the gap grew. But we were making progress slowly. Slowly. Ten steps, rest, my full weight drooped onto the ice axe until my lungs recovered. Another ten steps . . .

The rhythmic battle for altitude had started. I counted ten steps, I had set my body's clock; after a moment I forced myself to another ten steps. The worst was to stop and sit, for then the clock stopped working, the rhythm was lost irretrievably, and to wind it up again took a long time.

And in this manner, fighting with ourselves, we finally reached the summit ridge. The last section was in deep snow. Two rock towers on either side created a sort of wind tunnel. Normally a strong wind blows up this chimney from the Western Cwm, so this section is always climbed in a great billowing cloud, giving one wings and pushing one up towards the goal. At times the swirling snow clouds hid us from each other.

As Janusz and Zyga came down from the summit, we still had the last few steps to climb.

'Great, you made it,' we gasped, tortured lungs crying out for oxygen.

'It's not far, only another twenty metres, but we're not waiting for you,' they said.

We slapped each other on the shoulders weakly to reinforce the sincerity of our congratulations.

Onwards, just the last few most difficult steps, and we were on the great cornice-shaped summit. It was hard to know how much further to go, as it hangs over a precipice. I pulled out my heavy Exacta and we took photographs of ourselves holding a pennant of my first Scout Mountaineering Club and another with the red and white emblem of Katowice.

It was midday. I experienced no euphoria. I just knew that I had six hours of hard-fought tens of steps behind me, interspersed with rests forced upon me by my body at its limit. Time seemed to have slowed down terribly making us very lethargic and tunnel visioned. I cannot even remember what exactly we did on the summit. We took photos, for sure, because it is impossible to forget getting the lump of ice called a camera out of the rucksack. But approaching the summit, the moment we passed Zyga and Janusz descending and I still had those few more steps to go, all that is engraved more clearly in my memory than any photograph could portray. At the summit itself, only great exhaustion and a dominant thought existed: get down as fast as possible!

First we descended the chimney, where the wind now tried to stop us in our tracks. We reached Camp 4, then Camp 3 where Bilczewski and Baranek awaited us. Tomorrow they would go up to carry oxygen for the next pairs. Today they were excited by our successful ascent. They brewed up and passed round hot tea and some sort of soup. I sat and listened to the complex machine of my body, which had so nearly ground to a halt, calm down. I clasped the hot mug, given me by my good friends, and felt that only then was I beginning to warm up inside. I felt great, so that when Andrzej Czok and Janusz Skorek decided to go further down to the greater comfort of Camp 2 while there was still light, I felt disappointed. I told the others, 'I'll stay here with you one more night. Till the morning, okay?'

I did not say what I really felt. The weather was fine and it seemed a shame to leave so suddenly the mountain which had cost me so much effort. I felt so good there. I got into my sleeping bag and we chatted. Only then did it penetrate that all my efforts had resulted in success. I had made it.

Back at base camp there was celebration and sweet laziness, no need to gather oneself up, nights again for sleeping and not just waiting for the alarm. Freedom. Time to soak in the wonderful joys of the expedition. The festive atmosphere suddenly changed to one of sadness when the International expedition encountered tragedy. One day before we reached the summit of Lhotse they had climbed Everest. In the second group was the wife of the expedition leader, Hannelore Schmatz, who was to be the first German woman on the summit of Everest. She went up with two Sherpas and our friend from Alaska, Ray Genet. They reached the summit very late; going down, Ray Genet died from exhaustion at their first bivouac; Hannelore continued her descent the following morning with the two Sherpas. Then she just sat down and never got up again. She was dead.

We had seen the whole tragedy take place. As we climbed up to Camp 4, we could see dots moving around on the snow a few kilometres away. I can see them to this day, three dots moving down slowly. One stopped, they all stopped. I thought at the time they were resting. After a moment only two dots continued moving down. One of them was resting a bit longer. Then one of the two turned back up again. That the movement of those dots was interrupted by a human death I discovered only later by radio.

'Mr Messner is coming! Mr Messner's expedition!'

Two panting Sherpas came running up. If they had known Polish they would no doubt be shouting, 'Out of the way, herrings!' meaning Shift, you rubbish! On our way down we had stopped to camp near Namche Bazar. Filled with glory, we had already pitched our tents and stretched out on our backs to recover from the heavy rucksacks. Soon it would be dark. Just then this advance group of two Sherpas arrived, announcing the imminent arrival of the expedition.

They pitched his tent, remaining inside for a long time, laying everything lovingly out; they hung up a lamp and prepared his bedding. We watched this unusual performance, pretending that we had seen it all before, but fascinated. After a few more minutes the main body of the expedition appeared. He was coming.

I saw Reinhold Messner for the first time. He behaved like a normal human being. As he took off his rucksack, our food was already steaming away on the fire. We invited him for tea and a bowl of typical all-in-one mountain soup. He sat with us.

'Where have you been?'

'We've been on Lhotse,' we replied modestly, noticing this only provoked a polite smile, neither approval nor admiration. 'What are your plans?'

'Ama Dablam.'

I was taken aback a bit. Ama Dablam is only 6856 metres high. As this mountain talk got into full swing, I – who was really just a novice in this group – decided to put in my two pennyworth.

'Two years ago we climbed a new variation on Nanga Parbat. At a slight col, not far from the summit, and almost 8000 metres up, I found a torch.' As I said this, Reinhold Messner, who was being accosted on all sides by my older friends, became silent and listened to me carefully.

'A torch?' He looked at me intently.

'An ordinary torch. I could not understand how it had got there, as this was a new route.'

'Nine years ago I reached that col, after climbing the South Face with my brother, who later died on the way down. It must be Günther's torch. That is exactly where he changed the batteries.'

Nine years later I had found that torch. This created a link between us. I could not take my eyes off his wonderful equipment, including suits lighter than down, which the Sherpas were carrying up for him.

'I have a request.' Messner turned to me. 'I'm writing a book about my ascent of Nanga Parbat. I would be grateful if you could find that torch. A memento of my brother, you understand. Anyway, write a few words about how you found it.'

'All right,' I replied.

We exchanged addresses. We then wanted photos taken of us with him, but it was too dark. Looking at them today, it is impossible to tell who is who. In the morning they went up, we down.

A Warsaw newspaper, reporting that a Silesian expedition had gained the summit of Lhotse, added in a short commentary: 'The gaining of some summit nowadays can no longer be considered a great achievement, even if it is an eight-thousander.' This summary of our achievements hurt me. It took some time for me to admit that they were right. New times had arrived in Polish Himalayan history: the high-jump bar had been raised a lot.

On 4th December I was back home. The very next day I telephoned Andrzej Zawada in Warsaw.

'Congratulations, Jurek!' he said. 'I have a proposition for you. Would you come with us on the first ever winter attempt on Everest? We leave in two weeks' time.'

This telephone call marked a turning point for me. It proved that someone out there was now convinced that I could climb a high mountain. But the home situation was complicated. Celina, my wife, was in an advanced stage of pregnancy, the baby was due in early January, and the birth could be difficult. I held the receiver, Zawada's words whirling in my brain.

Everest in winter. Just a few weeks ago I had been there but not allowed to set foot on it. I might never get another chance ... I was beginning to weaken. Then from Andrzej's torrent of words I gleaned what could be a second chance after all. He was also talking about a spring ascent of Everest. First a winter ascent, but then, so as not to waste all the vast organisational effort of getting a team up to Everest base camp, he wanted to carry out a second attack.

So I said, 'Listen, I cannot take part in the winter ascent, but I'm a candidate for the spring attempt.'

'I have to be honest with you, I'm not really certain if this spring ascent will materialise. I'm just sort of planning it. Should the winter attempt fail, then we would try afresh in spring. I'm not even sure if we will have the means ...'

I deduced that Andrzej, who did not lack imagination, was using the spring idea as a safeguard against lack of success on the first ever winter attempt on Everest. Should the winter ascent succeed, the spring attempt would lose all its meaning. I could not however change my mind.

'Andrzej, as I have said, I have no option.'

I put down the hot and sweaty receiver. On 15th December the first group flew to Nepal. Without me. There are, after all, more important things than the Himalaya. The most important things. On New Year's Eve my son was born. We called him Maciek.

2

Everest the Polish Way

The South Face, 1980

I waited for news of the winter attempt on Everest which took some time, because Leszek Cichy and Krzysiek Wielicki only reached the summit on 17th February. Their success aroused my enthusiasm, but at the same time deepened my anxieties. What now? Would there be a spring expedition or not? With Andrzej Zawada's parting words in mind, the chances receded. But I believed in him. That guy had imagination, he was not small-minded, but capable of visionary planning. I was not let down. Zawada decided to follow up the success.

After the winter ascent must come an ascent of Everest by a new route, he decided. So he left two expedition members, Zyga Heinrich and Waldek Olech, at base camp to look after the equipment, and the rest returned home with him. He had not come back just to bask in glory, but to get more money – somehow. The major organisational hurdle was crossed when Julian Godlewski from Switzerland offered to support the expedition. At the beginning of March I flew out with the first group. Andrzej stayed behind to look for more money. He had heard that he had landed himself unwittingly with big problems regarding formalities.

It was discovered that his winter expedition had made illegal direct contact with Poland. That is forbidden in Nepal, the rules are very clear on the matter. Each item of expedition news must go via the Department of Tourism who pass on the information to the outside world. It so happened that during the winter expedition, one of the team, clearly getting bored in base camp, talked to anyone he came across on the ether, including short-wave radio buffs from Poland. It was to them that he passed on their most important piece of news: 'The first time that the summit of Everest has been gained in winter. By Wielicki and Cichy. Please note, there is an embargo on this information till nineteen hundred hours. Over.'

Nineteen hundred hours was relevant as it was just after the official time for regular contacts between base camp and the Nepalese Ministry of Tourism. But it unfortunately turned out to be a Saturday, which there was treated like a Sunday. There was no one in the Ministry. Minutes passed. The expedition tried to establish contact over and over again, but without success. In Poland radio hams, excited by the success, waited patiently till nineteen hundred hours, then let the news go round the world. They even got it onto the evening television news, the delighted newsreader making the announcement as a late extra. The next day, at the appointed hour, base camp made contact with the Ministry of Tourism who, instead of a courteous exchange of greetings, demanded an immediate explanation.

Now, just when Andrzej Zawada thought the whole clash had been smoothed over, the Nepalese authorities were withholding permission for the spring attempt. We were in Kathmandu with no permit, no leader and not enough money. What a silly situation. Over a week passed. We reckoned this was a sort of punishment being meted out by the Ministry of Tourism who would only give us our permit when it was too late to climb anything. We decided to handle the situation Polish-style: We would not simply wait till Zawada arrived with money. We would act.

We decided to organise a normal tourist trek to the base of Everest, for which an immediate permit can be obtained for a few dollars. We arrived at base camp officially as tourists. The camp was organised and ready for action, Zyga Heinrich and Waldek Olech were already there, patiently waiting. We could start the assault immediately. And we did.

There were two other expedition camps there beside ours, one Catalonian, the other Basque, both already climbing. But they had something which in our situation could not be ignored: liaison officers. Luckily neither of them even thought of checking our permit. Our arrival at our base camp, followed by our starting climbing all seemed perfectly natural.

In effect we managed without a permit, without a liaison officer and without the expedition leader to establish Camp 2. We had fixed ropes up the Khumbu Icefall and were setting up Camp 3 by the time Andrzej Zawada appeared in base camp with a permit in his pocket and a liaison officer at his side in mid-April. Had we waited for him, doing nothing, we would have sacrificed the chance of an ascent. After 15th May the monsoon starts and defends the mountain better than any regulations can.

Mount Everest, a new route on the South Face, 19th May, 1980

There were ten of us climbing at this stage: Gienek Chrobak, Krzysztof Cielecki, Andrzej Czok, Rysiek Gajewski, Zyga Heinrich, Janusz Kulis, Waldek Olech, Kazik Rusiecki, Wojtek Wróż and myself. Lech Korniszewski and Jan Serafin were doctors.

We put up fixed ropes in the traditional style, but Camp 3 was already on the new route. We wanted to attempt on the South Face between the 1700-metre high South Pillar and the South-East Ridge. Everything was taking us a bit longer than it should as the weather was playing games. Every few days it snowed heavily, more and more snow piled up on the mountainsides, and the risk of avalanches was ever greater.

To establish Camp 4 involved a major struggle. A pair of climbers went into the lead, fixed a hundred metres of rope and returned. The next day a second pair left camp to dig out the rope from under deep fresh snow – and return back down. The next day another pair fixed another hundred metres of line . . .

Wojtek Wróż and I were the first to arrive at the site of Camp 4, clear a platform and set up our tent. We realised that an important phase of the expedition was now behind us. Almost every expedition has a period during which everyone is climbing, everybody is hard at work, but nothing appears to be progressing. A breakthrough is needed. Sometimes fixing a hundred metres of rope is enough for the breakthrough, and suddenly the impetus returns in a surge of progress. We set up camp below a rock barrier, which would be the key to the Polish route on Everest. It was high and almost vertical, but more important it was above 8000 metres.

Andrzej Czok, Zyga Heinrich and Waldek Olech were the first to attack the band. They covered forty metres of difficult terrain and came down. Rysiek Gajewski and I were next to have a go. We managed to fight our way up the hardest section of the barrier. For a long time I could say that that was the hardest climbing I had ever done in the Himalaya. On an Alpine difficulty scale of I to VI it would rate Grade V, in other words Very Severe. To climb this at that altitude took so much out of me that at one stage the effort made me simply wet my pants. At times my vision blurred. It all depended on an eight- or ten-metre section of vertical rock. We climbed a whole rope-length, forty metres, in some parts hard, in others easier, but over all Very Severe. But it was those eight or ten metres that really decided the whole issue. It led us on to easier ground, above which were snow slopes. We fixed a rope and descended all the way to base camp. It was the turn of the next pair. They climbed easily up the ropes over ground which had been fought so hard for, then they fixed ropes up much easier slopes to about 8300 metres, the proposed site for the final Camp 5, and came down.

Now we prepared ourselves for the summit attack. It was already mid-May. Time flew by relentlessly. We should really be finishing the expedition. If we were to play the game along traditional lines, we should be fixing ropes to 8600 metres. Only then would it be safe to gain the ridge from which the summit attack could be launched.

The mess tent was crowded, every comment made accompanied by a tangible tension. I said, 'We cannot afford to fix another 300 or even 100 metres of rope at that height. It was hard enough just to carry it up to 7000 metres. Then we have to come down after we've fixed the rope and that will drag it all out terribly. Time is running out. I think we have to go for the summit in one big push from Camp 5.'

I felt the majority agreed with this assessment. Andrzej Czok, sensing the atmosphere, decided to follow up on the idea.

'We go for the summit, obviously, without oxygen . . .'

It was not the best of moments for this proposal. The murmurs united in a very clear protest. I cannot any more remember who voiced the feeling: 'That's out. Going without oxygen reduces the chances. We are talking now about the whole success of the expedition.'

Andrzej fell silent. I said nothing; to mention making an oxygenless ascent at this stage had definitely been premature. So far the most important subject had not been raised. Who was to go? Eight, even nine of us, had in theory a chance of going to the summit. Among those nine were all the stars of Polish Himalayan climbing. Wojtek Wróż and Gienek Chrobak had the first ascent of Kangchenjunga South and many other Himalayan successes to their credit. Their ability was proven. There was Zyga Heinrich, admittedly with few summits behind him, but on every expedition he worked like an ox, and he had recently climbed Kangchenjunga Central. It would take a while going through the rest of the group. Andrzej Czok and I were relative youngsters in that gathering. We had Lhotse behind us, but we had heard more than once: Lhotse? An easy mountain. Anyone can be lucky once. We were not considered by this élite group as ones capable of anything. We did not count.

So who was to go first? There was a hush. I cannot remember who broke the silence saying: 'In my opinion, Wojtek Wróż and Chrobak should go, or maybe Heinrich and Olech.'

More murmurs, whispered comments passed around, the mood became tense.

'I feel four should go,' I joined in. 'I personally would most like to go with Andrzej Czok. There must however be a team in support, in case we fail.'

Thus started the serious discussions. It was tough, very tough, like that short section of wall several kilometres above us where my vision blurred. Nobody said it straight out, no one adopted a superior stance over anyone else, but to us juniors one thing was clear in the mess tent, the prevailing message was, Easy, lads. We are the ones who have priority . . . That anyway is the way we sensed the mood.

Out of the torrent of words and ideas passing around, one idea became dominant, the one put forward by Zyga Heinrich. He was calm. He made his comments not on his accepted seniority but on logical arguments. Zyga acknowledged and valued the fact that Andrzej and I had been the most active and worked hardest on this mountain. Again a silence descended in the tent. Now and again a resigned sigh could be heard. All that time Andrzej Zawada had just been listening. The time must come when it would be his turn to say something. Everyone turned their eyes to him.

'I think,' a deadly silence reigned as he spoke, 'I think that Kukuczka and Czok should go first, because they are in the best physical shape. Behind them should go Zyga Heinrich and Olech, because they deserve it. You will go as a four.'

There are times when it is very important for one person to take a decision. The person should also enjoy everybody's respect. I do not say this just because on this occasion I had been chosen. Anyway the discussion had not yet come to an end. Zyga came back to the issue which all of us had already assumed to have been decided.

'Let's think carefully again about one thing. Let us come to our senses. I still suggest that we should go up again to fix ropes on the upper section, it will make it much safer.'

'There's no time,' I opposed him. 'Either we make a summit attempt now or we can face up to having to pack our bags and go home empty-handed.'

I felt morally entitled to put the matter like that, now it would be Andrzej and I tackling that last section of the route. We were the ones who had been up there, very high, for long enough to know one thing for certain: we had to hurry.

Zyga did not protest. It was agreed that we would go as a foursome. Andrzej Zawada, Janusz Kuliś and Jacek Rusiecki accompanied us to Camp 2. It was just then that a huge avalanche swept down from Lhotse, carrying off one of the Sherpas with the Catalonian expedition, who was buffeted 500 metres down a couloir. Though he was found, he died three days later.

This had a depressing effect, especially on Zyga.

'We've not got a chance, what we want to do is too dangerous,' he said.

No one resented him saying this. Andrzej Czok and I carried on. Zyga and Olech left a day behind us, now acting only in a support role.

Reaching Camp 3, I felt that the almost sixty-day period of exertion at altitude had worked wonders. The section which used to take us eight hours now took two and a half hours. I listened to the rhythmic beat of my heart. Everything was fine.

We reached Camp 5 uneventfully, re-ascending the fixed ropes and, pitching a special lightweight tent, snuggled into our sleeping bags to return to the topic which had been nagging away at us from the start. The question of oxygen.

At base camp everyone had been pressing us to get out of our heads the idea of an ascent without oxygen. It would reduce the chances of success for the whole expedition. Climbing Lhotse without oxygen was seen as no argument in favour, there were no major technical difficulties on the North-West Face of Lhotse. Everest was much higher and we did not even know if we were up to it at all. It was already dark by the time that we had finished debating the issue and decided that there was a lot to be said for either argument. I fidgeted around uncomfortably in my sleeping bag, at last saying to Andrzej: 'Let them have it their way.'

Andrzej muttered something about it being unfortunate, but if we did happen to fail as a result of not using oxygen, nobody would ever forgive us. All the same we felt disappointed. So we prepared the breathing equipment which had been brought up earlier. We put on the masks and slept with them on. Our sleep was undisturbed, our lungs could have their fill. We were not troubled by nightmares. We had even managed to add an extra eighty metres of fixed line before settling down for the night.

We left at five a.m. to follow this line upwards. The going was hard because of fresh snow. Initially the problems were not too great, but digging our way in that deep powder sapped our strength. Leaving the tent I had set my oxygen flow at one to two litres per minute. That is very little, it is what the body needs when sleeping. If we had to tackle a more difficult step I turned up the flow to eight litres a minute. Getting up to the South-East Ridge we came across ever greater difficulties on rock. Progress was slow, we were taking much longer than we had planned. It was two p.m. by the time we reached the South Summit. Ahead of us there was still a long, sharp ridge.

Now I began to feel that my lungs were unable to keep up with the pace. Just as I reached for the control on my cylinder, I heard Andrzej exclaim: 'Oh blast! My cylinder's empty.'

I fumbled anxiously with the controls of mine. I turned it up to max. but it brought no relief.

'Mine too,' I stated resignedly.

We had achieved a lot already. We had, after all, reached the South Summit and rejoined the normal route. For a moment we tried to see into each other's eyes, and read our feelings. Only then was the question voiced.

'So, then. We go on?'

'Of course. We're too near the summit to retreat now.'

This was concise, manly talk. We radioed our position down to base camp and told them our predicament and that we had decided to carry on. We had come to the conclusion that it was no longer any concern of the others. They were our lungs, our patches of blackness whirling in front of the eyes, ours to be or not to be. The others down below did not press us. Then we discarded the empty cylinders and breathing equipment and started on up.

We had ahead of us only one hundred more metres of height gain on this ridge. In good conditions it should not take more than forty-five minutes, at the most one hour. I tackled the Hillary Step. It was very airy and the ridge was steep-sided. We climbed for two hours. We only reached the summit at four p.m.

We radioed base who were worried because the last sign of life from us had come from the South Summit and they had been against tackling this giant without oxygen from the start. What they had lived through from the time I said that final 'over' on the South Summit we will not know. We could only guess as we again made contact, this time to tell them that we had reached the summit. In their voices, coming from so far below, we detected not only congratulations and happiness but also great relief. The echo of their words made me aware that something had happened, that I had at my feet the highest mountain in the world.

On that highest summit, you have to stand for a long time resting on your ice axe, while your breathing returns to some sort of normality. You have to heave the horribly heavy Start camera and the equally heavy Praktica out of your rucksack. Photos must be taken, all involving the maximum of effort, the maximum of determination. The flag left behind by our base camp neighbours, the Basque expedition, must be brought down as a souvenir. They had only carried it up there a few days ago by the normal route and then they had taken down the maximum-minimum thermometer and papal rosary that had been left there by the triumphant Leszek Cichy and Krzysiek Wielicki after their winter ascent. We left behind a rolled-up Polish flag, and also took down some rocks.

So all that a person does on the highest summit is extremely prosaic, but costs a vast effort. And during all this the thought passed through my mind, out of which all euphoria had long been drained away, Everest maybe. But it's just another mountain, just the same snow cornices as on other summits . . .

We started down. It was already five p.m. and I was beginning to feel exceptionally exhausted. I moved as if in a mist, feeling all the time as if I were beside my own body.

I used to take part in athletics competitions and once, during a race, as I approached the finishing line I had black patches whirling in front of my eyes and began hallucinating. This was similar but it went on the whole time. Above all however I felt the lack of oxygen, and the mist

24

appeared before my eyes when I didn't always manage to take my calculated seven or eight breaths, for every step.

It was getting grey when we arrived at the South Summit. We retraced our route in order to find the tent. After a while it was pitch black and we descended gropingly, at all costs not wanting to lose our trail. We reached a snowfield where fresh snow had blown over our tracks. Now we only had our instincts to guide us, and dreamt of one thing, finding the top of the fixed rope which must be there somewhere, then dragging ourselves back down to the tent. To be sure of success we decided to wait for the moon to rise, then continued down, stumbling from exhaustion.

On an icy section my foot skidded from under me. I was tumbling without any control in deep snow down some couloir for a dozen metres before I managed to stop myself. As I tried to get myself up and out of this white eiderdown, my hand felt something – the rope! It was pure luck that I had landed up exactly there.

We descended this lifeline to our tent. It was after nine p.m. and we were terribly thirsty, but as we melted snow and boiled up some water, exhaustion overtook us and we fell asleep. It was not so much sleep as a nap interrupted by nervous thoughts and dreams. Suddenly I woke, I could feel something choking me. I opened my eyes and was certain I was being oppressed by a great swelling sort of weight. There was simply nothing to breathe with. I panicked. Avalanche flashed through my mind. Andrzej woke too, and both of us started to struggle and fight. Terrified, we managed to dig ourselves out of the tent to stand in the snow, without our boots which were still somewhere inside there.

It turned out that snow was gradually creeping down the slope onto our tent. Luckily not an avalanche, but just a steady, slow irresistible mass gradually and with a silent insistence burying anything in its path. It could have been worse.

One thing was certain. There would be no more rest for us that night. Instead of sleep, one of us burrowed into the tent while the other stayed outside endlessly brushing off the weight. Then we changed places. When dawn arrived I felt much more tired than I did the previous night, when we had arrived and crawled into our sleeping bags, completely stunned with the exhaustion of reaching the summit, and feeling it was not possible for a human being to be more shattered. At last it became light enough for us to find our boots. We put them on but did not have the energy left for anything else. Then we started off down.

In Camp 4 Zyga and Waldek Olech were waiting for us, holding a thermos of hot tea. I lapped it up greedily. This was the first drink we had had in our mouths for thirty-six hours of superhuman effort and exhaustion. We guzzled and guzzled while that tea slowly helped us recover from our stupor. We could carry on again, to base camp congratulations, hugs and joy. We had done it.

Reeling slightly, like some hero who has not quite recovered after fifteen rounds in the ring, I detected from the mood around me that all was not well. Andrzej also had this impression. Beneath the surface of these congratulations and smiles there was something that as yet we could not pinpoint. Something which was upsetting the festive mood.

After fifteen minutes all became clear. Andrzej Zawada, when he heard that we only got back to the tent at ten p.m. after our summit push, came to the conclusion that the whole episode had been too risky. He reasoned that if a pair of climbers, who according to him were the strongest in the group, took so long, another pair, even given the same physical strength, might not be able to make the summit. So he had said, enough. This was the end of the expedition. We were all going home. It often happens that when a successful ascent crowns a fight against a mountain in which everyone has expended a lot of effort, they are all ready to go home. But with us it was different. Everybody had wanted to go to the top and there was no question that in the case of this group of the best Polish alpinists these ambitions were totally realistic.

So everybody was bitterly disappointed, and maybe I'm just deluding myself, but a fraction of this bitterness surely rubbed off on to me and Andrzej. Because we had made it. This was not a topic to be mentioned aloud at base camp. But it stuck deep inside me, like a splinter which can cause pain at any instant.

After a few days there was a distinct breakdown in the weather, the monsoon was coming, it started tipping down snow so much that any chances of further action were truly eliminated. Maybe it was this snow that effectively managed to tamp down the roused ambitions. Anyway the decision was now more often commented on. Andrzej Zawada was considered to have been perhaps right after all.

At the airport reporters awaited us. There were gold medals for Outstanding Achievements in Sport. Something was happening around us all the time, our achievement had been noticed. For the first time in my life I tasted fame. A typical event for me was my first day back at work. I was greeted outside the gate as a conquering hero. The management came out, all the workers came out, there was a placard: 'We greet the conqueror of Everest.' In this very same institute just a few months earlier I had had to keep a low profile, taking care not to expose myself to anyone's displeasure, going around trying to get a signature for my unpaid leave permit from one specific director rather than another because the other could simply kick me out of the office. There were those standing outside the gate now who had said before: 'You know, I have a two-week holiday. This fellow is not seen for two or three months on end. Does he have to keep going on these expeditions?'

It was good.

But let us not forget when all this was happening. A few months before, Cichy and Wielicki had come back in the glory of a great victory. Their historic ascent of Everest in winter was deliberately blown up. It was badly needed, and came for the government as if a gift from heaven. A second major Himalayan achievement in so short a space of time caused the propaganda specialists to be more watchful. After Andrzej and I had enjoyed just a month of praise, I received some bits of leaked information through a well-placed friend. Someone Very Important had said:

'Now listen, enough about these alpinists. A winter ascent of Everest, now another, you know. What are they up to, you know? This has to be quietly forgotten now. Is there nothing else to write about?'

And so it was. It was after all July 1980. Soon it would be August, the one which would soon be referred to as The August in Poland, when Lech Walesa led the Gdansk shipyard strike that gave birth to Solidarity.

3

A Plastic Ladybird

Makalu, North-West Ridge solo, 1981

While I was battling with Everest, my club in Katowice was planning an expedition to the distant mountains of Australia and New Zealand. The trip was not approved because the group was too weak and 'unable to guarantee the achievement of any sporting successes', to quote the traditional wording of official decisions. Faced with this situation, the leader approached Krzysiek Wielicki and me to join the expedition in order to strengthen its composition. I reckoned that after the Himalaya a break like this, to lower but technically difficult mountains, would do me good. Krzysiek was of the same opinion, so we agreed.

We were meant to depart in December 1980. In November, when all preparations were complete up to the last detail, new, rather mysterious and unexplained problems began developing, as a result of which the expedition was simply removed from the programme of events of the GKKFiS, which is the General Committee for Physical Culture and Sport that decides how much money – złotys and foreign currency – is allocated to each expedition.

It turned out that some public-spirited fellow-countrymen, not knowing that all our money in those days was raised by hard hours on factory chimneys and walls, made a complaint. These climbers do nothing but spend public funds on trips. It has got to the stage that even in these days of great economic hardship they go off to the other end of the world. After all, everybody knows it's a nonsense to go there because there are no mountains in New Zealand.

So I had to pack an album of pictures of New Zealand into my bag and set off for Warsaw to the GKKFiS. Here we luckily managed to intercept the Highest Authority and while He scurried from one office to another we managed to show Him that there are mountains in New Zealand and that some have Himalayan proportions with faces approaching 3000 metres high. I trotted behind Him with my open album and I talked continuously. It sunk in. Luckily the corridors of the GKKFiS offices in Litewska Street are long.

We did go after all and climbed various routes in the Mount Cook National Park on Mount Dixon, Mount Cook itself, and the ridge traverse from the Western Col to Mount Hicks, as well as some new routes, including one on the West Wall of Malte Brun. It was a very interesting trip. We were the first Polish group to climb in these mountains, and we also managed to break the ice with the very conservative local Polish community.

We returned to Poland by way of the Blue Mountains of Australia in April 1981 to be caught up immediately in the whirl of plans and preparations for the future. Even before leaving for 'the other end of the world' I heard that Wojtek Kurtyka was looking for someone to go with him on a spring expedition to Makalu. Who is Wojtek? Well it is really hard not to know him. He belongs to the real top group of Tatra, Alpine and Himalayan climbers; he has made first-class ascents in Norway. In 1980, he climbed Dhaulagiri with Ludwig Wilczyński, Alex MacIntyre and René Ghilini, making an East Face variation on the original route. He is well known not only in Polish circles. I did two new routes with him in the Alps, one on the North Face of the Petit Dru and a year later on Pointe Helene on the Grandes Jorasses.

Now he wanted to attack Makalu and was wondering who to take with him. He had already approached a few people, including Andrzej Czok. Much earlier he had discussed the matter with me. Would I be possibly interested? But he had not made me a definite proposition. In Poland Wojtek was pioneering alpine-style ascents. He was not interested in the old-fashioned great expeditions, he only wanted to work in a small team. I had told him then that this approach suited me best too and, should he ever be organising anything like that, he could count me in. But as I never received a concrete proposition, I went to New Zealand.

And now, back home, one day a letter arrived from Nepal. From Wojtek.

'Jurek! Come over. I've been under the West Face of Makalu with Alex MacIntyre, René Ghilini and Ludwig Wilczyński. It did not work out, we only got to 6700 metres. But I'm certain that it can be done. Or maybe the South Face of Lhotse? I still have some money left in the Cracow club funds, the rest you will have to raise somehow and bring here to Kathmandu. I'm counting on you! Wojtek.'

It was already May. In effect I had to organise the expedition single-handed. I urgently started looking around for money. It was too late to contemplate chimney work, a month was not enough to find a job and then complete it. I had to find sponsors. Maybe I could borrow money from the club or the WKKFiS, the regional committee in Katowice. I went for the latter and, by knocking at the appropriate door, received a promise of help. On top of that there were about 200,000 złotys belonging to Wojtek in the Cracow club funds. That should be enough.

Rysiek Warecki helped me with the organisation, but we did not realise how much work lay ahead of us. A totally new and apparently insurmountable hurdle appeared before us – shopping in 1981, in shops completely emptied of goods. It seemed an absurdity. There were problems with everything. Even with the once ubiquitous jam. Two years earlier, when we were organising the Lhotse expedition, we chose the best that was available in the stores. We chose foods that would last best in Nepalese conditions, certain tinned meats rather than others, a wide variety of tinned foods. Now we were grateful to find anything. We started trudging around various offices trying to get some allocations. Doing this we discovered that the situation in the country was not as bad as would appear – even for the most sought after goods. Somehow we managed to receive the allocations and then to our amazement came the surprise. Although there was no food in the shops, the warehouses were full! In Janow, for example, I had to collect an allocation of raisins and dried fruits at the PSS and MHD stores. When I entered the great warehouse and saw it crammed full from the floor to the ceiling with groceries I was dumbfounded.

'What is all this?' I mumbled. 'It's impossible to get any of this in any shop.'

'These are government reserves,' replied the store manager seriously.

I saw this everywhere, wherever I went on my search, trying to pick up some more supplies. The worst encounter I had was my visit to the great refrigerated stores under the Supersam supermarket in Katowice which were packed with every imaginable meat product. I went there to pick up canned meat. I left the underground storerooms in broad daylight, pulling behind me a trolley full of canned meats and ham. Passers-by started to become aggressive.

'You selling that?'

'Where d'you get it?'

'Give it to me, I'll pay you well!'

My one thought was to get back to my car as fast as possible with this trolley, throw it in the boot and drive off. But I began to think I might not make it. The crowd gathered, people were pushing, questions and offers became more pressing, impatient, hostile. When I was finally in the car and pulling at the starter, I felt as if I was in the mountains, trying to get away from an approaching avalanche. As I moved off I pushed my foot right down to the floor, the murmurs of the disappointed crowd fading behind me.

But that was not the end. I arrived back at the block of flats where I lived and I now had to transfer all my amassed treasures from the car to the cellar which served as the expedition store. Meats, hams, jams, honey; as far as possible I tried to pack things up into sacks so as not to cause distress to any passers-by, but sometimes I did not have enough time to do this. So during all these activities I was accompanied by simple fear.

Somebody could come one night, break into the cellar and steal all the food. Later rumours reached me that people in the area were talking. 'That Kukuczka on the ninth floor is some sort of blackmarketeer. I'm surprised the police have not taken an interest in his activities.'

Eventually we managed to get everything packed, through customs, and sent off. At last, Rysiek Warecki and I were freed from envious looks and flew to Bombay, followed by a train journey across India, transferring our loads by rickshaw onto a ferry across the Ganges, then by a rickety hired truck. At the Nepalese border Wojtek was waiting for us with a handful of forms required for the importation of our equipment and food into Nepal.

In Kathmandu only one thing spoiled the atmosphere: our foreign climbers had not appeared. René Ghilini was no longer interested in the expedition and would not be coming. Soon a telegram arrived from England. Alex had financial problems and would probably be unable to take part in the trip. And so the originally planned Franco-Anglo-Polish expedition became the Cracow-Katowice expedition. But without the foreign exchange that the others were going to provide, we began to wonder how we could set off to the mountains. Luckily, after a few days we received a telex from England. Alex had found some money and could come after all. We breathed a sigh of relief. We would have 2000 dollars from Alex, plus another 200 that Wojtek had left over from his spring trip. Not all that much, but it was something. We would have to make do with what we had. We cut down to the bare minimum the amount of food and equipment we would transport to the base camp, and as a result only needed to hire twenty-five porters.

The walk up to Makalu is one of the longest approach marches to a mountain giant. Normally it takes twelve days, we took about ten. For us the route was demanding not so much of physical as nervous energy. This was thanks to the liaison officer we had been given. This young lad had never before been in the mountains, but he nevertheless had a very accurate idea of what was due to an expedition liaison officer. As the earnings of an officer delegated to an expedition were some five times the salary for sitting in an office pen-pushing, you had to have someone backing you to get this lucrative posting. It turned out later our liaison officer, whose name was Khatka, certainly did have some inconveniently good backing. But one thing at a time.

Right from the very start we realised that we were going to have trouble with him. He came along with some other character whom he presented to us as his friend.

'He was the liaison officer on an American expedition. Gentlemen, ask him what he got from them.'

We ignored this opening. We pretended that we were simply not interested. For one thing, we knew exactly what we were required to provide him with and, for another, we had no intention whatsoever of trying to compete with Americans. We were, quite simply, too poor. But Mister Khatka did not change his tone.

'If you gentlemen do not want to ask, then I will tell you myself. He was given by the Americans excellent clothing, and not just that. He was given a stereo radio cassette player. I only mention this so that you gentlemen will know, because I hope that our cooperation will turn out to be equally fruitful.'

'If we work together well, then we will try, as far as we are able in our circumstances, to show our gratitude,' we replied, gritting our teeth silently.

As time went by, so Mister Khatka's disillusionment with us became more and more evident. When it came to giving him his equipment, as outlined in the regulations, he did not really like any of it. He began fussing.

'What sort of a jacket is this? It does not even have any stickers . . .'

He grimaced at the two pairs of trousers allocated to him, one of which had to be woollen, at the three pairs of warm socks, at the sleeping bags, at everything. What was worse he ran off with all his kit to lodge a complaint at the ministry. When at last he signed a declaration that he had received all the equipment, we sighed a great sigh of relief. Now nothing stood in the way of us being given our briefing by the ministry, which in effect meant their blessing to start the expedition. The final straw came when Mister Khatka informed us, while we were still in Kathmandu, that the doctor had prescribed that he should drink one beer every day and that we should allow for this in the expedition budget. We received this cheeky request with stoic calm. Once or twice we even stood him a beer while we were still in Kathmandu but our blood was beginning to boil. We were standing on our heads to try and keep the most essential costs down to 2200 dollars, so beer for the liaison officer was completely out of the question. A report about our expedition had appeared in one Bulgarian newspaper under the heading: 'Expedition, or argument for 2200 dollars?' The fact that we had set off for the Himalaya with so little money was so hard to grasp that it was suggested there must be some scandal associated with the expedition.

Buying anything during the approach march was also not to be contemplated. We did once or twice buy the cheapest possible vegetable to add to our supper, so as not to deprive ourselves entirely of vitamins. But in a teahouse, where it was possible to have a meal for five rupees, our Mister Khatka was demanding a beer that cost thirty as a special medically prescribed addition to his diet. We told him he would not get it and that was that. He seemed to calm down, as if he realised the beer was a lost cause, but there were more problems to come. We next caught him trying to stir up trouble with the porters. But he did not take into account the very important fact that he was on an expedition for the first time whereas we between us had been many times and we knew about all the customs and regulations.

When he saw the mountains, his eyes almost popped out of his head. Although we were still walking through lush meadows he demanded that all the porters were issued high-altitude equipment. What is more they must, he insisted, be paid extra for high-altitude work. The porters nevertheless carried on and we eventually reached our base camp at 5400 metres. It was here Mister Khatka's downfall began. On the second or third day he failed to get up for breakfast. When we called him, he crawled out of his tent blackened and dazed.

'What has happened?' we asked with concern.

'It was very cold during the night,' he blurted out, gasping greedily at the fresh air. It turned out that he had spent the whole night burning candles which covered everything in soot. He had been sitting in the completely sealed tent, and he came out effectively half-choked.

He complained, but now tearfully, 'It is not possible to live here. I am ill. The base camp must be located lower down.'

We retorted, 'If you want to go down, then go. That's fine. But leave us in peace.'

We equipped him with a tent, gave him food for his return journey and sent him off down. I was strongly tempted to kick him up the backside as he left, but managed to regain control of myself in time.

Anyway we were now free to begin acclimatising on a minor 6000-metre peak right beside our base camp. On our return we saw that we were no longer on our own. An Austrian expedition had arrived and set up their tents beside ours. We did not want to hurry as we were anxious to let our bodies become gradually accustomed to working at ever higher altitudes. After a few days we attempted an ascent of Makalu by the normal route for acclimatisation purposes. Conditions were difficult, the snow knee deep, the terrain dangerous and prone to avalanche. We reached 7800 metres which took us several days, before going back down to base camp.

There we found we had guests. Reinhold Messner and Doug Scott had come to visit us in our tent. They were also acclimatising prior to an ambitious plan to traverse Makalu, up the South-East Ridge and down the North Ridge. We treated them to mountaineers' tea, slightly fortified with alcohol from the medicine box. I sat in the corner listening to mountain tales. Wojtek is well known and respected in the Himalaya, he had met up and chatted with Messner more than once in these highest mountains. Doug Scott also knew him, for Wojtek had climbed with an English group in the Hindu Kush. So while Wojtek and Alex looked after entertaining the guests, I looked after the cooking. I did not get myself involved in the conversation, preferring to listen, particularly as I had searched through all my things in the cellar for Günther Messner's torch that I had found beneath the summit of Nanga Parbat, but I had not found it anywhere. If I had realised that it was not simply a piece of junk picked up during an expedition, but a valuable Messner family relic, I would have given it a place of honour in my house. But it was too late. They finished the tea, said goodbye and departed.

After a short rest we started preparing ourselves for our assault on the West Face. First we went carefully through our equipment again. Ropes and pitons must be matched to the face and what we might encounter on it. Wojtek and Alex already knew the wall. They were there in the spring, so made the main decisions. We weighed everything carefully on the spring balance, ending up with about twenty-four kilos per head, or rather per back. We packed. On top of everything we added six days' food, calculating the climb should not take us longer than that. And we set out for the wall.

The first camp was at its foot. Here we were still able to eat a very big, solid meal. With meat. I write this with a smile because Wojtek seemed to have forgotten how very recently he had played, quite belligerently, at being a vegetarian. Now he was backing down, announcing that it was impossible for humans to achieve anything in the mountains without meat. When he wrote to Poland to me, he had insisted first and

*Makalu, showing the highpoint of the attempt on the West Face and
Kukuczka's solo ascent of a new route on the North-West Ridge,
15th October, 1981*

foremost that I bring sausages and ham. Somehow we had managed to
do so and, thanks to that, we were now able to eat well, as was necessary.

From now on we moved without a tent, only a three-man bivouac
sheet. We started climbing, hard from the very start, if not difficult, then
exposed. We spent most of the day in the shade, the sun only reaching
us in the afternoon, so it was terribly cold. Getting up in the morning
in the extreme frost became a torture. Packing one's things in the sun
is so much more pleasant, it provides that extra bit of warmth and
heartens one, everything seems a little more cheerful. On Makalu's West
Face one could not count on its smile.

Our first bivouac was in a crevasse under a sérac, still in that depressing
shadow, which did however have its advantages. It was not snowing but,
what was more important, the wind, which all the time was battering the
mountain from the North-East, did not reach us there. The Austrians
ascending the normal route complained bitterly about the wind, but we
did not feel it at all. In fact the weather was really very good for us.

The comparative ease of the glacier came to an end, and we now had
to surmount a fairly difficult rock barrier. Then we had to climb ever
steepening ice slopes. This was done without any protection, because

the rope, for the sake of speed, stayed in the rucksack. A measure of security was achieved by placing the ice axe firmly into snow or ice and by making sure that the crampons were biting into sometimes glassy hard ice.

Wojtek surmounted a very difficult rock overhang, we followed him. Then came stretches of completely glassy hard ice. From Wojtek's accounts of the spring attempt, this whole area was glassy ice. Now large areas were also plastered with a coating of frozen snow. The teeth of the crampons bit deep into this, allowing for good progress. Climbing on glass is very exhausting. Before making a step up you have to kick your crampon into the surface before it grips adequately to support you. Luckily only a few of these patches remained. In the spring the glass had been a curse which lent a hand in the failure of the expedition.

Our progress in the first two days went exactly according to plan. Also the bivouacs. Eventually we reached 7600 metres, then 7800 metres, just below the main difficulties of the route. Above our heads was a 500-metre rock barrier, 300 metres of it very hard and partly over-hanging steep blank rock. Wojtek was sure that the key to the wall lay in a chimney on the right and that it was only possible to make a break-through there. Albeit somewhat less convinced, I agreed. In the morning Alex started the attack. From the very start it was artificial climbing, swinging up from piton to piton, there was no other possibility. At the end of the day we had bitten off thirty metres of the wall.

It was hard to disguise the fact that our fighting spirits had started to flag a bit. Even if we climbed a further thirty metres the following day we would not have made much impression on the wall and our rations, which were already sparse, would only last us another two days after that.

There comes a specific moment when no one talks to anybody else, but we all observe one another, watching the will to win gradually die. The pace drops, everything goes slower, with greater resistance. We were waiting for someone to say, 'Enough! We go down.' It happened as Alex was battling over an overhang. Wojtek broke the silence.

'I see no chance. We won't do this. Even if we manage to climb a hundred metres, it is still a very long way to the summit.'

We talked about the barrier and how, much higher up, it lay back a bit. It should be easier there. But the point at which it lay back was still such a long way above us. I tried to say something. Anything.

'Hell, we still have food for one more day's work. Maybe we should try a different variation? Let's climb another fifteen metres, we may find it becomes easier higher up.'

I could see that Wojtek was not convinced. It is always difficult for

36

me to accept the concept of retreat. But with Wojtek, when things go more and more slowly, he can suddenly say: 'That's it, we can't got any further, we go down,' and there's no further discussion. For me it is more difficult, I have to exhaust all the possible arguments before I can finally accept the decision. Once I was accused of deliberately stalling, so that later I could put it around that it was not me who gave up but my partners, who left me with no alternative. Such accusations can cause a lot of distress.

Well, it does not matter. We had to retreat anyway. As Alex was starting off down, and Wojtek and I were finishing off packing, I said, 'Listen, we have lost against this wall, but not necessarily with the mountain. There is still a chance to reach the summit.'

This was met with stony silence. We simply went down then, the three of us, one behind the other to our previous bivouac. It was hard going down backwards, one step after another. Descending can be as exhausting as ascending. We spent the night at the bivouac. There were more difficulties down to the base of the wall where we bivouacked again. Only the next day did we reach base camp.

Moods were bad. It was much the same among the Austrians, who were exhausted by the incessant icy winds on the normal route. In our camp Alex was mumbling something about it being time for him to start packing. Less than a day had passed and already he was gathering up his belongings.

'In fact I've already been too long on this trip. I have a lot of things to do when I get back home to England. I can't put them off for ever. Anyway, to be honest, I see no chance of getting up the mountain in the prevailing conditions,' he explained.

The Austrians also decided to give up the fight. They packed but had to wait for their porters to arrive. News arrived that Reinhold and Doug were already on their way back to Kathmandu. Our own porters would arrive in a week. A feeling of sadness and hopelessness descended.

Seven days . . . I looked up, high into the mountains, where the wind was howling around the ridges. I still could not accept that we were returning with nothing, and without a summit. I walked to and fro and finally suggested to Wojtek that we try again by an easier route I had been thinking of earlier. If we hit good weather we could make a fast ascent. Wojtek was for sticking by his original decision. He is one of those people who operate at a high pitch while he has an aim before him, then everything unwinds. To get himself worked up again, to change his attitude is difficult. But I did not let him rest.

'Just once more. Quickly. Three days might be enough, at most four. We might have luck with the weather.'

37

Wojtek had his own arguments.

'Firstly, there is no good weather. You can see that everybody is retreating because of that hellish wind. Secondly, I have slightly frost-bitten feet. I really do not see any chance.'

Then I said something that I had not really thought through carefully. 'In which case I shall try on my own.'

That took him by surprise. He thought a bit before he answered.

'Hm! If you are definite about it, then try, it's your decision, but I see no chance. Go. We are not here in the mountains to impose on each other rules and restrictions. If you want to try, go ahead. You can make use of my equipment, take anything you need.'

'Thank you. I have to think the whole thing out,' I replied. It was not an easy decision. Simple fear came into it, fear of the unknown, of being on one's own, the realisation that I was going into a situation where I had to rely entirely on myself. I knew that success could only be achieved if everything fell into place perfectly. I was already half-packed. I kept looking at the sky, but there was no marked change in the weather. I decided not to put it off any more.

'I'm going tomorrow morning,' I stated decisively.

But when I opened my eyes in the morning, I was not feeling quite right. Only after breakfast, at about ten, did I begin to get ready. So I left at a very untypical hour, somewhere around midday. I thought to myself, I'll approach the face, bivouac there and see how things go the next day. If it continues bad I'll simply turn back, if there is a chance of better weather I'll carry on. When I got to the foot of the wall, it was only three. There was still a lot of time. So again I talked to myself: If I am here equipped for a bivouac, it makes little difference if I sleep here or halfway up the face. There, to the right of the normal route, there must surely be a bivouac place. So I start on the wall.

I moved up a steep snow ridge until evening. Conditions were excellent, the snow frozen hard, there was no need to wade through it. I made rapid progress on this new route but found no good place for a bivouac. There was a full moon shining brightly, so I carried on as far as I could till about eleven in the night, when I reached a small flat area, very near where my route to the right cut across the normal route. It was a place often used for camps. The only drawback was the wind which blew fiercely all the time. I could not now unfold my bivouac sheet. Whenever I tried to take it out the wind pulled it out of my grasp like a sail before I could insert the mast. After struggling for two hours with this wretched wind-tugged piece of material I gave up. At the same time I noticed something sticking out of the snow. I stared at this thing, I moved closer. It was the middle of the night, but by the light of the full moon, I saw what was sticking up was the top of a completely buried tent. After two hours I managed to dig out the top section and part of the torn entrance. It was enough for me to drag myself in, and I did not change my position till the morning. At least I was sheltered from that penetrating, bitter wind.

When it became light I looked out, then curled up back into that second-hand tent abandoned who knows how long ago. In this weather I do not have much of a chance, I told myself, and not pursuing the weighty matter further I went back to sleep. I was so tired that I slept till eleven. When I awoke I took my time. There was always plenty of time for me to go down, if necessary. By the time I had made myself some tea and packed my things ready to go down it was already after midday.

I crawled out of that tiny tent and decided that the world was a nicer place after a hot cup of tea. The sky was blue, but it was still blowing, blowing terribly. But as I examined the horizon more closely I noticed tiny clouds clinging to the summits which I had not seen the day before. This smelt of change, I told myself. And then, so as not to tempt providence, I added, but is it for the better or for the worse?

At least there was some sort of a chance. Maybe I was imagining things, but it seemed to me that the wind was easing very slightly. So packed up, with my rucksack on my back, wearing crampons, and ice axe in hand, I walked around a bit, aimlessly. Up or down? Up or down? Suddenly I felt the urge to go up.

I made for the col, the Makalu La (7410 metres), lured in that direction all the more because during our acclimatisation attempt we had left a tent there. A real tent. That last night had convinced me that there was no point trying to go any further in such a strong wind with just a bivouac sheet. Reaching the Makalu La by my variation on the original route, I found the tent and pitched it. In the meantime the clouds had grown. I did not spend any time thinking about that. I was now looking forward to a normal refreshing night's sleep, in a real tent, in a sleeping bag. When I woke in the morning I saw that the clouds had formed themselves at one uniform level, below me, they were no longer rising up, and the wind had eased. In fact it had almost stopped blowing. I left my miserable bivouac sheet behind and packed up the tent carefully, put on my sack and continued up the virgin North-West Ridge. I had no idea what I would find ahead. I could only guess.

At 8000 metres I dug out a platform and pitched the tent. And now I felt like withdrawing all the compliments I had addressed towards the weather in the morning. It was still blowing. Maybe not as hard as yesterday but hard enough for the struggle with the tent to wear me out completely. I was only doing simple things which I could have done with my eyes closed, but there was nobody to help me hold down that flapping sheet even just for a moment. I was alone. When at last that nightmare was over, I got inside and started brewing up some badly needed tea. Just then I experienced a quite inexplicable feeling that I was not on my own, that I was cooking for two people. I had such a strong feeling that someone else was present that I felt an overpowering need to talk to him. But most of all I was so utterly exhausted that while brewing up the tea I lost interest in whether it was for one or two people and fell asleep.

The next day I left fairly late, at about eight o'clock, travelling light with just a camera, ten metres of rope, three pitons and two ice screws. Off I went. I only had this one chance. Either I made it today or I would have to retreat. Unfortunately, as I got higher, the conditions deteriorated and I came across deep, collapsing snow. I reached the ridge crest, followed this to a rock step. How should I tackle it, on the left or on the right? On the left I saw there was no way, it was completely vertical. The rock step itself involved Grade 4 or 5 climbing. Without a rope I felt frightened. I made an attempt, climbing a slight corner leading rightwards. Maybe this would go? But I only had ten metres of rope. I decided to push on using so-called fixed belays. I attached the bottom of the rope to a piton and went as far as I could tied to the other end of the rope till I could fix another piton and attach the rope to it. I then climbed down, untied the rope and tied myself on to the bottom and thus continued. By luck the ten metres of rope I took was just long enough. If I had had half a metre less I would not have been able to get up that wall. And so I went on and on, till the ridge became easier. There were small crevasses to step over but I was getting closer to the summit.

There was one thing that I could not get over. At about one in the afternoon, in the blue sky above Tibet I saw several twinkling stars! I sat down when I saw them, never having experienced anything like it in my life. I closed my eyes for a few moments, I opened them – there they still were. I rubbed my eyes, thinking some snow might have stuck to my lashes. No, the stars were still there in the blue sky; neither a result of over-exhaustion nor because I had been hit over the head with a heavy object. Then I remembered a climbing film called *Stars at Midday* which had featured Lionel Terray, the great French climber. He had seen them too.

It was growing late, but the knowledge that my chances of getting to the summit were now real and ever nearer overcame any fear I might not make it back down to the tent by nightfall. I carried on up. At about half past four I was just below an easy step, the last one, beyond was the summit. I took a short rest. Just a few more steps.

The moment of arrival was the fullest and the most wonderful experience. At the summit I found two pitons belonging to a previous expedition. I placed mine between them. I took out of my rucksack a plastic ladybird, which I had carried as a good luck mascot from my one-year-old son, Maciek, in Katowice, and left it beside the pitons. Then I took a photograph of my club flag on my ice axe. And down.

I desperately wanted to get back before dark but, despite the good weather, the wind continued to blow relentlessly and at that altitude spindrift and snow endlessly whirled around me. I was going down in a cloud of it. I could count on the moon but the full moon was several days ago, so it only rose at ten. Night came. Now I had to look for each foothold, to move one foot carefully at a time. I decided to abseil down the rock wall, rather than look for my original route. I just wanted to get it over with, as long as there was enough rope. I felt around and found a crack in the rock, hammered in my last piton, fixed the rope to it and just hoped that it would reach down to the little saddle. It did not quite reach the snow. Holding onto the very end, my feet still did not touch the snow, but I had negotiated the vertical step.

After a few moments the moon appeared and helped me see the lie of the land better, though I still had difficulty finding the tent. In the morning, despite my utter exhaustion, I was nevertheless very happy. I now only had to concentrate on completing the descent. At about five in the afternoon I met Wojtek who had been looking out for me.

'So, how was it?' he asked.

'I got to the summit.'

He was taken by surprise and a few seconds passed before he said, 'Congratulations. To be honest I really didn't think you would make it.' The base camp seemed deserted. Alex had gone. Reinhold and Doug were long gone. Only the Austrians were still there, sitting around waiting for their porters. They too were amazed by my news and their doctor took a sample of my blood. After testing it he shook his head. It was very thick, for someone coming off a high mountain is dried out like a prune. I can see this now, on the photographs that were taken of me. That man, grey and thin, is me. Makalu had taken its toll. But that is to be expected in the mountains.

The Austrians invited me for a meal, but all I wanted to do was drink, endless supplies of soup, tea and juice. In the crowded noisy mess tent sometimes I answered a question, then I would relapse into my own thoughts. Through my exhaustion one thing did sink in fully: that great mountain I had climbed alone was now behind me. Then another thought, this was my third eight-thousander, and I was the only Pole to have climbed three. A feeling of warmth washed over me.

In Kathmandu Mister Khatka was waiting for us with his renewed accusations that we had not paid him enough. We refused to be hassled.

'One moment,' we explained to him like to a child, 'you received five days' food to get you back down to the nearest village? You received seven days' travel allowance for your journey on to Kathmandu?'

But our liaison officer would not listen. He almost threw himself at us, he would deal with us, he would not sign our debriefing. There was no way out, we had to go to the Ministry of Tourism ourselves and give them a complete account of Mister Khatka's behaviour and his demands.

The official listened to us carefully and said, 'In this situation, gentlemen, you have the right not even to pay him his wages. Not a cent. That is what I would do if I was in your position.'

We did actually have money set aside for his wages. But if the Ministry of Tourism official actually made such a recommendation, we began to wonder. The next day this same official came looking for us urgently. He was clearly a worried man.

'Gentlemen. I think you should pay that scoundrel his money. He comes from a very influential family. He can give us a lot of trouble. We have already had a lot of pressure placed on the Ministry of Tourism regarding the debriefing of your expedition.'

So we paid Mister Khatka everything that was due, not a rupee more. We had had enough. But clearly not Mister Khatka. After a few days a Nepalese journalist came to visit us, requesting our impressions of the trip for an article. Later the same journalist invited us home for a meal.

'Do you know a guy by the name of Khatka?' he asked.

'Do we just! He was, unfortunately, our liaison officer. Why?'

'Well, he came to our offices and asked us to publish an offensive and libellous article. He claimed that the ascent of Makalu was totally impossible and that you certainly did not get to the summit.' Our host put Khatka's claims forward as if they were a joke, but he observed our reactions carefully, adding, 'What is more, he has left a copy of his report at the Ministry of Tourism.'

We shrugged our shoulders. The libellous report never appeared in the newspaper, because the journalist had a better understanding of Himalayan climbing than did our Mister Khatka. But this did not alter the fact that a rumour had been started in the Ministry of Tourism. The questions started all over again.

'Well, how was it, sir? Did you reach the summit or not?'

We lodged an exhaustive account, but the matter was left in the air. It ended up with my ascent of Makalu not being officially acknowledged.

Instead there was just some shoulder patting. No problem! No problem. I detected a note of condescending sympathy, as if they wanted to say: whether you were on that summit or not does not really matter. But it would make life for us easier if you admitted perhaps you weren't.

I lost my cool. 'I did not make that ascent so that I could then prove to you that I had done it. I do not care what you do, I have already told you everything and I have nothing to add, not a word. As far as I am concerned the matter is finished. If you want to believe me or not is entirely up to you.'

That was the end of it. The debriefing of the expedition was completed, we could now go home. But my solo ascent of Makalu remained under a cloud, thanks to Khatka's libels.

A year later at home one evening, when everything was quiet, I reached for the mail. There was an envelope bearing an exotic stamp. South Korea? I opened it first, unfolding a single sheet of paper. On it were written a few sentences in poor English:

'Dear Mr Kukuczka,
    We congratulate you on last year's (October) ascent of Makalu I. I am happy that I was able to verify your report personally. I am a member of the Korean 1982 Makalu expedition. We found on the summit a small toy or mascot in the shape of a small tortoise, black spots on a red background; in its place we left one of our carabiners. Miss Hawley informed me that it was a member of your expedition who had left this, that is why I am writing to you. Please reply to our expedition address,
                    Yours faithfully, Huh Young Ho.
address: Huh Young Ho
        191 Wha San z dong
        Te chun city, Chung Buk Seoul, Korea'

I bore our Korean friend no grudge for changing a ladybird into a tortoise. After reading the letter again, I got up and looked into Maciek's room; I had taken his ladybird away from him a year ago without even asking permission. He was asleep.

4

A Stolen Mountain

Broad Peak, West Spur, 1982

When martial law was introduced in December 1981 our spirits, as those of all Poles, collapsed. No one knew what was going to happen next. Everything was closed, nothing worked, it seemed that everything had to be started all over again. But was it worth starting anything? We felt trapped. Clubs were closed, nothing was being organised, I felt as if I was in a cage.

What was to be done? I was not the only one who was asking this question. After August, like so many of my compatriots, I had joined Solidarity. In this youthful and spontaneous movement I had felt a breath of fresh air blowing through the stifling atmosphere that existed in our country. I had signed, declared my support, and left for an expedition. I had contributed so little towards keeping the movement alive.

In the first days of martial law I felt a great apathy and guilt. Then in December 1981 came the Wujek incident when the authorities opened fire on striking miners, killing nine of them, just a stone's throw from where I lived. Total collapse and an all-embracing indifference came over me.

Eventually we detected that there were some openings developing. We noticed that sportsmen were leaving the country to take part in events abroad. We also were registered as sportsmen in the GKKFiS, so there was a chance. Wojtek and I closed our eyes to the situation at home and put all our efforts into getting an expedition going. At the same time Wanda Rutkiewicz was organising a large women's expedition to go to K2. Maybe we could tag along with her on her permit for K2? We would not trouble her in any way organisationally or financially. It was too good a chance to miss. We wanted to go just as a pair, climbing alpine-style, as we had on Makalu. Women's expeditions do not have a long tradition and it was Wanda who was the pioneer. She considered that women are discriminated against when working alongside men in mixed groups, that they were unable to demonstrate their ability to equal men in their achievements. Maybe she saw mountaineering from a sportsperson's point of view, as in the past she had played volleyball competitively. That is why, I suspect, she wanted to divide alpine achievements into women's and men's.

In 1975 she organised an expedition to Gasherbrum III. This theoretically Polish women's team had its sexual purity blemished slightly by being supported by a team of men who were there ostensibly to give the women greater security in a Muslim country. During the assault on the mountain, there were exclusively women's partnerships, but mixed partnerships also developed. So the outcome was not exactly as was intended. Initially the men were to have a completely different set of objectives, in a different area. That does not however alter the fact that the expedition was very successful: the first ascent of Gasherbrum III (7952 metres) and the ascent of a new route up the eight-thousander, Gasherbrum II. Wanda Rutkiewicz and Alison Chadwick-Onyszkiewicz were involved in the ascent of Gasherbrum III. Gasherbrum II was climbed by three ropes, one of which was a women's team of Halina Kruger-Syrokomska and Anna Okopinska. The men's achievements during this expedition were given a rather lower profile, for the expedition took place in the International Year of Women, and Wanda, as leader, was entertained by Mrs Bhutto, the wife of the Prime Minister of Pakistan. Everything was in the spirit of equal rights for women.

In climbing circles all this was viewed in a variety of ways. Most often with a slight smile. That is how I myself viewed those events then, and still do now. Why am I writing about this now, when I am just about to link up with another women's expedition? I think it very important to establish clearly one's attitude to the main concepts, aims and ambitions of such a women's team. This was my one and only chance to get away that year for an expedition. There was also to be an expedition to K2 led by Janusz Kurczab, but he had already completed his team selection, and Wojtek's and my wish to climb alpine-style meant there was no room for us in his group. Janusz felt that our approach was fine if ascending an uncomplicated seven-thousander. He would not even contemplate however the ascent of an eight-thousander in this style. Any co-operation with him on the understanding that we joined his expedition but worked entirely independently was simply out of the question.

45

So we started talking with Wanda. At that time I did not know her personally. But Wojtek Kurtyka got on with her quite well, they both came from the same club in Wroclaw. It was he who suggested to her that we should join their trip on the basis of totally independent action. Wanda accepted, which was a great credit to her, and proved she was quite broadminded. There was also a simple element of business in the whole arrangement. We undertook in exchange to organise the walk-in arrangements. Naturally we also paid our way at all stages of the trip. The only thing we could not help with was the payment for the permit to climb K2. As far as the Pakistani authorities were concerned we were part of the women's expedition, added on to their personnel list as photographer and reporter or something similar, with the role of giving protection to the ladies on their journey through a Muslim country.

Despite martial rule the expedition became a reality. What is more it turned out that the number of expeditions leaving Poland in those grey days was greater than ever before. There were simply no other chances to get out of the country. So a variety of tourists were included on expedition lists so that they had a basis on which to obtain passports to travel. Groups became larger, sometimes thirty or forty people would leave on an expedition. These would be friends from the club who simply enjoyed travelling in the mountains. After all, Alpine clubs were not simply composed of hard-core climbers. These people also raised money by working on chimneys, in order to go to the Himalaya and walk up to base camp.

We only put a small amount of our equipment in with the main group, most we carted around with us. We all met up in Islamabad to start on the journey into the mountains together. Together with Halina Kruger, I piloted the expedition equipment for 500 kilometres in a hired truck loaded to bursting point; three days' driving in overpowering heat over the rutted and windy road euphemistically called the Karakoram Highway, often carved out of the mountainside and very precipitous. I talked a lot with Halina on that rickety old truck, because earlier we had hardly managed to get to know each other. She was one of the main driving forces behind this expedition. Wanda had slipped half a year ago on Elbruz, fallen several dozen metres and broken her leg. She was taken to a Russian hospital, which she managed to escape from very quickly and return to Poland, where they put her leg together properly. Then she ended up in Austria where they got down to serious treatment. This all took a lot of time and she was effectively coming on this trip with only a partly healed leg.

At the K2 base camp there were three expeditions, all of them from

Poland. The women's expedition set itself the aim of ascending K2 by Abruzzi Ridge, the normal South-East route. It would be the first women's ascent of this, the world's second highest mountain. Janusz Kurczab, whose group included some Mexicans, had set up his base camp on a different glacier, a day away from us. He hoped to climb a new route on the South-West Face of K2. With him were Leszek Cichy, Krzysiek Wielicki, Wojtek Wróż and Alek Lwów. A strong team, possibly the strongest Poland could muster.

Then there were Wojtek and me. Our aim was a new route on the East Face of K2 or on the South Face. At first Wojtek was set on the East Face. He had been to K2 several years before and he had noticed possibilities here and this would be the first ascent of this very fine wall.

It was my first visit to K2. The mountain made a big impression, especially from Concordia, the meeting place of the two great glaciers. From there it is possible to see the whole of the South Face like a great beautiful pyramid. The effect is electrifying. The mountain completely overwhelms one. That sight of it generated in me a degree of anxiety which I had never before experienced, and that never left me for an instant.

What would happen? Would we succeed or not? The K2 myth acts on one strongly. Looking at it one cannot help but think of all the failed attempts to reach the summit, the myth of a hard and dangerous mountain, defended by frequent sudden changes in the weather. Like other myths, it came from the numerous tales of impassable barriers, of accidents, more often fatal than on other mountains. I'd seen the mountain on a hundred photographs. Now I was really there, standing opposite it.

To see the east side of the mountain we would have to walk round it. But all the time I had eyes only for the south side, which attracted me much more. It was so elegant. That is after all important. Like a girl you have just met, she must first of all be attractive. Later these impressions are superseded by others. It was the beauty of that face which captured my gaze. Such factors must also affect the choice of a route. But only the East Face existed for Wojtek. For several years it had been his fixation.

At base camp we had separate tents near to the women's camp and after only a few days we established a joint kitchen. Separate cooking would simply have been rather silly. Their expedition had a cook, but he only knew how to wash up and make rice. So we placed all our food into one communal lot and carried out kitchen duties on a rota basis.

One idea we did have to give up was that of acclimatising on the normal route up K2. That would have been the most convenient for us but this was totally unacceptable to the girls as it would go against their concept of a purely women's ascent of the mountain. Or maybe they simply did not want us getting in their way on the Abruzzi Ridge? Anna Okopinska took a particularly strong line on the issue.

'There is no room here for messing about. Either this is a women's expedition or not.'

As treading on their route would lead to impurity, we decided instead to go up Broad Peak by the normal route, to acclimatise. This was all legitimate according to our permit, which allowed us to travel in the area of K2 with the purpose of taking photographs and gaining acclimatisation.

Four days after establishing base camp we reached 6400 metres on Broad Peak, and left a depot, then came down to rest. The next time we would go up as high as possible before descending. That should provide us with enough acclimatisation to tackle our main objective – K2. So we started off up again, regained our depot and spent the night there. The next day we established a camp at 7300 metres. In the morning we left with the intention of pushing up as high as possible – not excluding the possibility of climbing the summit.

Just before the col at 7800 metres I felt as if I was beginning to choke. I was getting weaker. Now I was certain that I was not yet fully acclimatised. Wojtek was feeling better, his organism adapting more quickly, but he saw what was happening to me, so when we reached the col he asked, 'So, how's it going?'

'I feel grim. I would soonest go back down.'

'Damn, what a shame. We're so near the summit. I think I'll carry on.'

'Fine. Go . . .'

I sat there watching as gradually Wojtek drew further away. Soon he was on the ridge and I was feeling a bit sorry for myself. Blast! There were only a few hundred metres to go. Maybe I should fight this weakness and push on up at least as far as I could manage? Once I had got up and started moving again I found it difficult to tell myself to stop and go back. The summit is only 8047 metres high. It really was close now. What was more, the route was technically easy from there on. There were a few small steps and gaps, but the general angle was gentle. I found it hard to give up. A summit acts like a magnet. It attracts, one has to get there. I become very stubborn in these situations. I carried on, despite the fact that it was costing me a lot. The last few metres I covered with as much difficulty as if it had been a mountain of 9000 metres. I had no strength left, I was out of breath. I went ten metres and rested. I did not always sit, aware that getting up from the snow

48

might cost me too much more energy. More often I simply leant heavily on my ice axe.

Half an hour from the summit I passed Wojtek on his way down. It was getting late. Maybe I should turn back, he advised kindly.

'No, it's too near. Somehow I'll get there. Go down and get a brew going,' I gasped with difficulty.

I attribute my reaching the summit solely to strength of will. Nothing else. I'm now convinced that a twelve-day acclimatisation period is simply too short for me. It must take me longer than Wojtek. On the summit I only took a photograph of my ice axe and of the moon above the ridge. Then I took a panorama. Finished. I collected a rock as a souvenir and began my descent. I had been on the summit of Broad Peak illegally.

I have always considered permits for climbing a mountain completely unnatural, even stupid. When I go off into the mountains, be they those in Pakistan or in Nepal, I simply feel that I am at home, a shared home. I go up into the mountains because I like doing it, because I want to do it. And when I am there on the mountain I feel it belongs to me. Any rules and regulations brought in to say that I am allowed to go this way but not that way are simply ludicrous. It is like trying to say: this is my air in my garden, you cannot breathe it. The only valid reason to place controls on climbing a mountain is if ten or fifteen groups want to visit the same peak at the same time. I also seek some solitude in the mountains, a contact with nature, on a one-to-one basis, even though my climbing partner is nearby.

Mountains generate a continuous conversation with myself. To carry on or turn back? Do I still have it in me? These are all experiences one goes climbing for. How is it possible then to legislate a mountain? Writing these words I have sadly to admit that, in the case of mountains in Pakistan and Nepal, one never feels truly free. Sometimes, however, the situation can be created where one follows one's own inclination, since behind the rules there hides some bureaucrat who has never been in mountains and does not understand them.

I'm writing this so that you may understand how coming down off this 'stolen mountain' I had no feeling of guilt whatsoever. Rather the reverse. The circumstances had added spice to the result. This really was my mountain. I had climbed it. It remained even more mine because I could tell nobody about it. Believe me, this is a much deeper satisfaction.

This approach was not born in me here in the Himalaya. Often, even as a young lad, I would set myself various tests. To compete with someone is quite natural. If you run a hundred metres, you try to be first, not last. But I also felt the need to prove to myself that I could achieve other things. Once I set myself a six-day fast. I did not eat or drink anything, just to see if I could last out. Nobody knew about this. Not only did I not want to tell, but also I could not tell anyone. I did it. The satisfaction of knowing that I could do it was all that I needed. It's a bit like a beautiful girl. If she is yours, if you are happy with her, the satisfaction is so complete that you have no urge to tell everybody about it. It is your secret and hers only.

I have encountered situations where someone has been bragging about climbing this or that and I have sometimes thought I did that earlier, in better style and more quickly. But I do not say anything. I must admit that at such times I also think you are much weaker than me anyway. Knowing myself is what is essential and now and then I set myself tests of keeping silent like that because I know what I can do and the knowledge is sufficient. That was how it was coming down from Broad Peak exhausted, but inside me carrying a genuine deep satisfaction.

I arrived back at the tent after dark, so tired out that Wojtek made no mention of the fact that it was my turn to cook the meal. At this altitude one must drink. Without it one very soon becomes as dry as a prune. We had not drunk anything all day long. The next day we started off down to base camp. At about 6400 metres, we saw a group of three climbers coming up. It was Reinhold Messner and two Pakistani climbers, Nazir Sabir and Sher Khan who were climbing Broad Peak by the normal route.

Messner knew Wojtek, but he still did not recognise me, so he started the conversation with him.

'I have some bad news for you. One of your women has died on K2.'

We tried to find out who, and how it happened, but he just shrugged his shoulders helplessly. He knew no details or names. As we did not have a radio, we could only receive information on our descent to the base camp. We were anxious and a bit crushed by this, a death so soon, so suddenly, for no known reason. Messner squatted down beside us. The usual mountain conversation started up.

'Where are you coming from?'

'We've been doing an acclimatisation trip. We went up to the area of the summit,' Wojtek answered evasively.

That was not enough for Messner. He examined us for a few seconds silently, then asked directly: 'So were you on the summit or not?'

'We were in the area,' Wojtek stressed. Messner just smiled.

'Yes, yes. Understood.'

'And, if I may ask you, please, do not talk too much about having met us here.'

'Fine, fine,' he made light of the situation. After an hour's rest we parted, they to go up, we down, exactly like my first meeting with him after Lhotse, when our expeditions passed each other on my way down.

At base we found out that Halina Kruger had died. At Camp 2, on 30th July, she had died suddenly in a few seconds of a pulmonary or maybe a cerebral embolism. Her friends and Janusz Kurczab's expedition were already in the process of retrieving her body. We joined this Himalayan funeral procession, bringing her down to base camp, to be precise to the only place nearby where it was possible to dig her a decent grave. Everywhere else was either glacier or rock. Among others buried in this place is the American Art Gilkey who died on K2 in 1953.

On 1st August we buried Halina with her ice axe. We made a small mound over her, placed a cross on it and carved an appropriate memorial on the metal lid of an equipment container. We took every care even in these primitive conditions to ensure this was a suitable ceremony for a friend we were already missing, who also was a Pole and a Catholic. Wanda read out a farewell to her, someone else said a few words, then there was a communal prayer. It was the first time for me to attend such a funeral.

This death weighed heavily on everybody. It brought up that question eternally asked in a difficult situation: what should we do now? The girls were wondering whether or not to pack up and go. The discussions lasted a long time. Eventually Wanda gave everyone a chance to vote and the majority decided to continue the expedition. Only Anna Okopinska, who was Halina's partner, found it impossible to accept the fact that she would never again go with her to the Himalaya, or even the Tatra, and said she was going home. One memory has stuck with me from those sad days, and that is the picture of Anka, in the very early morning sitting alone, away from the campsite, trying to gather herself up again.

In the end she remained. I'm writing this so that the reader may find it easier to understand that women when faced by tragedies in the mountains behave basically in the same way as men do.

After a few days' rest we set off for the East Face of K2 on a reconnaissance but on reaching a point from which we could see the face, I declared that I could see no possible way of getting up in the prevailing conditions. Three-quarters of the way up the East Face there is a sérac barrier whose configuration changes. Sometimes there are many sérac avalanches, sometimes fewer. Wojtek's proposed route led through this 200-metre high barrier by way of a narrow steep pillar resembling a spur of snow, which itself depended from the sérac walls and its thickness varied. In some years the pillar vanishes completely. This year the séracs were big and threatening. Setting out on this route would be far too risky. At the point where the pillar should be there is just a vast sérac wall. There must have been a massive avalanche here recently. Even if we managed to gain the base of this ice cliff, and we decided that the conditions were safe enough to climb it, we would still be faced with exceptional technical problems on this slightly overhanging ice wall.

So we returned and decided to go for the South Face. Deep inside I was happy. I have already said how I liked the look of the South Face, how it lured me. As we planned the route we realised we were faced with a similar problem here. At half height there was a sérac barrier which must be by-passed safely. From a distance we saw two possibilities: one on the left, one on the right. We decided to skirt it by going below the right end where the wall was at its lowest. There was still an element of risk involving 'twenty minutes of fear'. We would have to run beneath this section at a time when the séracs were most stable, in the very early morning, before sunrise. We could not see exactly what the situation was just left of this sérac barrier because it was hidden by a rock outcrop, but I suspected that the sérac might be very low at that point.

Reaching a good bivouac at 6200 or 6400 metres took us two days. The going was hard, there are various walls and ridges to climb. Along the way we found bits of old rope indicating that others had tried this route in the past. This was probably an Austrian expedition, but I am not sure. We now had tangible proof that others had been lured by this wall which is hardly surprising, seeing as how it rears up imposingly right in front of one's nose. One can hardly miss it.

We slept to the side of the barrier. The following day, still in the dark, we prepared ourselves for this dangerous traverse. We managed to get across the 'twenty minutes of fear' and reached unthreatened ground, but as we carried on up easier ground new problems appeared. It was snowing hard, visibility was deteriorating fast. At 7200 metres we stopped and dug out a platform, to put up the tent and get inside, worrying what was to happen with the weather. Even before we put up the tent we had already had a minor exchange. Wojtek had looked around him, he spent a long time looking up in the direction from which the clouds were coming.

'I do not believe that the weather will improve,' he assessed.

I knew straight away what he was aiming at, so I pre-empted him.

'We can wait a while. As we are here now, we may as well bivvy here. If we turn back we will still have to bivvy somewhere.'

This way I managed to win the night there, but the weather did not improve. I did everything to stall Wojtek, pointing out the weather could change for the better at any time. But I gained nothing by this. The previous day's conversation returned like a boomerang.

'Well, so now? We go down?'

'Let's wait at least one more day. We can lose nothing. We will be better acclimatised.' I grasped at absurd arguments, knowing that if it did not stop snowing a new avalanche danger would emerge.

So we waited and waited, and when midday arrived Wojtek decided, 'This makes no sense. We are wasting our energy.'

I knew that we did not have a chance, and with a sad heart, agreed to go down, recross the 'twenty minutes of fear', and make the full-day trudge down through the deep snow to base. It was not just we who had ground to a halt. The women had established another camp at 6800 metres but, despite several attempts, all efforts to progress further had foundered because of deep snow and very strong winds.

We decided to have another go. Our bivouac equipment was now at 6400 metres, so we waited for good weather. After about a week there was an improvement and we returned to where we had left the tent erected. We floundered in sometimes two metres of fresh snow but on arrival we could not find the tent. We tried to reconstruct in our minds the place where we had pitched it. We dug in the snow, burrowing into it like moles, but our tent had simply vanished. In the tent were our sleeping bags and all our other bivouac equipment.

We spent half a day digging, growing more and more desperate as the prospect of sleeping out, as we were, came closer with every hour. At last we found it at the end of one of our tunnels.

Next day we regained our previous high point of just over 7000 metres. But again the weather deteriorated, and we had to go down.

Before the descent I had another exchange with Wojtek. In those long hours spent in this great snow eiderdown, a thought kept coming back to me, not giving me any peace. It concerned the variation to the left which we could not see properly from the base camp.

'Come on, let's try and get a better view of it. If we get beyond the corner it might be harder but it'll certainly be safer. We won't have to go across these "twenty minutes of fear".'

Wojtek was not convinced.

'There's no sense in it. If the weather gets better we could have a quick look, but I think it will be quite hard there.'

And so it stood. We retreated to base camp, where we waited for two weeks. The weather did not relent. Each day reinforced our fears that we did not have much of a chance. Kurczab's expedition reached 8300 metres and also decided to retreat.

We all went home. Out of the three Polish expeditions we were the only ones not returning empty-handed. We had climbed Broad Peak by the normal route, hardly a great sporting success by present-day standards. For me this was however my fourth eight-thousander, which made me the leading Polish Himalayan climber.

But because of Broad Peak we had problems in Islamabad. There had been some sort of a leak. We suspected a French journalist who had accompanied the expedition.

In Islamabad, in the Ministry of Tourism, Wanda was being grilled. 'Were those two on the summit of Broad Peak or not?'

'I know nothing about this. I know they were on Broad Peak because they wanted to acclimatise and take photographs.' Her explanation sounded plausible. We were down as photographers on the expedition list and by far the best view of K2 is from the normal route up Broad Peak. Wanda wasn't allowed to sidestep these difficult questions at the Ministry of Tourism debriefing which in effect marks the official conclusion to the expedition and, more important, gives permission to leave Pakistan. But somehow she survived.

On our return, Janusz Kurczab presented a summary of the year's main sporting achievements at a meeting of the Polish Alpine Club Governing Committee. The season in the Karakoram he summed up something like this: 'The women's expedition reached about 6800 metres, at which height it came to an end because of bad weather. We reached 8300 metres and also had to retreat because of horrific weather conditions. There was also a third expedition, from the start doomed to failure, because a two-man expedition has no chance to climb a wall like that . . .'

He did not breathe a word about our ascent of Broad Peak. It was after all a stolen mountain.

Soon after that Reinhold Messner's book appeared, with a title something like *Three Times Eight*, because he had climbed three eight-thousanders in one year. In it he wrote, 'On my way up Broad Peak, somewhere around 6400 metres, we met Wojtek Kurtyka with another Pole, coming down from the summit . . .'

To this day I wonder. Maybe he simply forgot about our request at the time of our meeting.

5

A Mountain on Credit

Gasherbrum II, South-East Spur,
Gasherbrum I, South-West Face, 1983

T he heat beat down from the sky, sweat blinded us, our hands were visibly shaking. Wojtek and I unsealed one drum after another, because that was what the Indian Customs Officer had demanded. We were furious. We had not foreseen this. Crossing the India-Pakistan border had never before presented such problems. The border crossing formalities at Amritsar go something like this: first you pass through Indian customs, then there is 200 metres of no-man's-land through which no vehicle can pass. Beyond is a barrier, defining the Pakistani border. Only once had we been able to persuade them that a truck, hired in India, could be driven up to the barrier so that we could transfer our gear to a Pakistani vehicle. This time we achieved nothing. We tried to chat up the local border guards, but they did not even want to listen.

So we had to unload all the equipment, then hire porters who had special permission to walk across the no-man's-land; and for carrying our luggage those 200 metres to Pakistan we had to pay them almost as much as it cost to hire the truck we used to cross half of India.

On top of all this they had decided to carry out a thorough customs check. So the truck was unloaded. We took one drum down after another and laid them on the blistering hot ground in a row like soldiers. Then the customs man told us to open each one in turn. As this game went on, Wojtek, who has a considerably better command of English than I do, tried to bluster a bit.

'Come on, man. What are you looking for? We're leaving your country, not entering it.'

But the customs man just grunted back that those were his orders and to keep unsealing the drums. He did not dig to the bottom of every one, but he did insist we opened them all. Then he admitted defeat and went back to his superior officer to report.

'What? You've checked them? So quickly?' snapped back his superior, whose uniform was adorned with innumerable distinctions. 'Return immediately. We will check it all again. This time properly. Together!'

They started all over again. The superior plunged his paws into everything himself. Had they been given a tip-off? As he approached the last three drums, I turned away, sat down in the scant shadow of our truck, lit a cigarette and decided to think of nothing. I awaited the worst.

Then I heard Wojtek, now clearly furious, shouting, 'What the hell are you looking for? You want to see everything? Fine. Be my guest.'

I looked up to see him reaching for the first of those last three drums, pulling out one sleeping bag after another, brandishing them and flinging them to the ground. This was the end. In those last drums, among those bundles of sleeping bags and down jackets was the whisky. There was much more than regulations allowed. I knew that this was punishable, so did Wojtek, but the funding of the march-in relied exactly on this whisky.

Suddenly I realised that Wojtek's great bluff was working. In a show of uncontrollable fury he had ripped the first bundle containing whisky out of the officer's hands. How he had managed it I did not know, nor how the bottles did not break, nor even give a suspicious clink. But the customs men had decided to abandon the search. The extremely fierce superior officer had changed his tone. Clearly satisfied, he went off in the direction of his small office with Wojtek who reappeared carrying a scrap of paper stating that the customs check had been completed. The junior officer saluted in a friendly manner, and the porters leapt forward to carry our load across no-man's-land. Now we had to go through the Pakistani customs check.

'Do you have any alcohol?' A serious question. We were entering an Islamic country.

'Alcohol? Schmalcohol!' we responded jocularly. It is important to answer very definitely. Once, at this same border crossing, a friend had unwisely admitted to having one can of beer left and was summarily ordered to pour it down a drain. A shiver went down our spines at the thought that we might have had to pour all our foreign exchange down a drain. But we were in luck. Soon we were off into Pakistan in our next hired truck. On the long monotonous journey there was time for reflection. How little is needed to become a criminal. To think that a few kilometres back I could be sitting, casually sipping a beer in a restaurant. Here public drinking was punishable by public flogging. In addition it was the time of Ramadan, and if caught eating in a public place during the day, you could be lynched.

We were off to the Gasherbrums. The expedition had not really started, but already we felt as if we were returning from a long absence. It was on the K2 and Broad Peak expedition that Wojtek and I had found four days free in which to carry out a reconnaissance of the Gasherbrums. They fascinated us. In particular we were attracted by the South-West Face of Hidden Peak (Gasherbrum I), and before leaving Islamabad had lodged an application to climb this with the Ministry of Tourism. We felt certain we could get another summit done at the same time, but we did not have the money to pay for two peaks. Now we were back in Islamabad and the first thing to do was visit the Ministry of Tourism for the promised permit. But instead of reaching for his rubber stamp or our dollars, the official asked, 'How was it, gentlemen, last year on Broad Peak? Did you get to the summit or not?'

'What summit?' We tried to make light of the situation. 'Last year you asked our expedition leader about all that and she explained . . .'

'I know. But it would be good, gentlemen, if you too could make a statement about this. On paper.'

They had us cornered. We were there to climb the Gasherbrums, but they could dig their heels in and not give us a permit. Wojtek wriggled like an eel, he talked, he explained, and finally spawned a report which satisfied them and saved us. The official, tired by the sweltering heat and the incessant hum of the great overhead fan stirring the papers on his desk, and with the prospect of a good meal at the end of a day's fast, accepted the explanations as adequate. Soon we had the permit in our pocket and were allocated a liaison officer. It was the end of May and we could start off for the mountains.

By Urdukas, at the snout of the Baltoro Glacier, we met with unseasonal snowfall. At the end of May and in early June there should not be any. But it became really wintery. The porters were not prepared for this. Most were wearing light tennis shoes, so they sat down and refused to carry on because the snow was up to their knees.

Government regulations require expeditions to provide porters with food and footwear for their journey to base camp. We had given all ours a pair of tennis shoes which many had sold straight away. How could we now, in the heart of the Karakoram, equip them with thirty pairs of winter boots? The food itself was a big enough problem. Just to feed the hard-working porters took thirty kilos of rice and flour per day. This is how even a small expedition ends up quite numerous because, for twenty people carrying equipment, six more are needed to carry their food.

Now our porters had thrown their loads down in the snow, they shouted and gesticulated. One thing was clear. At any moment we could end up on our own in that icy wilderness. If they were not prepared to carry on this could be the end of our expedition. We were still a very long way from our mountain. A day of inactivity passed.

'Listen, Wojtek,' I said, 'we have to convince them somehow. Maybe we should pay them more, or increase their rations?'

Wojtek understood the gravity of the situation, but he was thinking along different lines. 'Maybe it would be better to let them go back down, wait for a week till this winter spell is over, then come back up again? After all, they are probably very cold, we must try to understand them.'

Wojtek likes to show his kind-heartedness at the most unexpected moments, thus adding to our problems. Waiting for a week could result in us eating a lot of food destined to keep us going on the climb. Allowing the porters down for a week would be the equivalent of having to organise the walk-in all over again. No. We had to do everything to persuade them to carry on.

Wojtek offered no opposition. We paid off some of the weakest porters, the rest we tried persuading, offering them better rates. But this produced no results. A whole day of negotiation went by, another loomed. Then, like a blessing from heaven, a German expedition arrived coming down from Broad Peak. One of their members had died, so they were going home. Their liaison officer came over and, intrigued, studied our battlefield.

'We have problems,' I explained. 'We cannot, after all, force them to . . .'

'What problem? Where is the problem?' The officer was aroused. 'You pay them, so they have to do what you say. Where is your liaison officer?'

This question rather altered the direction of the conversation. Our liaison officer, a real army officer no less, had gone down two days earlier with a leg problem. To be honest, this was rather convenient from our point of view. Our plans in fact hinged on his absence, but now we had to explain the situation carefully for our, and his, benefit.

'He has gone down for health reasons.'

The officer wasted no more time and took the matter into his own hands. One shout and all the porters leapt to their feet. He talked to them and, although we did not understand a word, I am sure each one was either a whiplash or a carrot. In three days we had reached base camp.

A Swiss group was already there. We met Stefan Werner, the leader, and also Marcel Rüedi and Erhard Loretan whose names meant little to me at the time but who turned out to be leading Himalayan climbers and strong contenders in the competition to be the first to climb all fourteen 8000-metre summits. They were climbing the Gasherbrums by the normal route.

We pitched our tents and the first thing we did was start writing a letter. The more discerning reader, who has been following these memoirs carefully, and who by now understands Wojtek and me a bit better, should be able to guess why. We wanted to climb two peaks: Gasherbrum I and II. We could have asked for permission for both in Islamabad; we would certainly have been granted permission, but we would have had to pay on the nail, and this was not on. So now we played the absent-minded millionaires who had simply overlooked putting in an application for the second mountain until now we happened to notice we were beneath it. As nothing was likely to stop the Ministry giving us a permit, we would of course complete the rest of the formalities on our return to Islamabad. This was the tone of our application and we addressed the letter in the first instance to our liaison officer, who was just then in Islamabad. There was no reason why he should not give it his blessing and pass it on. We were certain this letter would reach the correct desk in the correct office in the Ministry of Tourism in good time. We were also convinced that the positive response to our application would not reach us before our departure from base camp to start our climb. The mail-runner grabbed the letter and dashed off down. At last we could start giving serious thought to the real mountain work ahead.

With the objective of Gasherbrum II firmly in mind, we began to acclimatise on 24th June with an ascent of the hitherto unclimbed Gasherbrum East (7772m). We did not have a permit for this peak either, but lying almost en route to Gasherbrum II makes it permissible. After a short rest we tackled the much bigger task of climbing Gasherbrum II by the unclimbed South-East Flank.

We did this in three days. Our first bivouac was at the Gasherbrum La, the second beneath Gasherbrum East, the third on the way down off Gasherbrum II. We returned to base uneventfully. Now we prepared ourselves for the main objective. Gasherbrum I or Hidden Peak (8068m) was waiting for us, or more precisely its South-West Face.

The Swiss had gone. A few days before we had invited them to sample a Polish feast of Silesian knuckle of pork with sauerkraut. It must have tasted good, because they repaid us royally. They had vastly overestimated the amount of food they needed and, rather than take it down and transport it back to Switzerland, they left us twelve drums, almost

Gasherburm II, a new route by the South-East Spur, 1st July, 1983

300 kilos of first-class hams, confectionery and cheeses. It seemed only yesterday, Wojtek and I had agonised over how much food to take, anxious not to spend one dollar too many. Would 100 grams of sugar a day be enough, or should we take 120? Now we could roll around in the stuff.

There were now just the two of us at base camp and once more it began to snow. It snowed for one whole day, then another. Each morning we came out of our tents, looked at the sky, and could see nothing but snow.

During this period of inactivity meals played a central role. We took turns making them, and dreaming up new dishes like chapatis and sardines with a rich Swiss cheese sauce. It snowed for five days. We

Gasherbrum I (Hidden Peak), a new route on the South-West Face,
23rd July, 1983

would eat our breakfast chapatis and talk about everything – politics, our country, our homes. We planned future expeditions in minutest detail. Then it was time for lunch. More food. We had so much of it, dried meats, bacon, chocolates, sweets.

But our hopes of climbing the mountain receded. We had calculated that in the course of fifteen days we could easily climb the mountain, get back down and break camp. Instead it was snowing. Ten days passed. The hours between meals were the most difficult. We sealed ourselves in our personal tents and read all the books we could find to the last word. We knew the instructions for erecting the tent off by heart. Wojtek was learning French, I was learning English. How long to supper?

Two weeks went by. We had said all there was to be said to each other, and had started getting in each other's way. I had to put on my anorak and go for a walk. The waiting and inactivity were crushing my spirit. I was beginning to allow myself to think we had no chance.

Once, when the sun did break through, we looked in the direction of the bowl beneath the South-West Face of Hidden Peak. To get to our face we would have to cross this bowl which is surrounded on three sides by icy slopes, down which avalanches pour every day. How much snow must have accumulated there? Would it be possible to cheat that great white mass? Then the clouds rolled back in, nothing could be seen, the snow continued.

The nights were worst. I sometimes woke with a start to find myself covered in a cold sweat because I had a recurring dream. I was crossing this bowl and, suddenly, something was flying towards me. Then I would regain my senses and go back to sleep. During the day I stopped thinking of the mountains and started thinking about home. What was happening there? I was beginning to feel homesick, yearning after a normal everyday life. I asked myself a question to which there is no answer: why is it that, when I am there, I long for the mountains and when I am here, and forced into inactivity, I long for domestic life?

Any day the porters would arrive, at the latest by 20th July. We would be packed and we would go down. The 18th passed and it snowed. On the 19th the sun appeared. The clouds and snow rolled away and vanished, the weather became so beautiful one knew immediately it was not just a short-lived spell but a longer period of settled weather.

Silently we stood and looked at that sunbathed mountain wonderland, our eyes drawn to one place, the bowl we would have to cross at the foot of the South-West Face which had swollen up with the vast amount of extra snow. Then, as we watched, from the highest point in the bowl an avalanche began, a white hell that had accumulated over twenty days on those precarious steep slopes. I had never seen so great an avalanche. It only came to a stop several kilometres away on the far side of the valley. It was a cataclysm. A great cloud of spindrift billowed high in the air. We stood dumbfounded, in awe but at the same time relieved. All that could have fallen on us. But it had gone, and it had swept the bowl clean. It would always be dangerous. But it had stopped being as dangerous as it was half an hour ago. Tomorrow we would go up.

There was just one problem. This was the day the porters were meant to arrive back at base camp. How could we inform them that we were on the mountain and tell them they should wait? They could simply come and clear away the whole of base camp, treating it as abandoned. Or they could come, decide there was nobody around, and go back down. To reorganise them would take an extra ten days at least. So how could we leave them a message? Even if any of them could read, we certainly couldn't muster any Urdu script. After some thought, we decided to draw a letter. On a big piece of paper we painted the base camp tents and, beside them, people. Above this we painted the mountain, on which we drew arrows indicating our route up and down. By the arrows we drew five moons, meaning we would be away for five nights. They should understand.

We left out the food they would need in invitingly opened drums, and a couple of hundred metres from camp buried our documents and money and a few goodies which would come in useful on the walk-out, among these the last tins of my favourite pork knuckles.

This was all a bit of a risk. We could come down from the mountain to find nothing there. We could lose our tents, all their contents and the rest of our equipment. But these would only be material losses, and risking these meant that we would not sacrifice our chance of climbing the mountain, which was, after all, why we had come there.

That night, as on every expedition, was very difficult and largely sleepless. One was adjusting this, sewing on that, checking the other for the hundredth time, only lying down at midnight to a shallow half-sleep, interrupted by nightmares, before preparing to leave well before dawn.

We set out for Hidden Peak at two a.m., running as fast as possible with our hearts in our mouths across that hellish dangerous bowl while it was still frozen. When we reached the wall, we experienced a moment of great relief. We were alive and in one piece. The snow slopes gradually steepened and became ever icier. The higher we went, the harder the ice. We reached the foot of the rock barrier where we had planned to bivouac fairly early. But how could we carve out even a small platform for our tent here? Our axes bounced off the hard ice.

'Maybe we could try getting over this barrier today?' I suggested to Wojtek, because anything seemed better and easier than pecking away at this ice.

'It looks hard, but we could try.'

He started climbing, while I belayed him from my stance attached to two ice screws. Gradually he moved up. I heard him swearing. There was nowhere to bang in a piton. I watched him struggle, trying once, twice, his calves trembling with the effort, because he had been standing on a tiny rock platform with barely the tips of his crampons supporting him for a long time. The day was drawing to an end. Wojtek left the rope in place and came down. There was nothing for it but four hours of ice cutting before we could get into our tent, which even then hung over a several hundred metre drop.

It was my turn in the morning. I quickly reclimbed the rope to Wojtek's highest piton where I could see that the only possibility of progress involved scraping all the snow and ice off the rock to search for holds and cracks. The slow work started and at last I found a mini-crack into which I hammered the smallest of my pitons. This gave me little real protection but enough psychological reassurance to tackle the next section of climbing. A few risky moves led to easier ground. I found a stance, belayed myself to the rock, then shouted to Wojtek, 'Climb when you're ready!'

That night our bivouac was at 7200 metres on a flat natural ledge on which we were able to pitch our tent in a few minutes. I brewed pot after pot of assorted drinks and served up delicacies such as bacon on dark bread. We warmed up and filled our stomachs. It was like being in God's kitchen. We fell asleep.

Wojtek started brewing again well before dawn so that we could begin climbing at first light. We were going straight up now alpine-style for the summit. But we were beaten back. The variation we were trying became impassable at a rock barrier which we could not climb at that altitude. We turned back, determined to make another attempt. But which way? Wojtek had his ideas, I had mine.

As we were abseiling down the ropes to our tent, Wojtek's crampon fell off and disappeared without trace. On an ice face one cannot play at being a stork and use one leg only. When at last we managed to get back down to the tent and settled in for the night, Wojtek came out with words I could have expected.

'The food's running out, I'm without one crampon. Enough. Tomorrow we fix the ropes and abseil down.'

I could not accept this. After those horrific twenty days waiting around, and having been so close to the summit, how could we retreat?

'Food's no problem,' I said. 'Even if it does run out, we can last one day without it. Much worse is the blasted crampon. How about if I lead? I'll cut steps in the ice where necessary, and you, well, you follow as best you can ...'

I was fully aware of the feebleness of my proposal. Nevertheless Wojtek muttered his approval, and we fell asleep.

It was still dark as we set off again. We were trying another variation, further to the right in order to get round the ugly rock barrier which had so completely stopped us yesterday. I went ahead, Wojtek climbing behind me. Effectively we had three legs. Wojtek's leg without the crampon was a considerable nuisance, making each step very difficult. Somehow by first light we had climbed 200 metres. Suddenly, I looked down and at my feet. I could not believe my eyes. Wojtek's crampon.

This was astounding. Finding a needle in a haystack would be mere child's play in comparison. Our new route had just happened to take us past the spot where his crampon had landed after falling off somewhere high above us on a different route. The recovery of the crampon raised our spirits so much that we managed the rest of the climb to the summit uneventfully, and a new route on this unclimbable face had become a reality.

It is a really elegant summit, a classic snow pyramid. I mainly remember the beautiful weather, which allowed us to sit there for almost an hour. We were well acclimatised, so we could just sit and rest, contemplating the beauty of the panorama and reliving the successful climb. I was able to take some very fine pictures. It was simply great on the summit of Hidden Peak.

We found an ice axe which I have to this day. In its place we left a piton and sling. Ten metres below the summit I dug out a rock and put it in my rucksack as a souvenir.

The descent was a comparative anticlimax, and all we were worried about now was what had happened at our base camp. Had the porters reached it or not? At the foot of the face we could see our tents in the distance, so the worst had not happened. As we got closer we saw people moving around. Phew! The porters were there. We exchanged greetings. Had they understood our letter? We gathered that they were not too sure what it all meant but had decided to wait anyway. One porter added that he had seen us on the wall through binoculars, so they knew we would be coming back. With great dignity they explained that they had not touched any of the food left for them. However, our secret cache of goodies, which we had hoped would raise our spirits on return to base, had vanished without trace.

After seven days we reached Skardu, from where a bus took us back to Islamabad. Here we met our liaison officer, and gave him an account of all we had done in the mountains. He in turn told us that he had sent on our letter to the Ministry of Tourism with a covering note. So officially it appeared that all was in order. Officially. But at the debriefing meeting with the Ministry, the officials were not satisfied with our documentation and report. They asked us to repeat all the details. We did. Then came the dreaded question.

'Why did you climb Gasherbrum II without a permit?'

'But we wrote to you about that. Surely you have our letter? We waited at base camp for your reply, but we could not sit there inactive for ever. We had to be ruled by the weather. We were sure we would obtain your permission, so we simply went up.'

'But gentlemen! You cannot *do* that!' Then, seeing that, after all, we had, they let us go and contented themselves with grilling our liaison officer. He parried all their questions with unflinching calm. Why should he not agree? Our request did not clash with anything. There was no other expedition in the area, no other expedition even contemplating going into the area. And it would be 2000 dollars more for Pakistan as soon as we returned to Poland and paid up.

The matter was not so easy for the Ministry to resolve. We were kept waiting ten days for the completion of our debriefing, without which you cannot obtain an exit visa from Pakistan. Normally it takes one day, the next day one goes for the visa and that's it.

But at last we were free to go, though given to understand that the matter was still to be cleared up with our unfortunate liaison officer. And so the whole matter somehow came to an end. Or that is how it seemed to us. Just in case, we asked the Polish Embassy in Islamabad to say a good word for us and guarantee that we would pay our dues.

We returned home with spectacular successes in an otherwise uneventful season: two new routes on two eight-thousanders, climbed by a two-man team, in pure alpine-style. It was a totally convincing vindication of the alpine-style approach, because a big traditional expedition would probably not have had the flexibility to cope with such ascents, and certainly, if a second expedition had to be mounted to climb the other eight-thousander, it would have all cost several times more.

This was the gist of our report to the GKKFiS, to which we added a request that our debt for the Gasherbrum II permit be paid off. And maybe all would have ended happily if it had not been for one dissenting voice at the meeting of the Sports Committee of the Polish Alpine Association.

'But they climbed Gasherbrum II without a permit. Now everybody will start climbing mountains without permits, and expect us to cough up the fee. Where is the money for such extra unplanned expenses to come from? There is a dangerous precedent here.'

Somehow we managed to defend ourselves. In the end, on the basis that this was really exceptional, the committee gave its verdict that, in this case, the bill was to be paid. To this day I am not sure if the decision was reached on the strength of our unquestionable sporting achievement, or for fear that the matter, if left unsettled, could cause future Polish expeditions a lot of problems in Pakistan. The most important thing was that the bill was paid.

But the matter was not allowed to drop. Next the GKKFiS got its teeth into it. Remember that all this was taking place in 1983, when the word 'permission' made people stand to attention. Added to this was the fact that Wanda Rutkiewicz's episode had not yet died down, Wanda had had problems with accounting after her women's K2 expedition. This was an example of a typical Polish absurdity. She was told by some bureaucrat to account for how she had spent several thousand dollars obtained from foreign sponsors. She replied that she had already accounted for these two years ago to her sponsors.

'But this was an official Polish expedition of the Polish Alpine Association. So we have to know where this money came from, you know, and what happened to it, you know.'

Wanda got herself involved in such a tangle of formalities as a result of this. How can one account again for what was finished and over two years ago? Especially to a jerk who always knows better.

Now Wojtek and I had come along and this same fellow, who maybe once in his life took a cog-railway ride in the Tatras to admire the view, growls at us, 'We will not overlook this. You will be punished.'

We knew that with these officials there is no joking. They punished Wanda by stopping her leaving the country for two years, this being the simplest method of repression during the state of war. We could expect the same.

Andrzej Zawada also had problems with expedition accounts. Every expedition leader does. Here is a typical situation. Some time after the expedition's return an official visits the leader and says something like, 'You took out ten tents with you, and you come back with five. Where are the others?' So the leader explains: 'One fell into a crevasse, two were swept away by an avalanche, one got torn.' But the cog-railway climber is very shocked at this.

'You can't go losing half your tents like this. What did you do with them? They should have been repaired and brought back to the country!'

He tries to explain again. 'We could, of course, have brought the torn one back to Poland, but it would have cost us four dollars per kilo for that useless rag.' But the accountants know better. Sometimes, for the sake of peace, some old rotting tent material is dug out from club stores just to shut these controllers up. It's the sort of thing one has to be prepared for all the time at the planning and at the accounting stages.

For our expedition the amount in question was two thousand dollars. We were already preparing for our next expedition, and now we were being threatened with its suspension. I have a suspicion that it was the president of the Polish Alpine Association, Andrzej Paczkowski, who somehow managed to bring reason to and pacify the GKKFiS. He suggested to them that maybe they should just withhold our Gold Medals for Outstanding Sporting Achievements and leave it at that. That sort of punishment was very popular in those days. It made an impression among the officials. But we were not stopped from going to the Himalaya.

Yet I could not help wondering which other climbers could be stopped from leaving their country. Did leaders of expeditions from the West also have their cog-railway dictators, to tell them to bring back old rags for accounting? I could just imagine, in my mind's eye, what would happen if Reinhold Messner were called to account before one of them.

67

6

A Run-Over Snake

Broad Peak via North and Middle Summits, 1984

'If we just tagged on to your K2 trip, how much would that be?'
  Stefan Werner thought for a while: 'About one thousand dollars each.'

Werner is Swiss and organises commercial trips to the Himalaya. Clearly he understands the value of money; he must have been giving us a discount. Lightning mental computer calculations ensued, translating dollars into Swiss francs into złotys, plus a mental picture of all the ghastly rushing around which is involved during the organisation of any trip. There could be only one answer.

'We're coming. Put our names down.'

The Swiss conditions were unusually attractive. Wojtek and I would have had to pay out that sum of money just to get a permit, for which we would have had to wait for heaven knows how long. All we would have to buy were a few things still available at home for złotys and then make our way to meet Werner in Islamabad. Another big plus was that Werner did not mind at all what we would be doing in the mountains, for Wojtek and I were determined to continue operating as a pair. Janusz Majer from Katowice was also planning an expedition to the same area. Four of them were off to Broad Peak. So we decided to join forces for the basic preparations. A joint effort would be much easier.

But nothing was ever easy when preparing for expeditions in Poland, especially as there were shortages of everything and in particular meat. Here one interview has etched itself indelibly into my memory which occurred in a Very Important Office, and upon which rested the permission to buy extra meat supplies. After a long battle at the entrance I eventually found myself in the presence of The Director who, lounging

68

behind his desk, greeted me curtly with, 'And so what exactly is all this about?'

So I, respecting the time and the pressure of work the Director-Upon-Whom-All-Depended was under, stated my case succinctly.

'We are soon to go on an expedition to the Himalaya. We have to take meat. We are unable to obtain the amount we need against the expedition members' ration cards. So we are counting on your office considering our request favourably, as you have done in the past.'

As I was speaking I could see something unpleasant happening to The Very Important Director. He frowned and did not even allow me to finish what I was saying.

'Well! It is high time to put an end to this. When I want to go for a trip into the mountains, I save my ration cards for a whole year and then I go and buy my canned meat supplies. And you come here asking for some special allocation!'

And he simply threw me out of his office, where I had to reappraise the situation fast, because without that meat there was no way we could depart for Pakistan. Writing off the director, I decided to try to sort out something with the lady who wrote out all the special allocations. The next day I paid her a visit with chocolates, flowers, a souvenir pennon from our club, and a request for her to understand that this was not just a trip, not just my holiday, but something really important.

'Leave it with me,' she said. 'I'll fix it somehow.'

How she did it I don't know. Maybe she buried our authorisation in the middle of a fat pile of requests for the director's Very Important Signature? It does not really matter, the main thing was that it was done.

Our equipment set off in a Mercedes 506 truck. For a few dollars a day and a chance to see the Baltoro Glacier, its owners, Rysiek Warecki and Tomek Świątkowski, undertook to transport our equipment as far as humanly possible. Everything went like clockwork. We flew in to Islamabad, a day later Rysiek and Tomek arrived behind the wheel of their Merc. Stefan Werner was already there. Then came an unpleasant surprise.

The Ministry of Tourism simply would not agree to our names being added to the Swiss expedition list. Could it have been anything to do with our climbing Gasherbrum II on tick the year before? I suspect however that the real reason was far more basic. There was an increasing pressure against international expeditions, and against adding in extra individuals onto expedition lists. A climber would arrive with one expedition and then transfer himself to another and thus end up climbing two peaks in one year. This went against the interests of Pakistan. In Islamabad they naturally preferred that for every summit climbed there was a completely separate expedition organised, which paid for a separate permit, for its handling agent, its porters and so on. This was hardly surprising. Pakistan is not a rich country.

Neither Werner nor we could do anything about getting us on his K2 expedition. But we did have a permit for Gasherbrum IV and, as a sop, we were granted permission for Broad Peak under Janusz Majer's permit. So we just changed teams.

This was not what I had hoped for. I had climbed Broad Peak already, admittedly only by the normal route, and strictly unofficially, but I had done it. At least this time I would be legal and could attempt a new route, maybe a traverse of all the summits. Anyway we would start on Broad Peak and then move on to Gasherbrum IV.

Gasherbrum IV is 'only' 7920 metres high, so it is not an eight-thousander and it was not going to count towards the collection of all fourteen eight-thousanders which I now had in my sights. But it does attract everybody, like a magnet, towards its beautiful, famous and hitherto unclimbed shining face, soaring skywards not far from Concordia, and passed by every expedition bound for K2 and the Gasherbrums. From the moment I first saw it it gave me no peace. Wojtek and I decided we had to try it after Broad Peak.

But first there was the journey to base camp, and a last-minute change of plan as Rysiek and Tomek announced that they had to go back home but would return to collect our equipment after the expedition and take it back to Poland as agreed. This put us in a bit of a spot. It is 600 kilometres from Islamabad just to Skardu. Now we either had to hire a Pakistani vehicle at great expense, or drive the Merc ourselves. Luckily one of our party, an Austrian, Edek Westerlund, had a commercial vehicle driving licence. We left Islamabad at 4 p.m. and drove all night. Up to 4 a.m. I was driving, then Edek took over while I scrambled onto the luggage and managed to get a few hours' sleep. At 8 a.m. I was driving again. The local people drove in a spine-chilling manner, and the road was nightmarish and exhausting, on one side the mountain, on the other a 200-metre precipice with a mountain torrent at the bottom. It was called the Karakoram Highway but, stuck behind the wheel, we were in no mood for jokes.

I drove accidentally over a snake sliding across the road; I grimaced and wondered if it was a bad omen, like seeing a black cat crossing the road is in Poland.

I got my answer 150 kilometres from Skardu. The road was blocked by an avalanche which might take four days to clear, so I turned the vehicle round and we headed off for the nearest town, Gilgit, forty miles away.

Leaving those tiring mountain hairpins, we found ourselves in a totally different country, a green valley through which the last few kilometres of road led dead straight towards the town. I relaxed, driving down the centre of the narrow strip of asphalt. Our vehicle felt slightly overloaded, but off the Karakoram Highway hairpins this did not matter. Only now and again a small stream bed was crossed by a narrower bridge which required care. I drove onto one of these and routinely turned the wheel slightly right to gain the middle of the road. Suddenly, my hair was standing on end. The vehicle had not responded to my adjustment.

Everything took place in fractions of a second. One wheel hit the side barrier of the bridge, knocking the steering wheel out of my hand. We were going straight into the ditch. Luckily on its far side was a steep slope which the vehicle ground into. I braced myself in the driver's seat and got away unharmed. Rysiek Pawłowski, who was dozing beside me, regained the maximum control of his senses in an instant as he flew out of the window, carried out a classical judo fall, and somersaulted to his feet, a bit bruised but otherwise in one piece. But how about the others? I had a nightmarish vision of what could have happened if the heavily packed rear compartment were to break through the flimsy wooded partition and hurl our equipment onto our sleeping companions. But voices full of protest and indignation reassured me as one by one they clambered out.

The vehicle was not so well off. At a first glance it appeared fit only for the scrap heap. In Gilgit we took stock of our situation. Luckily Gilgit was where Sher Khan lived, a first-class Pakistani climber who had accompanied several Polish expeditions. His father was a retired air force group captain who sat on the local council and had wide ranging powers. It was Mr Sher Khan senior who hired a crane from the local army unit which dragged our wreck out of the ditch and towed it to the town. It was he who discovered a 'workshop' whose owner promised to take care of our wreck. And so our Merc found itself in the 'workshop', in other words in the centre of an oil and grease-stained courtyard, where two men stood, one with a hammer and the other with two spanners, telling us with total conviction that our vehicle could be salvaged.

'It will be done,' murmured one calmly. 'We will just need a few parts.'

They had two months to do the job, while we were off climbing. Edek Westerrund was soon to return to Austria and promised to send what was required from there. We sat down to compose a telex to Rysiek and Tomek in such a way as not to shock them but at the same time to request them to come and help with the repair work and decide the future of the wreck. It was after all their vehicle. Only yesterday we had been close to selling it as scrap metal, but now we were beginning to believe the owner of the workshop. Let him have a go at repairing it. And so the problem was not so much solved as postponed.

To get to the mountains we needed another vehicle. That cost money. A lot. We should have to cut down our equipment to a bare minimum. Having our own truck we had not thought too much about load limits, which meant we took a lot. But not everything was essential, so we set about a thorough re-packing and selection process, cutting everything down to a bare minimum – food, tents and sleeping bags, as well as climbing equipment. And because we would need funds to hire another truck and also to pay the mechanics for the resuscitation of our Merc, all the things we did not need we sold. We became an instant bazaar, selling pots and pans, mess tins, sleeping bags, everything. It was beginning to get alarmingly out of control. One man came up and said, 'I hear you have some things to sell. Show me them.'

So we showed him some things, but he was not interested in any of that because he had just noticed our soap. He grabbed the soap and stuffed some rupees into our hands. People arrived in throngs and jostled round. Our crowd situation was rapidly becoming illegal. You're not allowed to trade anywhere you want to in the streets. We were petrified that sooner or later the police would roll up. At last however everything was sold, the bazaar was closed down and we set off for the mountains.

Wojtek and I set up our base camp beneath the South Ridge of Broad Peak. Broad Peak was one of those mountains on which the only route climbed was still that of the first ascentionists. This was of no interest to us as we had already climbed it. Our plan was to carry out a traverse of all the summits, starting with the hitherto unclimbed South Ridge. Starting this fine route by the South Ridge was the great attraction, and we examined it carefully from our tents, seeking out the best way of tackling it. From a distance it all looked attractive but rather unclear. A little dip, a ridge, a wall, a little saddle and so on. It was high time to see what it really looked like from close up.

The first reconnaissance trip was like pouring a bucket of cold water over our enthusiastic heads. From the word go we had to put up fixed lines and use ropes to secure ourselves. On our next attempt we decided to bivouac on a steep icefield. It got dark, we cooked some food, guzzled it ravenously, then shifted into our corners of the tent inside our sleeping bags.

As we did so something began to drum against the tent sheets, innocently at first, as if someone had tossed a handful of rice against our

Broad Peak
1 The normal route by the West Spur, 1982
2 Traverse via the North and Middle Summits, 1984

tent. Instinctively we snuggled up to the side walls, turning our backs to the intrusion as if to hide ourselves away. After a few moments we felt the rice becoming bigger and there was more of it. There followed two dull thuds. Then nothing. Silence. I opened my eyes, which I had instinctively closed. So did Wojtek, and we discovered stars above us. Our tent had been ripped open. In its centre, exactly where a few moments ago I had been squatting cooking, lay two big rocks the size of a human head.

Quite an experience. What were we to do? Where could we run? It was night, and we were stuck in the middle of a fifty-degree ice slope. While it was still light we had decided that this was the best spot and spent three hours hacking at the ice to make a platform for the tent. There was no alternative. After crawling around hopelessly for a bit among the remnants of our tent in the darkness and frost, I said, 'Ah well, a bomb rarely hits the same crater twice. Let's try and stick it out.'

Wojtek did not answer. We wriggled back into our sleeping bags and, in our original positions, sat it out till the morning. But that night we not only lost our tent but also our spirit. We had to get back down to base camp. After all, we no longer had a roof over our heads.

On our next attempt we reached a height of 6200 metres, where we

73

were halted by a very steep ice slope, so hard that, even with crampons, it was difficult to find purchase. Things were becoming disheartening and Wojtek laid out the alternatives as he saw them. Starting the traverse of Broad Peak by this route was a bit too hard. We could of course climb the South Ridge as an end in itself, climbing on to the main summit and finishing there. But if we still wanted to do the traverse, the summit would only be the halfway point.

As he spoke I got the feeling he had lost enthusiasm for our original plan, and for this ridge in particular, and what he said next confirmed this.

'Let's start from the North Face. The traverse is, after all, more important than this route.'

I was of a different opinion but said little. We descended in silence. In base camp we began thinking things over again from the beginning. It took a long time, because I found it terribly hard to accept any change of the original plan. Wojtek's arguments failed to convince me, I could not part just like that with the South Ridge which is such a beautiful sporting challenge. We must have talked for two days. Then Wojtek simply dug himself in. Any further reasoning did not reach him. In the end, very unwillingly, I burst out, 'If we are sentenced to each other, then have it your way! Let us go from the north side. We must do something.'

We set off. It took us five days altogether. The first and northernmost summit did not give in easily, we were met with some very difficult climbing. The central peak was easier, and we completed the project without encountering any further problems. We were perfectly acclimatised, thanks to our abortive struggles during the reconnaissance of the South Ridge. Wojtek was right, the traverse from the north side was easier. But how beautiful it could have been if we had started it from the south.

We began our descent from the summit, happy and relaxed, by the fairly straightforward normal route, on which we found many traces of an Italian expedition and Janusz Majer's group. Traversing above their Camp II at 6400 metres, I lost sight of Wojtek. I stopped and waited. Minutes went by, a quarter of an hour, he had vanished. What had happened? Wojtek was not a person to hang around.

He appeared just as I was about to start back up to look for him. His eyes were still bulging with fright. When he had calmed down, he told me how he had come across a fixed line, which he'd held onto for extra balance. It was old, it had been hanging from a piton for a long time and it broke. Wojtek had started sliding down an icy slope, he tried to save himself but his crampons just scraped against the hard icy surface.

With a final effort he managed to dig them in and stop just above a vertical drop.

The finger of God demands care in the mountains to the very last moment. I remembered the snake run over on the road, and then the refusal of permission for K2, the lorry crash, now Wojtek's narrow escape.

Completing the traverse of Broad Peak was only half of our plan. Now Gasherbrum IV awaited us and its famous shining wall. For many years it had been a climber's dream, but one synonymous with impossibility. It attracts the eye like a beautiful girl, but just one glance also brings the realisation that it must be desperately hard, that nowhere in that wall of ice and rock is there an easy section. No one was willing to predict when and by whom it would be mastered. When I saw it for the first time my instinctive reaction was that it was unclimbable.

Later, when I had passed below it a couple more times, I began to examine those 3000 metres of rock and ice more confidently and see that maybe there was a chance. It took me a long time to begin contemplating its ascent, Wojtek spent a long time talking me into it. The Shining One is, after all, quite a shining undertaking, which gives no peace of mind. The day came at last when I told myself I could see a possibility. That couloir led up very high, it could be climbed quite quickly on ice, then a 200-metre steep rock wall, but after that the angle lay back. I had the route firmly engraved in my mind. I believed in it.

Now we were ready, after a few days' rest, with our rucksacks packed for five days of climbing. We had eight hours to go from base camp to the foot of the wall. The sun shone, the weather seemed fine, but maybe not settled. For a few days now the clouds had built up to raise the question: would the weather break? But how long can one wait? One morning we simply decided to set off.

As we approached the shining wall it seemed to grow, and grow . . . I noticed a change coming over Wojtek; he slowed down. He said nothing, but I sensed that something had happened to him. Then he sat down.

'Do you know what? To hell with this. I'm not happy about this wall. And this weather . . . Let's go home.'

I was furious. After all he had done to convince me over the years, that he should be the one to back off now.

'Wojtek! Fine, we go back,' I exploded. 'But I do feel that we need to get a rest from one another.'

We returned to base camp. It was the end of the expedition. Janusz Majer, Krzysiek Wielicki, Rysiek Pawłowski and Walenty Fiut had ascended Broad Peak as a group of four by the normal route, thereby achieving their target. Krzysiek Wielicki had also created another record. He had climbed and descended Broad Peak, a mountain of over 8000 metres, in a mere twenty-three hours. That was not climbing but running. Phenomenal!

We prepared to walk out. For the first time in my life I felt an urgent need for solitude and decided to spend some time in the mountains alone. Wojtek probably had similar thoughts. He set off somewhere to the right. I started walking ahead. I chose a seldom used route in the region of the Masherbrum Glacier, hoping to reach the Masherbrum La and from there take a shorter route through the villages back to Skardu.

I did not imagine that during my solitary walk I would experience so much. First of all I was unable to walk past Biarchedi, not very high, about 6700 metres, but a virgin summit and just a one-day detour from my route, 'and then it will be off my mind'. And so it was. Being completely alone, I experienced the mountains completely differently. Lacking a companion, I talked to myself and to the mountains. I felt a part of this great world. But most important, I was doing what I wanted to do.

After climbing another mountain, I turned my attention towards the Masherbrum La. Maps of the region are rather inaccurate, some parts of the Karakoram being hardly known to this day. As a rule one seeks as much information as possible from the local people. So before leaving, I had asked our cook about this route. He said he had been on this pass once and assured me with great conviction, 'You can take a rope with you just in case, but at most ten metres. There is a small step. But nothing serious.'

However, I found myself in such a labyrinth of crevasses and séracs that I wandered around in them for a whole blessed day, my heart in my mouth. I could not get down, I could not retreat. Crossing crevasses is not really such a great problem if there are two of you. One holds the rope, the other jumps or lowers himself down. But I was on my own. If I decided to jump I had to be sure to reach the other side. If I lowered myself into a crevasse, I must be certain I could get myself out of it again.

That pass took a lot out of me. When at last I dragged myself out of the maze of crevasses and séracs, I found myself looking down the snout of the glacier. Quite often a glacier creates a slight terminal or lateral moraine behind which there is a little patch of green grass and flowers, even at 4000 metres. That is what I saw. After two months in the Karakoram, where there is only ice, snow, or black rocks, where one forgets that a world of colours other than white, black and grey exists, that greenness shook me.

But between me and that green paradise was a labyrinth of ice blocks, many the size of a house. Here a great block hung over you, there was a yawning crevasse. And it was getting dark, and I was on my own, my heart pounding, knowing full well that any instant one of the elements of this jumble could collapse. But I was inching closer to the bottom of the icefall. Then a bit further was that glowing greenness. But a fifteen-metre wall separated me from it, down which I could not climb – full stop. I looked for a way round. There was none. But the cook had said ten metres of rope was enough.

I swear if I should ever meet that cook again, I will tell him very clearly what I think about his knowledge of the area. But this did not help my present position. I decided to put in an ice screw. I attached one end of the rope, the other swung five metres above the ground below.

Jump?

Five metres is at least a first-floor window. Even if I managed to land without twisting or breaking something, there was still another unknown – what I would be jumping onto. All I could see from above was a jumble of ice, stones, dirt and snow. Underneath all that could be a crevasse. But I could see no possible alternative. First I dropped my rucksack which landed with a dull thud. Then I threw down all other heavy items before putting on my abseiler and very slowly letting myself down the full length of the rope. The moment so beloved of cheap action films arrived. I let go the rope, still clutching tightly onto my ice axe. I was falling. My cramponed feet hit the icy ledge, luckily there was no hidden crevasse. It was solid. I stuck in my ice axe and knew that I was back on all fours again. Slowly I gathered up my things and put on my sack.

I did not ever want to repeat such a jump. But in a few seconds I would receive my prize – the meadow. It was as if I had carried out a jump into paradise. I lay down on the green turf, and closed my eyes in ecstasy, I felt as if I had come into a world of eternal, glorious spring, which I had reached from another planet. I lay on my back in the grass and a feeling of well-being spread through me. Then I pitched my tent and got into my sleeping bag. Such moments are worthy of the greatest effort, the greatest risks and the greatest hardships.

But such wonderful moments do not last for ever. In the morning I folded up my tent and carried on down. After a full day's walk I reached the first shepherds' village. The people living in their crude mud huts in that remote corner of the Karakoram were content to live on what their work provided. They had grown used to a landscape unchanged in a thousand years. Now, from the glacier above, a stranger had walked down the rocky path into the centre of their village. I was surrounded by the dirty faces of women and children, looking at me first with fear, then with curiosity. I spoke and smiled, but I was unable to communicate. I made gestures which anywhere in the world mean food and drink. At last they brought a clay pot full of sour milk. I drank every drop of it. I sat for a few minutes, gave the children some sweets and then continued on my way.

After a few more hours I reached a rather more civilised village which a jeep called at once a week. Passing by the school I was stopped by the teacher.

'Come, you will sleep with me.'

At last I could speak to somebody. My kind host plied me with the same question all the time.

'Where have you come from? Why are you on your own? Where are your friends?'

'I have come across the Masherbrum La. I am on my own,' I replied patiently.

'But how? Where are the others?'

'There are no others. I came on my own . . .'

'But that is impossible.' The teacher was adamant. 'Only once before have people crossed that pass, five years ago, but that was a group of American climbers. Apart from them, no one ever has managed to get over that pass.'

I gave up. He still didn't believe me. But his incredulity gave me a deep satisfaction. By accident I had achieved something which was probably as hard as the traverse of Broad Peak.

I decided against waiting for a week on the chance that the jeep should arrive, I said goodbye to my hospitable, but to the last moment unbelieving, teacher and set off walking down green valleys. It was hot, but a pleasant heat only encountered at altitudes of 2000–3000 metres. All along the road there were apricot trees. I stuffed myself with them. I could not hide my sheer joy in the simple fact of being, in knowing that the world can be wonderful because of its greenness and flowers, and that one can have a full stomach. Then I was brought down to earth again.

In Skardu I met Wojtek. In Gilgit we found the truck beaten back into shape, welded, standing on its own wheels . . . but still not working. The new parts had not arrived, there had been no acknowledgement of our telexes from its owners. I supposed that Tomek and Rysiek back home bore a grudge against me for having smashed up their vehicle.

We also bore them one for not having completed their original contract. But the strained atmosphere was not going to be helped by the fact that for two months we had received no sort of a reply from them, not even the proverbial 'kiss my arse'. Nothing.

We eventually received permission from the Pakistani authorities to sell the wreck. To the money thus obtained Wojtek and I added a further 700 dollars and the owners of our unfortunate Merc, which I had driven over the snake on the road to Skardu, somehow forgave us.

Despite the great success of the traverse of Broad Peak, the season did not leave me completely satisfied. As well as the business with the truck and the loss of equipment, there was the uncompleted mountain programme and disagreements with partners whom I have always considered friends. It was also a lost season from the point of view of my 8000-metre peak collecting programme. All that created a depressing mood. It would be necessary to start all over again.

'There are two winter expeditions to the Himalaya being organised from here. What do you say to that?' I asked Wojtek.

'I'm not interested in winter expeditions,' he answered.

'It's a chance of doing two summits in one winter season.' These were Dhaulagiri and Cho Oyu.

'Rubbish! Impossible. There's not enough time, it's madness,' retorted Wojtek.

'But such madness could turn out very well,' I suggested hopefully.

'In that case we must go our own ways.'

'You know what? Maybe we should indeed part company for the time being. You go your way, I'll go mine.'

And that was how the 1984 season finished.

7

8167 Metres of Snow and Mists

I rang the bell at the familiar front door and thought how little had changed since I had stood there a few years ago, ready to make my proposal of marriage, armed with a bottle for my prospective father-in-law, flowers for my mother-in-law, chocolates for her sister. They welcomed me in heartily. Just like then. But now I had come about a very different matter.

'How is Celina?' they asked.

'She's in hospital. The doctor says that everything is fine. Any day now she should be giving birth. She's feeling fine.'

Our second child was due and because of this my plans had become complicated, and I needed to ask a special favour of my in-laws before I talked to Celina. I had the chance to go on another expedition. But I had only got back in September, in October the new baby was due, and in November I wanted to be off again. I would be unable to help my wife in those first and most difficult months of motherhood. For the first time I would not be at home for Christmas. Up till now I had taken part in one expedition a year, now it was a chance to make it two. My mother had already promised me her help, but without my in-laws' understanding, the whole thing would fall through. My mother- and father-in-law helped so much with our children that I just could not imagine leaving Celina without their support. So they had become the key figures in my future Himalayan plans. Everything depended on what they said. And they said, 'If it really is so important to you, then go. We will talk to Celina . . .' From that day, whenever I hear jokes about in-laws I refuse to join in the laughter.

On 26th October my second son, Wojtek, was born. From the first moment of his life he was radiantly happy. When I bathed him he smiled blissfully. The domestic atmosphere was so peaceful that broaching the serious conversation with Celina became a mere formality. She agreed, knowing she could count on her parents. As for me, any feeling of guilt about the desertion of my fatherly duties evaporated as I launched myself into a whirl of preparations.

In the club I kept my cards close to my chest till the very last moment. Why give the sceptics ammunition against me? I was, as they say, trying to play on two pianos. Andrzej Zawada, leading the winter Cho Oyu expedition, suspected I was up to something but offered no comment. Adam Bilczewski, leading the winter Dhaulagiri expedition, had not crossed my name off of the expedition members list, but I saw that he was not counting on me too much. They were already packing and due to send off their equipment at the beginning of November. When I arrived in Gliwice, at the last minute, with my two drums of equipment, I had the feeling that they were not treating my participation too seriously. They did not say so, but there are times when words are not needed. True, I had failed to put in the traditional contribution to this expedition, both on the chimneys to raise funds and in the organising. I just had not had the time. My club's contribution was to cover all my złoty-expenses and my air ticket. All foreign exchange expenses I had undertaken to cover myself. Though this arrangement was a bit unorthodox, I felt it was fair. A week later I telephoned Gliwice and found out that the luggage had gone and that only two drums were left behind. Mine. They had had trouble fitting everything into the vehicle, I was told, so the simplest solution had been: 'Well, he won't be going anyway, we can leave his stuff without worrying.' So there I was, left with my two drums, alone, in Silesia. This made me even more stubborn. I sent a very definite message to Adam Bilczewski: 'Please do not cross my name off the expedition list when you are in Nepal. I will join you. I am serious.' And from that moment I threw myself into the preparations for Andrzej Zawada's expedition to Cho Oyu.

At breakfast in Kathmandu I put my cards on the table. I explained that what I really wanted to do that winter was attack two 8000-metre summits, Dhaulagiri and Cho Oyu. But Dhaulagiri had to come first because the lads were already there, established at the base of the mountain. If I went on with Andrzej Zawada's team to climb Cho Oyu and then tried to join the Dhaulagiri trip I would simply be too late.

The breakfast table went quiet. I detected that this did not bode well for me. Then came an outburst, most of it critical.

'You must realise,' Zyga Heinrich said, 'that this will be a serious blow to *our* expedition strength. You know that we have a very hard route ahead of us, and now, right at the beginning, you are withdrawing your assistance from the hardest work, that of establishing the route. I don't want to flatter you, but we were counting on your help. Now you simply want to join us later, which probably won't work out anyway. In my opinion you are just creating problems which will go against the best interests of our expedition.'

The Canadians, who were part of the expedition were against the idea too. Others just shrugged. Oh, let him go, no problem. Andrzej Zawada, on whose agreement I was counting, listened and hardly contributed anything to the discussion until the following day, again at breakfast, he said, 'As to Jurek's idea, I've made up my mind. He can go to Dhaulagiri. We'll wait for you at Cho Oyu. It is a great idea, rather wild. But it might come-off.'

I beamed at Andrzej with gratitude.

The following day I packed the minimum of personal equipment, which still worked out to be around forty kilos, and set off by bus to Pokhara. I was a man in a hurry, which is not easy in Nepal in winter. I had planned a route to the Dhaulagiri base camp which was both expensive and risky, but if it worked would halve my travelling time. The risks concerned a flight in a twenty-seater Fokker which could only take off in perfect conditions, and the crossing on foot of two very high passes. The normal approach to Dhaulagiri is from the Mayangdi valley, but this would take much longer.

I arrived in Pokhara, bought a ticket and waited for the plane. I waited all day, the flight had been cancelled. A second day, cancelled. The third day I actually got to sit in the airplane before the flight was cancelled. I was beginning to worry. I had left Kathmandu on 20th December, it was now Christmas Eve and I was still stuck down here, far from the mountains.

Pokhara is the second largest town in Nepal. At the height of the season it is teeming with tourists, but in winter the little hotels are empty and the streets quiet, resting after the international summer invasion. To pass the time I hired a bike and spent all day exploring around the picturesque lake, near the town and admiring the view of the south side of Annapurna and Machhapuchhare. The snowy summits were as clearly laid out as if they could be touched. But they were far away, waiting, and I did not even know how one would approach them. The weather reminded me of a Polish September, but the evenings were cold, and the hotels where one paid a dollar a night were made of rocks stuck together with clay, with cubicles reminiscent of our old Silesian pigsties. In the rooms there were a bed of boards and a table. Nothing else.

This is where I was to spend my Christmas Eve, the most important of Polish family celebrations. I bought a few exotic fruits, opened a can of sardines and, instead of the traditional prune soup, boiled up some *barszcz* from a packet.

I had brought a Bible with me and the consecrated wafer which on Christmas Eve we Poles share within the family with mutual wishes of health and happiness. But in Pokhara there was no one to share it with. As I lit the candle I felt very sad at the first Christmas Eve I could remember spending away from home. A sip of the local spirit did not ease my sadness. I cannot hide it, I was very close to tears.

At five o'clock next morning I repacked my rucksack and my so-called hand luggage which had all my ice axes, crampons and carabiners in it, and while it was still dark I took everything over to the airport again. My baggage was checked-in, again I pretended that my hand luggage was featherweight, they wrote out my ticket and smiled. After all we were now old friends. Then the waiting began. I could hear them contacting the other airfield to enquire about conditions, then they put down the receiver and cancelled the flight again. I picked up my things and returned to the hotel. I had another day ahead of me.

By Boxing Day when I arrived with my luggage at the airport, I was convinced of the futility of the whole project. Then a miracle occurred. We took off! The flight took us up the throat of a long valley entirely surrounded by mountains, and our pilot had to execute some horrific manoeuvres into a head wind. Now I understood the reason for the delays. As the aircraft was thrown violently around, I decided this was the last time that I'd take a flight like that. I regretted not having started walking straight away. In those five days spent in Pokhara I could have reached my destination – and arrived in one piece. Whereas up there, no point in mincing words, it was hell. Apart from myself there were two tourists, an American soldier on leave, and some local people with laden baskets and live geese under their arms. During that nightmare flight their expressions mirrored mine. I got out of that plane on trembling legs, looking towards the pilot's cabin with the greatest of thankfulness. I felt like kissing the ground, but decided instead to find myself a porter.

I needed someone who knew the way, was not frightened of the mountains in winter, and who would not demand a small fortune for his services. I was not too worried about competition, I was sure to be the only one who wanted to go into the mountains at that time of the year, but it took two hours before a young boy was brought to me, who claimed not only to be a porter, but also a guide and if required he could cook as well. What is more, he knew the route I proposed to take. Ideal.

Without argument I accepted his conditions of pay which were twice the normal summer rate of pay. We set off, he carrying on his back a 25 kilo rucksack, I a 15 kilo one.

The first day all went well, we reached the last of the pastures at Tukuche, heading for the high Dambush Pass and the French Col. The first night in the tent was still below the snow line, but it was already very cold. I gave my porter food and the stove, but as I lay out my sleeping bag watching him out of the corner of my eye, I realised that if we continued like this we were not going to have enough to eat. With difficulty he made some tea, of which he was very proud. But, to hell with it, I took over the cooking. After all he was there to carry my things and lead the way.

The next day we reached the snow line. The two passes we were making for were at about 5350 metres, in other words high. It was now that I noticed with concern that my porter was dropping behind. I tried to set a steady, not-too-fast pace, but the distance between us grew. I waited for him and asked where the route went. He seemed a bit confused. It was a long time since he'd been here . . .

There remained nothing for it but to pull out the map that I did not trust anyway. The local tourist maps, to put it politely, are rather inaccurate. The situation was becoming serious. I was condemned to lead in that white wilderness, dragging along my porter in a not too clearly defined direction.

Another bivouac, this time in the snow, completely freed me of any delusions. As soon as I had erected the tent, my porter crawled into his sleeping bag and he was no longer capable of doing anything more. I had to feed him and look after him like a child.

The next day it got worse. We crossed the Dambush Pass and headed for the French Col, with me in front in the role of a snow plough, clearing the way. But still my partner kept falling behind. I repacked our loads, so that I was carrying much more than he. Step after step, counting them as if ascending an 8000-metre peak, we moved forward. But was it in the right direction? The word pass is rather confusing. This was not like a normal pass between two mountains, more a two kilometre-wide snowy wasteland. But we reached the French Col eventually and got onto the glacier on which the Dhaulagiri expedition base camp was located.

The glacier is three, sometimes four, kilometres wide, with great mounds of ice rising up, and wide crevasses cutting across it. Locating the camp in such terrain was not going to be easy. Wherever one looked all one saw was a white jumble. I began steering by instinct and by thinking where I would have set up a base camp, had I arrived in this glacial wilderness. I came upon a Polish tin can. Could that mean they had already finished their assault, packed up their things and gone back down? They had, after all, been here since the beginning of December and they were good climbers. What was I to do now? I wandered around ever more helplessly among the ice jumble, my porter following me.

Just then from a dip in the icy masses two figures appeared in the distance whom I recognised as Janusz Skorek and Andrzej Czok. I did not shout, jump for joy or wave my arms about, instead I just sat down and waited. When they were two metres away I jumped up and shouted out, 'Passport control! Do you have permits?' in the Slovak of the border guards of our Tatra neighbours. They stood as if turned to stone, completely stunned, until they saw who it was and we greeted each other heartily.

'Wonderful. If you're here, we won't go up the hill. Let's go back to base camp!'

It was what I wanted to hear. They hadn't yet climbed Dhaulagiri. My final worries evaporated. They had managed, they told me, only to establish the second camp. There was a lot of hard work still to do; they needed manpower, and were very happy that I had turned up.

Behind me still dragged my completely ruined 'guide'. That same day I sent him off down, suggesting he returned by the normal route which, although it was longer, did not lead over any passes with which he could not cope alone. I gave him some baksheesh, and watched with relief as he ran off, visibly happy that his little trip was over.

Advance base camp was only twenty metres away but I could easily have missed it because it was placed hard up against a great rock. Base camp was much further down in the woods. As they had set it up, there had been an avalanche above and the associated gust of wind had blown down all their tents. So the majority of the porters, who were meant to continue up higher, had categorically refused to go any further. Now they were still ferrying some of the equipment up to this great rock. Here it was quite safe, the glacier was wide and it was a long way to any steeper snow slope.

They had managed to establish one higher camp, above the North-East Col on the normal route. Nobody talked about the original plan of climbing a new route. I was not in a position to say anything, I just got stuck in to the work. They had not got all that high. The col, above which the climbing starts, was only at 5700 metres.

The next day was New Year's Eve. I had decided that it should be a rest day. The nights were cold, so cold that our New Year's Eve Ball only lasted a couple of hours. We reminisced, and I became rather sentimental, remembering the New Year's Eves at Istebna where I was

Dhaulagiri, first winter ascent of North-East Spur, 21 January, 1985

brought up and where traditionally we always went to greet the New Year. The last time, Andrzej Czok and Janusz Skorek had been there with me. These club events often turned out to be quite well supported and sometimes as many as twenty people would be living it up in one shepherd's hut. We would organise sleigh rides and fire rockets. We always greeted the New Year outside the hut.

Lying here with ice beneath me, there was no need to go outside. In fact we all felt so sad and cold we did not manage to wait up till midnight before crawling into our sleeping bags.

On 2nd January I set off for the mountains with Andrzej and Janusz. I was a bit worried about my acclimatisation. They had already been there three weeks, I had only spent a short time crossing a pass of barely 5350 metres. But I felt good for the time being and I kept up with them. Friends with previous winter experience on Everest had assured me there was almost no snowfall in winter, that the main problem was diamond-hard ice exposed by the wind. But on Dhaulagiri the problems were quite different. Yes, there was a strong wind, but it was accompanied by uninterrupted snowfall. Everywhere there was masses of the stuff. We only reached Camp 2 at midnight, as the fresh snowfall made it difficult to find. The next day we wanted to get a bit higher but the weather broke, with snow, mist and a blustery wind. We were to discover

Just below the summit of Makalu, 1981. After the Polish team gave up on the West Face,
Kukuczka soloed a new route by the Makalu La and the North-West Ridge.

Left, Kukuczka setting out for Everest in 1980, and above right, with Andrzej Czok (drinking) after their ascent of a new route on the South Face; below, east meets west at Makalu base camp in 1981: Alex MacIntyre (left), Kukuczka (centre), Reinhold Messner and Doug Scott.

Three formidable challenges: Gasherbrum IV from the Baltoro Glacier, above left, and, above right, the sheer South Face of Lhotse. Kukuczka reached 7800 metres in 1985, but was to fall to his death on a second attempt four years later. Below, a new route on the South-East Pillar of Nanga Parbat, which he considered the most difficult and dangerous of his climbs.

Camp 3 on Nanga Parbat above the deadly avalanche runnels became advance base camp for the assault on the summit.

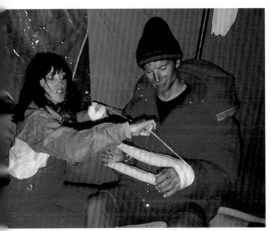

Base camp life: above, with climbing film-
makers Kurt Diemberger and Julie Tullis,
Broad Peak, 1984; left, finding a use for men:
Wojtek Kurtyka obliges Danuta Wach
of the women's K2 expedition led by
Wanda Rutkiewicz. Kurtyka and
Kukuczka made an unauthorised ascent
of Broad Peak to acclimatise for their
own first attempt on K2's South Face.
Below, Pankiewicz and Probulski at the
Kangchenjunga base camp, winter 1986.

Above left, Kurtyka on the South Face of K2 in 1982 with Gasherbrum I and Broad Peak beyond; above right, Tadeusz Piotrowski on the South Face in 1986. After making an impressive new route with Kukuczka, he lost his crampons and fell to his death on the descent; below, coming up to Camp1 on the South Face in 1986.

Above left, climbers on Shisha Pangma, 1987. Two new routes were achieved from the Yebokangal Glacier by the West Ridge and up the Central Couloir of the North Face; above right, some Polish members of the team, from the left, Rysiek Warecki, Kukuczka, Janusz Majer and Artur Hajzer; below, the summit ridge of Shisha Pangma.

Kukuczka achieved his fourteenth 8000-metre summit with the ascent of Shisha Pangma on 18th September 1987. All but one had either been climbed by a new route or was a first winter ascent; below, he celebrates with Artur Hajzer and Janusz Majer and a plate of commemorative doughnuts

that this was the norm. We got no settled spell, the wind was very gusty, it was extremely cold and there was so much fresh snow around that we regularly found ourselves up to our armpits in it – these conditions became our daily bread and butter. They were far more difficult than I had ever previously encountered, but I had to keep going. It was, after all, why I had come to these high mountains.

As usual I listened carefully to my body. On my first arrival at Camp 1, I had not felt in peak condition. My second visit was better. I know this because I always check my pulse, from which I can judge my acclimatisation pretty accurately. At the beginning of any trip my pulse is fairly normal, about 70 beats to the minute. But as my acclimatisation improves, my pulse rate drops. After three or four weeks of high-altitude action my base-camp resting pulse is about forty-eight. I always find this strange – why should it not increase?

We waited for two days at Camp 2, but there was no improvement in the weather so we went down. Others replaced us, then it was our turn again. Eventually we set up Camp 3, and from then on the assault started in earnest. I was in front all the time now. We set up Camp 4 at 7000 metres, aware that this was rather low but confident we could go for the summit from there. Andrzej Czok, Janusz Skorek and I started off very early in the morning, but at midday, when we were at about 8000 metres, we realised that we had no chance of making it. Janusz captured our mood very concisely.

'Bugger this for a laugh. I'm going home.'

We retreated to base camp. The weather did not change, clearings lasted at most half a day, then it snowed again with a bitter, penetrating wind. The one redeeming feature I noted was that when it clouded over the wind did not seem to be so strong. Although it seemed better, the price was endless digging around in deep snow and a visibility rarely exceeding fifteen metres. You had to rely a lot on your mountain instinct, all the time plagued by nagging doubts. Sometimes you simply did not know whether to go left or right to avoid a couloir which looked dangerous. One had to make continuous choices, sometimes one ended up saying, this is more dangerous but it is much faster.

The classical route up Dhaulagiri by the North-East Ridge is not difficult. It is a fairly typical route up an eight-thousander, probably easier than Annapurna. At first there is a very long and straightforward ridge, with no route-finding difficulties. But where the ridge merges into the rocky cliff doubts arose as to whether to stick to the ridge or move onto the face. In places the wind exposed old ropes which helped us find the way. At base camp we analysed the situation calmly. We knew that we had to establish another camp. Camp 4 was simply too low. But it was getting late, the middle of January. I looked at the calendar doubly concerned – still thinking about Cho Oyu. So I was very pleased when it was decided to move Camp 4 up higher while making the summit bid. There simply would not have been time to establish another camp from scratch.

As we planned our pairings a new problem arose. Janusz Skorek had been climbing with Andrzej Czok as a solid partnership. I had barged in on them, and from then on we climbed as a threesome. If we kept this arrangement, any team behind us would be considerably weaker. Logic suggested two pairs, and as Janusz had not been on top form in the last day or two, and Andrzej and I had been highest and were best acclimatised, we were the obvious candidates for the first summit pair. Janusz could see his summit chances receding, and there was friction.

Adam Bilczewski, the leader of the expedition, eventually took it on himself to make the decision.

'Kukuczka will go with Andrzej, and the other pair will be Janusz and Machnik who will go up first and move Camp 4 higher. Jurek and Andrzej will follow.'

Janusz did not hide the fact that this was not to his liking. But eventually he agreed and set out with Machnik to Camp 4. The weather was appalling, and they simply could not go any higher, so they descended to Camp 2.

Our turn. Andrzej and I left Camp 2 with Mirek Kuras in support. By now Camp 3 had been completely buried. We spent the night at Camp 4 which was really cold and we were not the least bit surprised that Machnik had a frostbitten finger.

In the morning we had a difficult task ahead of us, to move the tent higher. Just as I was dressed ready to go out I felt a great invisible mass pressing down on me. I lost my cool, yelled and jumped in panic towards the tent exit, but I could not get out. After a moment everything settled down a bit, the great force was still pressing down on me but I realised that we were all alive. Now I was beginning to suffocate.

'Give me a knife!' I shouted. I wanted to cut open the tent.

Then I heard Andrzej's calm voice. 'Take it easy, take it easy, relax, we'll manage without a knife.'

I began tugging at those blasted strings, breaking them, digging away some of the snow and at last . . . Fresh air!

Luckily we were not too badly buried. We crawled out of the tent, which had been erected on a ledge hacked out of ice above a vertical drop. We looked at the snowy battlefield left by the avalanche which had just brushed against our tent. Andrzej had not put his boots on, he had simply jumped out in his socks. Mirek could not find his gloves, his hands were getting cold. We managed to shove some of the snow off, and pulled out what we needed, but Mirek had lost the feeling in his hands. And there descended upon us that nagging doubt associated with the onset of difficulties. Shame. That's it finished.

The tent was completely flattened. Slowly, we began to sort ourselves out. We couldn't just bring ourselves to say, 'Well, that's that.' We dug out the tent poles and discovered that they were not broken, just bent. Luckily they were made from Polish duraluminium which is not as hard as it should have been.

'Hell,' I said. 'Maybe we can get these straight somehow.'

Digging out the whole tent took a further two hours. We put together the poles and decided that they could still be used. Only Kuras had to give up any hope of doing anything, because his hands were now so badly frostbitten that they needed urgent attention. We said goodbye to each other, he went down, we up. Step by step we gained height. Our world shrank to a few metres, I saw only my ice axes and the tips of my crampons. First the axe, then the hammer, then a pull up, kick in the crampon points, I'm a metre higher, again the axes . . .

By the end of the day we had reached 7700 metres and pitched our battered tent on a slight ridge, ready for tomorrow's climb. But our troubles were far from over. Only now did Andrzej admit that something peculiar was happening to his legs. When the avalanche hit us in the morning, the zip on his gaiters had broken, now he was unable to fasten it completely. He did not say anything but turned his back to me and determinedly massaged his feet. Soon a murmur of satisfaction meant he was regaining some feeling. They were much better, but from now on they would be at risk. Andrzej did not even think about giving up. Tomorrow, as early as possible, we would set off lightweight for the summit. With this resolution we fell asleep.

The ascent was very hard, snow fell all the time, we saw hardly anything, just sometimes a slight clearing allowed us to see at best 100 metres ahead. We found our way by instinct to the summit ridge, where it was windy but it did not tire us out. It allowed us to move. We reached a technically difficult section, steep on both sides. Suddenly, it was no longer just plodding up a snow slope, but real rock-climbing, grade 2 or 3, in places 4. Just like the Tatra. We moved roped together, placing running belays.

The ridge was jagged, with many pinnacles, clefts and saddles. Ahead I could see the highest point, the summit. But fifteen metres further on there was a higher point. A short rest, we regained our breath, and set off for the last few metres without stopping for a breather. Then we realised that, Hell, that point over there was higher. Off again. And so at three o'clock we reached a point that was definitely the highest. We even found an old bamboo cane there which had probably been used for taking measurements.

We were on the summit.

The wind was blowing, it was cold. Andrzej was plastered in ice, his beard was icy, an icicle hung under his nose. I probably looked the same. Andrzej started taking the radio out of his rucksack, but I grabbed him by the arm.

'Leave it. Let's go down a bit, we can contact them later.'

I took a few pictures and we set off down as fast as possible. Once we were a fair distance below the final ridge Andrzej stopped.

'We must contact them now. The lads will be worrying. We've not been in touch since morning.'

My main aim was to get down as fast as possible. It was getting late, and we still had quite a long way to the tent. But Andrzej was determined to make contact. At last he got through.

'We have made the summit, made the summit, over . . .'

Among the crackles we heard cries of joy and congratulations from below. Just then it dawned on me that I made a mess of the times, it was not three, it was four o'clock. I grabbed the radio unceremoniously from Andrzej.

'OK, lads, OK, we must finish. We have to hurry down to the tent, over.'

Andrzej stuffed the radio into his sack. Down, down, fast . . . But could we win that race against time? Without warning I found myself standing on a snow slope, and in every direction it was dark. We did not have the faintest idea which way to go. This way was too steep, that way too difficult, we went around in circles. The route should be easy enough, we should be simply following a ridge down, but at night even the easiest route can become absolutely impossible. I took a step, not knowing where I was going. Was that the ridge or just a small step?

'Andrzej, we will not make it. We are beginning to stray, that can only finish up badly. I think we've got to bivvy.'

'Let's just try to go down a tiny bit further.'

But I remembered that below meant getting onto steeper rocks, leading down to high cliffs. So I stuck to my decision. We dug out a niche, and tried to hide in it, but the snow was very powdery and it kept collapsing. An hour of this passed. It was still hellishly cold, but it did seem a bit clearer.

Andrzej looked around and said, 'I know where we are. We have to go down a bit. We will find an old hand line there, that will lead us to the ridge.'

'Let's go.'

We set off, we even abseiled down a short section of the rope, but I saw that the situation was becoming more complicated. We now knew nothing. Did we have to go down 100 or 200 metres? Would we go too far and then have to re-ascend? Andrzej agreed that we would, after all, have to sit it out.

We sat on our rucksacks, huddled close together, in minus forty degrees of frost. Of course we had nothing to eat, and there was no question of a drink. Just one thought: to last out till daybreak, to hold on, to survive. I fell into periods of lethargy; when I shook them off, sure that an hour must have passed, I would discover it was just a few minutes. At last a pale light developed and we started down. Now we could see where we were and in half an hour we reached the tent. Only then did we contact base again; the lads had been worrying. Adam Bilczewski later admitted to me that as a result of that night he took up smoking again – after seventeen years. But now he was happy.

All was great, until someone asked about Andrzej's feet. He answered calmly as if he was talking about someone else. 'They're bad. I have no feeling in them.'

So before we got the stove going to have a drink we took turns massaging Andrzej's feet which were swollen like melons. Their only chance was to get him down as fast as possible, but we were both so tired we kept falling asleep. When I woke I felt thirsty again. I decided just one more brew and we'd be off. We snoozed over the steaming pot, and had another brew.

We eventually left the tent at two o'clock. We could not have made it earlier. We were relaxed, ahead of us the route was straightforward. We should get down to Camp 3 easily, maybe even lower. But even on such an obvious route we had not reckoned with our current state of exhaustion. We took turns at leading, but eventually realised that we were not going to be able to make Camp 2. Let's hope we could get down to Camp 3. For a moment I sat down. Andrzej carried on and vanished from sight. In the spindrift we could see ten, at most fifteen metres. I got up and followed his steps, which suddenly vanished. A feeling of anxiety overcame me: blast, surely Andrzej was going down too low here?

I was standing at the point where we had to start traversing towards Camp 3. I shouted after him, but there was no answer. I tried to convince myself that he had already done the traverse and was now relaxing like a lord in the tent. I began traversing, then I saw that this was not the place where our tent had stood. I returned to the ridge as it was getting dark. I shouted but there was no sign from him.

I began to descend, and descend, feeling my way because it was completely dark now. Step after step and I knew I couldn't fool myself any more, I was going to be faced with a second bivouac.

I knew that I could last out, even though I was completely shattered. But I wanted warmth, I wanted a drink. I was afraid that another night like the last could end in a drama, but what else remained? Then I felt the ground dropping away below me. Maybe it was a short drop, maybe a hidden crevasse. But there were no crevasses here. Where was I?

Wherever I felt with my axe I found hard ice.

Terror overcame me. I could see one chance now to protect myself somehow from that terrible wind. I tried to dig myself into a niche. As I opened my rucksack I lost my torch. I was condemned to total darkness. I sat down on my rucksack and the great battle for survival began all over again.

Every now and again the wind eased and the spindrift cleared and I could see lights at my feet. Lights? Yes, it was not a hallucination but a real village lying 4000 metres below me at the foot of Dhaulagiri. I am there, with them. I sit in front of the fire. It is warm, I warm myself with tea, which I drink with a glass of the local spirit made from apple juice. I dream about this hot spirit . . .

Hallucinating on in my state of lethargy, I improved my niche of crumbling snow from time to time as the night passed. I had a sleeping bag inside my rucksack but I did not take it out. In the morning I had put it right at the bottom of my sack. If I was to take it out now I would have to unpack all those bits and pieces and I did not have anywhere safe to put them in the wind. I was afraid to lose my gloves and everything. I consoled myself with the thought that the sleeping bag was completely wet through, and just a lump of useless ice. If I had been able to think more rationally, I would have realised that just getting into its wet innards as I stood could have helped. But in those conditions logical thinking is not easy. A very specific stupor overcomes you which reduces you to very basic thinking: if I am sitting then I will remain sitting. Why change my position? Why lie down?

When dawn at last arrived I saw that I was sitting on a slope down which I could quite easily run. If I had taken the chance yesterday and carried on feeling my way down, I would have got down. In the morning one is always much wiser.

I reached Camp 2 just as they were beginning to stir. I gave a shout, and total happiness reigned. We were all together again. It turned out that Andrzej went down to somewhere in the region of Camp 2, the lads came out to find him and he reached the camp at ten p.m.

Janusz Baranek and Mirek Kuras were also there. They had been waiting for us in Camp 2 all this time, and Mirek had almost managed to get his hands back to normal again.

We packed up Camp 2 and went down. Lower the weather was fine, there was no wind and the sun was shining. But there were great drifts of snow. It was difficult to describe our descent as walking, it was more sliding on top of or among slabs of this fresh snow. In fact we did not manage to make Camp 1 and had to bivouac again. But at least there was some warm cereal and a last packet of soup to eat. And all the time we drank and drank and drank.

The following day we only reached base camp at four in the afternoon. The doctor examined Andrzej's legs and diagnosed third-degree frost-bite in almost all of his toes. He needed medical assistance urgently which was only available down in the valleys. We had to get there fast. The kitchen had almost run out of food. The rest of the team had been surviving on cereals, saving the last can of meat for us. So we ate our final supper, and next morning evacuated the camp and went down.

But I would be going back up . . .

The others had all their hard work behind them, they could relax. For me those 8167 metres of snow and mists on Dhaulagiri were the end of phase one. The final objective was still ahead. Down there the grass was green, there was happiness and a lot of hot rice.

I put my rucksack on, and set off. Back up the hill. Ahead of me, round two.

8

Broken Rungs

I took only what was absolutely necessary, tent, sleeping bag, gas stove, some clothes, some food. The rucksack still ended up weighing twenty-five kilos. I was off up to the French Col again, first stage to Cho Oyu. I had already developed frostbitten feet coming down from Dhaulagiri, but nothing in comparison to Andrzej Czok's and I had kept quiet when examined by the doctor whose whole attention was directed towards poor Andrzej. I reached the French Col with little difficulty, the going was good. But on the other side of the pass I encountered deep powder snow, up to my armpits, and started having my first doubts as to my ability to get through. Maybe it would be better to turn back and follow the longer but safer route the others were taking to Kathmandu? But I kept thinking of the time factor. I had to get through! It was already 25th January, and the Cho Oyu permit ran out on 15th February.

All day I fought that awful snow. At times I felt overwhelmed with helplessness. I had to kick a passage a metre at a time, leaving behind me a snowy tunnel, stumbling on, sometimes in a zig-zag, because when I saw rocks ahead I'd make for them, hoping there would be less snow there, but the rocks would prove to be just small islands and on the other side I would be floundering waist deep again. It was a mindless, wretched fight, which brought me to the edge of tears of frustration. At the end of the day I could still see the place where I had bivouacked the previous night.

The following day the battle continued undiminished. As I started to descend my relief was short-lived, for it was soon clear that during one month's absence the amount of snow had if anything increased. What

94

was more, it now reached much further down the valley. My hopes focused on the forest edge I could see in the distance.

At every bivouac I scrupulously bandaged my feet which were covered in ever growing blisters. I did something that I should not do, I pricked them. Despite my care, everything became infected and started oozing pus and rotting. I kept washing my feet but could do no more, and in the morning I would just put on my boots and carry on. At last I reached the forest. I was no longer following the route I had come up by, I was just crashing on down. But there was one hell of a lot of snow in that forest. I started to lose my orientation. The simple concept that I must reach human habitation somehow was no substitute for a map and compass. I descended to a vertical cliff. I retreated and tried a bit further right, then back left until I came across some animal tracks. If four-legged creatures could get down here, so could I. Luckily they were not the tracks of a snow leopard but those of a herd of deer. I followed them down to easier-angled ground, past a hut which showed signs of recent habitation, and after a few hours I reached the village of Morfa.

Everywhere eyes were riveted on me in disbelief as I made for the little inn where I had stayed on my way up.

My landlady did not challenge my explanation that I had just climbed Dhaulagiri and had left the rest of the expedition and crossed the French Col. In Poland one simply taps a finger against one's temple to express one's opinion of such a claim. But she was too polite, especially as I was a paying guest; I was allowed to hallucinate.

Only once did she counter, 'Nobody has ever got through that way at this time of year.'

It didn't worry me, I was feeling fine, sitting by the fireplace eating a bowl brimming with steaming rice, beside me a glass of Morfa brandy. Everything was just as I had dreamt of when I was stuck on the icy slopes below the summit of Dhaulagiri. Could anybody in the whole world be happier?

Then into that blissful atmosphere came the voice of the Nepalese Radio announcer: 'The Polish Dhaulagiri expedition ended in a success: Andarsy Chokoyo and Jery Kukuczak reached the summit, this is the first ever winter ascent of this mountain . . .'

I would barely have noticed. Our names were terribly distorted. But what drew my attention was the change that came over the face of my hostess. Only then did it dawn on me that they were talking about me. The next glass of Morfa brandy was on the house.

The following morning I ran to the landing strip to discover there were no flights scheduled for three days. There was nothing for it but

95

to hire a porter and set off on foot. The nagging pain in my feet returned, but I could not afford a rest. My porter was a young lad I was helped to find by a well respected local Sherpa who owned an apple orchard and had befriended Polish climbers before. Thanks to him I was not paying my porter an inflated rate, and the young lad kept going from dawn till dusk. That trek normally took seven days of fast marching. We reached Pokhara after three. I took a taxi to the bus station where by luck there was a bus ready to leave for Kathmandu. With not even time for a coke, I got on and the bus set off, arriving in the capital at ten the same evening.

I ran to the agency which had radio contact with the Cho Oyu expedition base camp, and stood by biting my lip as they tried to get through.

'Polish Cho Oyu expedition, Polish Cho Oyu expedition.'

If they were already very high, they could say that there was no point in my joining them. Then amidst the crackles a voice I recognised came across the ether. It was the Canadian, Jacek Olech, the only man left in base camp, and he sounded really happy to hear of my arrival.

'Catch a plane to Lukla immediately, we're waiting for you. Over.'

It was 5th February. The next day I managed to buy a ticket, no easy feat because every flight to Lukla is packed with tourists starting on the trek to Everest base camp. In the early morning I packed and took a taxi to the airport, my baggage was checked, then the flight was cancelled. Back to the hotel. Another whole day, I was beside myself. The next day it was the same thing all over again. Taxi, airport, check-in, flight cancelled.

I now had only one last day left. If the flight didn't go on the third day there would be nothing for me to go up there for, as I still needed a few days to get to base camp, then a few days for the climbing itself and, although I was in good condition, I was also worried about my feet, which felt numb and were still suppurating.

On the third day the plane took off. The moment I arrived in Lukla I grabbed a porter and made it clear I was not interested in staging. The first day we covered three stages. I was lucky because we were going to spend the night at his home, so he was also keen to get there. Next day we did another three stages before I looked round for some shelter for the night. By good luck I met a young Sherpani who ran a small hotel a bit further on. She had been walking down because there were so few guests in winter, but turned back for us, which was fortunate as I'm not sure we could have found our own way without her. So we enjoyed a second 'luxury' night, with a fire in the middle of the room and bundles of hay to sleep on.

Cho Oyu, first winter ascent of a new route on the South-East Pillar,
15th February, 1985

However, my porter's spirits sank the further we got from his home
and eventually he staged a sit-down strike. At that very moment, as if
from nowhere, a runner appeared, sent down by the anxious Andrzej
Zawada. Without saying a word he accepted the rucksack from his
exhausted compatriot. And so, on 8th February, at two in the afternoon,
I arrived at the Cho Oyu base camp, where I was greeted by Zyga
Heinrich who told me the lads were on a new route on the South-East
Pillar. The two Maciejs, Maciej Berbeka and Maciej Pawlikowski, were
already at Camp 4 and planning to move the camp up further to attack
the summit. Gienek Chrobak and Mirosław Gardzielewski were at
Camp 3 and would follow the Maciejs as a second assault group.

That evening when we made radio contact, I heard Gienek's voice
saying that he was packing it in because they would have to wait a long
time for the others. He had had enough waiting and might just try for
the summit by the normal route.

So there was no question of having a rest. I repacked my rucksack
straightaway and set off with Zyga for Camp 1. The next day we reached
Camp 2 where I would have to wait till the others reached the summit,
slept at Camp 4 and finally vacated it. We had ahead of us almost one
thousand vertical metres of difficult climbing.

I was a bit worried about our ability to jump a camp in one day on the way up, but we did not lose faith in our strength. After one day's wait I set off with Zyga in the direction of Camp 4 because Camp 3 no longer existed. On the way up we met the two Maciejs descending after their successful summit ascent. As we congratulated them, I felt a twinge of jealousy that they had already done it. It was tough. They described how we should go and reminded us they had to remove several lengths of fixed rope from some difficult terrain because they had needed it higher up.

Zyga and I were now climbing the sections without the fixed rope. It was like climbing a ladder which was in place but had some broken rungs. The hardest section was the last 160 metres leading to Camp 4. Here again the fixed rope was missing. Instead there were just ice screws and pitons left in place every twenty or thirty metres. The atmosphere became rather tense; it was decidedly late. We had to complete this ropeless section before dark. Beyond that it should get easier. But it was just here, where it was very hard, that complete darkness descended on us. I took out my torch and set about changing the batteries; then I dropped the torch. Once more I was left in the dark.

The terrain was, however, fairly obvious: a wall of ice where there's no point in searching around for holds, instead you drive your ice axe and ice hammer into the hard ice. I only cut a step out every few metres. Even in the pitch black it was somehow possible to climb. From step to step, slowly, pulling up on both ice tools, I was gradually moving up. My mind was actively stimulating my efforts, thinking about the tent above waiting for me, the hot tea and warm sleeping bag.

Zyga who had been belaying me for the last two hours must have been getting very stiff and cold. Too bad. We were on a steep face, there was no place to sit down and bivvy, we had to go up. At last I reached a sharp ridge where, if the worst came to the worst, two people could sit. My recent dreams about the warm interior of a tent had now been replaced by the simple necessity to survive, sitting it out till the morning. I dug myself into the snow, hammered the ice axe in and tied myself to it, ready to belay Zyga. I shouted to him that I was holding the rope tight for him to climb.

I waited. Total darkness, the wind blew, drowning all other sounds. I had no contact with Zyga. Only the rope told me if he was moving or not. Then it stayed tight for a long time. Something, damn it, must be happening.

I bellowed 'Zygaaaa!'

Maybe I was just trying to convince myself that I heard a voice above that howling wind. But hours passed before I at last heard heavy breathing not far below me and Zyga appeared.

'What took you so long?'

He was so tired that he could only answer in gasps. 'I ca-me off on the tra-verse . . .'

He was climbing when he slipped and fell three metres, pendulumed and hung on the rope. With the help of the rope he managed to drag himself back up to the traverse line, but he had had a long, demanding time. I was hardly surprised when he stated: 'I've had enough!'

'Just a few metres and you will be able to sit down.'

After a short while we were at last together. Everywhere it was desperately dark, the wind moaned.

'Let's get a bivvy organised,' I said calmingly.

We wrapped ourselves up in an emergency lightweight sheet and sat down close together for warmth on the stamped out platform the size of two chairs, our feet hanging over black nothingness, and shivered until daybreak.

In the morning I dug myself out of the snow and got up another fifty metres and there, just ahead of me, I saw the tent. We were only sixty metres below it. Our dreams about dry sleeping bags and a pot of hot soup were so strong that we decided to have just a short rest in the tent. But we were so completely exhausted that a moment turned into a whole day and night. When we woke it was 15th February. Our last day. We were at 7400 metres.

We left the tent with minimal packs and immediately the climbing was hard. The altitude was beginning to tell. More snow, luckily only up to our calves. Despite feeling quite well I was very tired. It seemed to me that I was climbing normally but from our pace I realised that I was not as fresh as I could be. Zyga on the other hand lacked full acclimatisation. He had been forced by an earlier injury to wait at base camp and had not had a chance to go higher. At 4 p.m. the situation became rather serious.

'What do we do now?' I asked. 'If we reach the summit before the sun sets, that's fine, but then we have to face a descent in the dark, with the threat of a bivouac . . .'

Then Zyga astounded me. He is known in the club to be a very sensible person. He was forty-eight, he belonged among those who, faced with unreasonable risks, simply give up. But now he answered, with great difficulty and gasping: 'We are too close to the summit . . . We go as long as we can.'

So we went. I had already learnt that it was possible to survive a bivouac at 8000 metres in winter. And the summit really was quite near.

We now only had one final bit of very hard ice climbing ahead of us. But the fact that Zyga thought like I did raised my spirits. This time I was not the mad one who always pushed on ahead. Belaying ourselves all the time, I reached a sharp ridge leading up to the summit, difficult and very exposed on both sides. A fight developed against exhaustion, the lack of oxygen and time.

In the red glow of the setting sun I reached the summit. Doing so I experienced a wonderful feeling, as one step took me into another world. The steep walls and the knife-edged ridges vanished, it was as if I had stepped out of a dark and dangerous canyon onto a plateau bathed in purple light. It was 5.15 p.m. A moment later Zyga appeared out of the shadows. Cho Oyu has a very untypical summit, a great flat area, the size of several football pitches, stretching out of sight. The weather was settled, just above the horizon was the red ball of the setting sun. I found two sweets, probably left by the two Maciejs. I took several photographs with the Super-8 camera given me by Andrzej Zawada. Then I took a few with mine. (The film for Andrzej turned out well; unfortunately my camera froze and all my Dhaulagiri and Cho Oyu photos were over-exposed.) Zyga took a few photographs too. It was so wonderful that we would have liked to have stayed up there much longer, but now only one thing was of importance, getting down as fast as possible into the gathering gloom.

Being not so well acclimatised, Zyga began to fall behind. Every so often he would sit down and I shouted at him: 'Get up! You've got to keep going.'

Then the situation was reversed, when I tumbled over in the snow and heard a cry above me, 'Get up! Go!'

An onlooker might have thought we were tormenting each other. But there were no onlookers, and the fight for every metre of descent was a fight with very high stakes, maybe the ultimate stake, as we climbed down and down with the last of our strength, both knowing that another bivouac awaited us. We had to get down as low as possible before being forced into it. When the last light vanished completely we were on a snow field, but we carried on down in the dark, rope-length after rope-length, taking turns at belaying.

I was ahead, belayed somewhat illusorily by Zyga, as the rope stayed very slack. I was descending backwards, hanging from my two tools. It was getting steeper. I dug in the ice axe again and felt space beneath my feet. I began to get worried. Surely there was no drop here? Maybe it is just a one metre crevasse? I cut out a ledge in the ice and stepped down onto it, first one foot then the other. I lowered myself a bit further and in that moment my ice axe came out. I tried to dig it back in but my foot slipped. I was falling . . .

I thought that's it. Then after a fraction of a second I crashed down onto something. I felt myself carefully; things hurt but I decided I'd live. I began to feel around me. I was lying on a ledge; I was well supported. I'd survived.

I shouted up to Zyga: 'Stop! There is a drop here! Go a bit further right!'

I could now see by the silhouette against the sky that the drop of about five metres petered out altogether to the right. Zyga traversed down to me and we decided to stop there. Below was a black abyss. We did not know which way to carry on in the darkness. We huddled down, our emergency bivvy sheets by now so badly torn they provided little protection against the desperate cold, minus forty for sure. I mentally congratulated myself on surviving the fall, before allowing my mind to turn to a horrifically real situation – my feet.

Before leaving base camp I had never mentioned my feet to the doctor in order to avoid unwelcome examination. Luckily, it never occurred to him that the soles of my feet were frostbitten, because I had marched in on my own two legs from another expedition and was happily carrying on. But I was continually fighting with my feet. Every night spent in a tent I changed the bandages and massaged them, but was careful that Zyga did not see me at it, as I did not want this to influence any of our decision-making or cause conflict. Now on this desperately cold bivouac I could do nothing for my feet. Somehow we survived that night and started off down to the tent. We had only been 200 metres away from it the night before. We spent the whole day there, though it was hardly resting at an altitude of 7400m, but we were too weak to go down any further that day. We had some food and some drink left, but were so shattered that we cooked and dozed by turns through the whole day and night. The following morning we thought everything would be quite straightforward now: we were going down, and during the day would reach base camp. But by nightfall we had barely managed to reach Camp 2. Normally it should have taken us two, at most three, hours. But I was terribly exhausted and Zyga in an even worse state. So we bivouacked at Camp 2, while down at base camp they were getting a bit anxious. They knew we had made it to the summit, and all that remained was the simple matter of the descent.

Yet again I assured them over the radio that we should definitely get to Camp 1, maybe even to base camp that day. But things seemed to pile up. We got up at seven a.m. rather than at five. Before we had cooked something it was already nine. By the time we were ready to leave it was accursedly late. We managed to get ourselves down to the glacier on which Camp 1 was situated. It was then that we saw tiny dots below us moving up, growing larger and larger. They had come out to meet us and help us. Once again we were descending at night; just before midnight on 19th February we reached base camp.

Everything was ready for the expedition to depart. They were just waiting for us. In the morning there was no time to rest. We packed up the tents and set off. I was acting like an automaton, but the lower we went, the more oxygen there was, and the more strength I had. Simply eating and drinking helped a lot; at last we managed to rehydrate. What was most important, the pace was now dictated by the porters, in other words we were moving more slowly. The stages were no longer from first light until dusk. We walked for four and at most five hours in a day.

I felt dried out, I was very thin, but I managed to move. I could move and think. After Cho Oyu I was aware that I was now being treated as the one who could offer a real challenge to Reinhold Messner. When they said this to me I grimaced involuntarily. Yes, I could give him a bit of a run for his money, but for me to be able to win the race they would have to imprison Reinhold in his alpine castle and give me permission to do just what I wanted to do in the Himalaya. That did not mean that I was not prepared to take up the challenge. Far from it. After all, ticking off two Himalayan eight-thousanders in one winter season had never been achieved before in Himalayan climbing. I was fully aware that this was a major achievement. This so-called race against Messner had developed almost unwittingly, I had allowed myself to become drawn into it without any real thought for the outcome; after all, I had started off so far behind my rival. The concept of racing up all the fourteen eight-thousanders by the normal routes just to tick them off simply did not excite me at all. What interested me far more was fourteen new routes. I would carry out this plan with fanaticism: a new route, or a first winter ascent. This game was worth the candle. It was big stakes. The race against Messner would merely give me the opportunity to carry out this plan. So I had something to chew over as I plodded along on my maltreated feet.

That evening I finally admitted to my frostbite and asked the doctor to have a look at them. Krzysiu Flaczynski threw up his hands in horror, and immediately gave me injections of antibiotics, put me on a drip, applied dressings and a poultice, and generally placed me in intensive care.

Now every evening the field hospital was prepared, normally in the corner of some Sherpa chicken house, where Krzysiu laid out his instruments, drips and syringes and started work on my feet, cutting away bits of dead flesh from my toes, washing them, putting on fresh bandages.

While this was going on a Sherpani would serve me with potatoes boiled in their skins in a great pot over an open fire in the centre of the room. They tasted like the greatest of delicacies. My starved body demanded more and more food. And I drank, drank, drank.

In the morning I had to carry on. Nobody could direct me to the nearest bus stop. But frostbite had one blessing: in its early stages there is no pain. So I walked down quite normally, further aided by pain killers. And thus we reached Kathmandu.

Because of my feet I flew immediately to Delhi, from where I was supposed to get back to Poland as quickly as possible. But now I was at the mercy of Aeroflot. Each day I limped into their offices to ask for a seat on a flight and each day I received the same reply: '*Niet*,' impossible. Nothing helped, neither visits to the director, nor a letter written to Aeroflot on my behalf by the Polish consul. Unfortunately, I could not sweep off to another carrier. On my ticket there was a red stamp: 'Not transferable'. It took ten days, during which time, instead of being in hospital, I was stuck with my suppurating feet in awful heat, in a small hotel at the Tourist Camp, surrounded by filth, stench and scavenging rats. By luck I met a doctor from Cieszyn there, who managed to reban-dage my feet each day. He was a wonderful man, but he had come to Delhi as a tourist, so he did not have a whole medical cabinet with him. I reached Poland in March and my toes had been saved.

I was so happy to be back in the midst of my family with the wife and children I had missed so badly and at first a warm satisfaction at manag-ing to carry out my crazy plan stole over me. Only one thing began to sour it. Although nobody came out with it directly, I could sense the criticism. It was felt in some quarters that I had ascended Cho Oyu by the ready-made ladder of others' labours. Well, maybe there was an element of truth in this. I did not have the satisfaction that comes from working from the very beginning of an expedition.

It was a fact that when I set off up Cho Oyu with Zyga the route was almost completely prepared. The ladder may have been in place, although there were a few rungs missing. The ones near the top.

9

Nanga Never Forgives

Nanga Parbat, South-East Pillar, 1985

After my winter expeditions to Dhaulagiri and Cho Oyu I sat at home waiting for an 'invitation to the dance' because I knew a Cracow group had been preparing an expedition to Nanga Parbat for a year now. But I wasn't going to ask. Not since I was sent off with a flea in my ear, when I tried to invite myself on to someone else's trip ten years ago, back in 1976. So I waited. I heard that my name had come up. But it was not yet a proposition. Then the expedition leader, Paweł Mularz, phoned me. I was in.

Making use of my contacts in Silesia, I managed to acquire all the scarce food for the trip and I set off for Cracow, my tiny car packed to the roof with excellent dried meats, sausages and hams. It was 3rd May, a poignant date to most Poles, because on 3rd May 1791 Poland adopted its first democratic constitution. It was a day for protests against martial law, and here was I with my Maluch packed to the gunwhales with highly sought-after tit-bits on a day when it could be expected to be rather 'hot' in Cracow. To add to it all, I had stopped along the way at a petrol station, took off my jacket and left it on the car roof with all my papers in the pockets, including my passport. I only realised this when I was coming in to Cracow. Customs Clearance took me two days.

I left two weeks later to chase after the expedition. It was an international team, but the real heart of it were Paweł Mularz and Piotrek Kalmus. First there was a thirty-hour bus journey from Islamabad to Gilgit, then on by hired jeep up the rocky highway. It was like looking at the rerun of a film I had already seen. For it was here, eight years ago, that I had first experienced the magical greatness of the Himalaya, but also the disappointment, the bitterness of defeat. I had come with the myth born from books such as *Man Conquers the Himalaya*, every page packed with superhuman hardships, fear and death. I returned free from this myth of the Great Himalaya. Conceit? No. I returned with a great respect but with the realisation that the Himalaya are also for normal people.

The only mountain to whose base one can get after a short jeep ride and then a two-day walk-in; the only mountain where the base camp is at 3300 metres, where there are fields, where it is green, one can pitch tents, have a camp fire, almost like a normal Scout camp; the only mountain on which one climbs through all the seasons from the height of summer to minus forty; a mountain which allowed me to play with it for a bit, allowed me to reach 8000 metres and then slapped me in the face. That's Nanga Parbat.

On it I discovered that the Himalaya are first of all a continuous, stupefying problem of transportation, with very little to do with climbing. Before one could think of climbing one had to spend days bent double under a heavy load, like a beast of burden, carrying up tents, sleeping bags, bottles of gas, food, go down and start again. With this came the thought, of which I am convinced to this day, that if we had gone there as a three-man team, we would have achieved just as much as with a full-scale expedition. One really can perform effectively in the Himalaya with just a small group.

I recollect the scene that took place between three friends after a night spent at 7400 metres, after our first attempt was repulsed at almost 8000 metres. We knew it was not far to the summit, but that there was a rock barrier in the way. The others involved were Marek Pronobis and Maniuś Piekutowski.

'So then,' I demanded, 'do we try again, are we going back up?'

'I'm not going to be able to,' said Marek with resignation. 'I still cannot feel my legs.'

'I don't see the point of carrying on,' admitted Maniuś.

'Let's leave Marek here for a day. He can attend to his legs while we make one more attempt.' I put forward this compromise desperately. We were packed, all that was needed was one word: up, or down. I knew I was not going to hear it, silence is often more expressive than words. Then I said in total desperation: 'Maybe I'll go up alone, you carry on down . . .'

Marek reacted to this. 'Don't be silly, you are the only one who is fit!'

He was right. Maniuś suffered some permanent frostbite damage to his hands and feet, and Marek lost all his toes as a result of this climb. I remember sitting down resignedly in the snow, while the others slowly plodded down pulling slightly on the eighty-metre rope I was belaying them with. I looked up: blue sky, no wind, silence, dream weather, the summit just there. I wanted to cry. A tug on the rope.

'No more rope! Come on down!' Marek shouted from below.

After a few days we had packed up the base camp and returned to the valley. It was the beginning of a wonderful autumn in the full beauty of golds and yellows. Above us, glistening in the sun, was the mountain and a great sorrow that we had to be going away when we had been so close to success. If I had decided to go off and do it alone, would I have reached the summit, or not? That question nags me to the present day.

'Quite nice weather.' The voice of the driver woke me from my reverie of eight years ago. We were getting close to the mountain where I had lost once already. Soon I'd be standing beneath it for a second time, but I had no complexes about it. I did not fear it more than any other mountain. To get rid of the knowledge that I had once failed on Nanga Parbat I simply had to climb the mountain.

All the same, I was slightly daunted by this expedition. The plan was ambitious: a new route on the South-East Pillar. That was the route we had planned to do back in 1977, but we had lowered our sights at the last minute. Now after eight years we had better equipment and much more experience. Tadeusz Piotrowski was with us, a Himalayan climber with a list of great achievements behind him, and the most knowledge about this route. There was also the ever reliable Zyga, the others were relative Himalayan novices. I was meeting the two Mexicans, Carlos Carsolio and Elsa Avila for the first time. What could these youngsters, born in a land of cactuses, be worth? We would have to see. I had assumed I would be climbing with Tadek Piotrowski and Zyga Heinrich, but even before we started our first reconnaissance walk this idea was knocked on the head.

'You won't be going together because you are all far more experienced than the others. If we adopted that arrangement the others would have a much reduced chance of making the summit.'

I was dumbfounded for a moment, it was the first time on an expedition that I had heard such logic. After a moment's thought, however, I saw the matter in a different light. I was taken by the sheer honesty of this stance, which certainly made sense to some extent. Major traditionally led expeditions normally adopt one of two styles of action. Either they attack the mountain with a small but very strong partnership which forges on ahead, the others all just acting in support. Or they form two or three teams which take turns at going to the front. I always preferred the concept of the single partnership approach, but here I accepted the alternative. One should try everything. We were, in effect,

Nanga Parbat, a new route on the South-East Pillar, 13th July, 1985

divided into three teams, Tadek led one, Zyga the second and I the third. One team was always out in front, while the other two were resting. The route was difficult and extremely dangerous. It worked its way up a face seamed with steep runnels and couloirs down which there was an endless flow of avalanches. Luckily these had scoured out their own permanent descent lines, so it was possible to predict the route of these raging rivers of mud on the lower slopes and snow above. But these gullies had to be crossed all the time. The problem revolved around the choice of the right moment to race across them. To this day I believe that this was one of my most dangerous expeditions.

Only Tadek Piotrowski knew the route. He had been on it three years ago with Andrzej Bielun during a German expedition led by Karl Herrligkoffer. He had been involved in the lead all the time, and one German had even managed with a supreme effort to reach the ridge, from which the summit was not so far away. So the route had always been completed. What was missing was the dot over the 'i'. Now the whole burden of route-finding fell on Tadek. Clearly, he should be out in front all the time.

The route was further complicated by the sparsity of good campsites. Base camp and Camp 1 were more than a thousand metres apart. To do anything one had first to cross those avalanche runnels. Camp 2 was established at 5330 metres. We put up fixed ropes, but one team had to spend all its time repairing sections damaged by stonefall. Then we discovered we did not have enough line, our calculations were wrong, and we had to buy more at the nearest town, Gilgit.

Fixing line from Camp 2 to the planned Camp 3 brought us the greatest difficulty. This section was so long that it took three or four hours to reach the end of the fixed ropes. Only two hours remained for breaking new ground and fixing a further ropelength or two, then several hours were needed for the return to Camp 2. But too much snowfall or a section of damaged rope to repair were enough to hold things up to such an extent that by the time we reached the top of the lines there was not enough time to do anything but leave the ropes hanging from the highest piton and go down. For a week we just thrashed around without achieving much.

How were we to crack this? We decided to go heavy, in other words carry all the equipment required for setting up Camp 3, but bivouac wherever we reached. Our aims were very fluid. Above the end of the fixed ropes we added another 200 metres of line up a very difficult steep icy face. When I reached the stance it was already night, the others climbed up to me by feel. We cut out a minimal ledge in the sharp snowy ridge, enough for a two-man tent, then the six of us piled into it and waited for the night to pass.

This was the breakthrough. Thanks to this push we were only 200 metres below our planned Camp 3. The next day we climbed these last 200 metres and established the camp at 6200 metres, below a twelve-metre-high sérac.

It began to snow. I looked with concern at the growing amounts and the vanishing tent tops. If we left them unattended the camp would disappear. I decided to stay up with Sławek Łobodziński while the others returned to base camp. We got inside the tent and started cooking. After a few hours powder avalanches were coming down around us, which was why we placed the camp beneath a sérac, counting on it acting as a shield. We were right, though we had not foreseen the sheer amounts of snow that would be coming down. Tongues of the stuff simply flowed round the sérac and approached our tent from the side, piling up against it. Digging it out and moving it to a slightly better place took several hours, in which we had hoped to be able to catch up on badly needed rest. The next day we had to move the tent again, even closer to the sérac. The day after the sun at last smiled on us again.

Going back down to base camp, I noticed a rucksack hanging off a rock not far from Camp 1. How did it get there? It should be on someone's back. It began to worry me. My concern grew as I approached Camp 1 and found the tents were empty. I was sure something must have happened, as it was not all that long ago that I had seen people moving up towards this camp. Hurrying on down, I at last saw two figures on the glacier and soon all was explained.

Just before reaching Camp 1 Andrzej Samolewicz had been caught by an avalanche, not a big one, but enough to sweep him down one of those avalanche chutes as if on a bob-sleigh run. He was badly bruised and scratched but otherwise alive.

His companion, Paweł Mularz, had hung his rucksack on the rocks when he went down to rescue him. Samol had had an extremely lucky escape. This was our first serious warning.

After a few days' rest we decided to fix ropes up to Camp 4, then a further 200–300 metres to a point where the angle eases, before going down to Camp 3. Not wishing to tempt providence by climbing those deadly avalanche runnels between Camps 1 and 2 too often, we decided that from now on we would designate Camp 3 our advance base camp and only go down that far for rests.

After a further two days we would again push up towards the summit, setting up Camp 5 along the way. This more alpine-style concept suited my temperament better. We packed huge sacks and waited our turn to slot into this twelve- to fifteen-day programme.

After a delayed start Tadeusz and Mikołaj Czyżewski set off with the task of fixing rope up the last section up to Camp 4. After a struggle with spindrift and hard ice, they fixed 200 metres and left the rest for us. Sławek, Carlos and I found Camp 1 had vanished, simply blown away by the blast associated with a huge avalanche all of a kilometre away. We found a couple of sleeping bags, a few mattresses and nothing else. Next day, zig-zagging around we managed to avoid numerous other avalanches and reach Camp 2. On this route we had to obey the tough game rules dictated by the weather. In the morning avalanches were less frequent, only when the sun warmed up the snow slopes did they start thundering down. By lunchtime it was a continuous heavy bombardment. So it was necessary either to get up extremely early, or to leave late in the afternoon when the sun had left the slopes and frost established its tight grip on the situation. We left Camp 2 before five the following morning, and carried on above Camp 3 to finish off fixing line up the final sections. Climbing up steep couloirs, where we expected to be able to do the work quickly, we encountered ice with unconsolidated snow overlaying it. The leader had to clear away the fresh snow before he could dig his front points and ice axes into the ice and place an ice screw. It was hard, time-consuming climbing. At last I reached an arête and followed it for a further hundred metres.

That was enough for one day. We returned to Camp 3. The following day we reclimbed the fixed ropes, then ploughed through deep snow past a band of séracs to Camp 4 at 7400 metres, arriving there after dark. In the morning I got up another hundred metres with Zyga and returned to Camp 3 for a rest day before going back up to Camp 4. Tadek Piotrowski, Piotrek Kalmus and Mirek Gardzilewski were meanwhile setting out from base camp. The theory now was that we four were to push for the summit and if our attack failed they would take over in a second attempt.

During the night of 10th July a violent storm flattened Slawek and Carlos's tent and blew till midday. We waited all day for an improvement in the weather. Tadeusz only reached Camp 1 with his team quite late. The next day they found themselves on the most dangerous section between Camps 1 and 2 at midday, and when I turned on the radio at the scheduled time of one p.m., I heard: 'Piotr Kalmus was swept down by an avalanche at 11.10.'

It happened just before Camp 2 while they were traversing one of the dangerous couloirs. The avalanche pulled him off the fixed rope. Tadek and Mirek sent out the alarm message as soon as they arrived at Camp 2. But they themselves were trapped in Camp 2 by the midday avalanches. Only those below could try and find Piotr to see if he was still alive. We too were completely unable to help, being a good kilometre higher up, condemned to follow everything happening below us on the radio. As nightfall approached, we became completely depressed, prepared for the worst. At four they saw a body in the debris but when they reached it all they could do was declare that Piotrek was dead. A tragedy had taken place. We had lost a friend.

That evening the radios were busy as Camps 1 and 2 discussed how to bring down his body, desperately hard work over difficult terrain.

We sat there on the outside of this mainstream of urgent consultations. What next? Do we carry on up or go down? Do we pack up everything and concentrate on the evacuation of the body, then take part in the burial of Piotr at base, or do they feel strong enough to cope with that themselves? It was too important a decision for one individual to make. It had to be a group decision.

I was in an awkward situation. It was well known that I act as the main spring for upward motion, the one most concerned about reaching the summit. They expected my standpoint to be: there has been a tragedy, the death of a friend. If however we reach the summit, although we will not erase the tragedy, the expedition will have achieved its aim, which was one of Piotrek's great desires

But I chickened out. This was all too hard for me to say. Zyga Heinrich was the climbing leader and I said I would go by his decision. Hiding behind Zyga was not only cowardly but risky, because Zyga, although one of the leading figures in Polish Himalayan and Alpine climbing, had rarely set foot on a summit. He is the sort of expedition member who can be quite satisfied carrying loads between Camps 2 and 3, knowing he is contributing his bit, but lacking that driving ambition to push right to the very summit. He lacked that free-ranging touch that allows one at a crucial moment to decide we'll take a small risk, for the sake of the summit. I had every reason to expect that he would now say let's pack up our things and go down.

He had surprised me once on Cho Oyu. Here he did it again. He took the radio from my hands and said: 'This tragedy must not be for nothing. Above, everything is ready, we are poised for our one and only chance to go for the summit. If we come down it's the end of the expedition. There will be no second chance. We should press on. Over.'

He was talking to Paweł Mularz several kilometres below us who was the most broken by the tragedy. Piotrek had been an old friend and he was for packing up the expedition. The radio discussion lasted two hours. It was finally decided that those below Camp 4 would go down to assist with the transport of the body and the burial, and we would continue with our summit bid.

There was just one more problem. It was obvious that not all six of us could go to the summit, we had too little food and equipment. So who would go down? Looked at from the viewpoint of strength and experience Zyga was an old hand and I could see us going on together. But who should be the third one? Carlos was ambitious, determined, but very inexperienced, and Sławek Łobodziński had climbed a lot in America, but not in the Himalaya. Yet these two had to some extent sponsored the expedition. Mikołaj and Samol were also on their first Himalayan trip. Eventually I suggested, 'Zyga, Sławek and I will go up first. Carlos, Mikołaj and Samol will wait to make a second team.'

Saying this, I was not convinced that they had it in them to make a second bid, and felt I was as good as writing off their chances.

Mikołaj must have felt this too when he said, 'In that case I feel I should go down.'

Only Carlos dug his heels in. 'I won't eat, please don't consider me in your food equations, but I will go with you. I have to go, it is my one and only chance to be the first ever Mexican to reach the summit of an 8000-metre peak.'

What could one do with such a stubborn man? It was on this trip that Carlos developed into a great Himalayan climber. We started recalculating, knowing full well that all this counting would not increase the amount of food by one crumb.

And that is how it ended up. Mikołaj and Samol went down and the rest of us went up. Four people are however a rather impractical group. A two-man tent is just adequate for three, but not for four, so there was more equipment to be carried, and we would simply have to go without food on the last day.

It was desperately cold as we established Camp 5 at a height of 7600 metres. We were saving gas, as there was little left. The next day we were going to go for the summit, still a long way away in the debilitating wind as we approached the ridge. It would not be just a stroll, those last 600 metres. Should we bivouac en route and be faced with two certain days without food, as we only had fuel enough for one night? Or do we go for the summit, take a risk, travel light, and move fast, getting back down to camp after dark? We decided on the greater risk. We would take just a bivvy sheet.

'Let's take that stove and the last bit of fuel,' Zyga suggested.

'If we are to travel light, then let us do just that,' I countered flatly.

We left early in the morning and the hard slow work began straight away on snow, ice and icy rocks. We came across a couloir of glassy-hard ice. All the time we had to belay. At about two o'clock, with still 200 metres to go before the final ridge, a steep wall reared up ahead at 8000 metres. I led, placing a rock peg or ice screw every few metres to clip into. I was moving terribly slowly. What was worse, clouds began to roll in.

At four a genuine snow storm broke out. My only security was a piton driven into the rock which was so charged with static electricity that I could see sparks jumping all over it. My instinct told me to get away from this piton, but it was my only point of attachment, my only chance of survival in that white hell split by lightning flashes and rolls of thunder. It went on for half an hour.

'There's no chance of reaching the summit today!' I shouted down to Zyga. 'Search around for some place where we can dig ourselves into the snow. There's nowhere up here!'

By the time I got down again the others had almost finished digging out a snow cave just big enough for the four of us to fit into close together and protected from the wind. Then, without a word, Zyga took out of his rucksack a stove and gas canister. It was exactly what we needed, and I blessed him quietly, after having earlier insisted he should lighten his load. There was only enough fuel to melt some snow, but even a few mouthfuls of warm liquid meant so much on a bivouac like that.

The night passed in a never-ending squirming around in a desperate and unfulfillable desire to straighten out one's stiff legs, unknowingly thrusting one's elbow into a neighbour's mouth. It must have been about $-40°C$ outside, but there was no wind in the cave, and wrapped in our emergency survival sheets we somehow managed to pass the night.

Next morning we slowly got ourselves organised and reclimbed the first eighty metres of fixed rope. I led again, relieved to find the next section slightly easier than the previous evening's. Now the worst obstacle was that damned hard ice, and of course the altitude. I ran out the eighty metres of rope, made a stance and, preparing to give the others a belay, I dropped the rope!

This left me attached to an icy slope solely by my crampon points and my two ice axes. Luckily Zyga was tied to the other end of the rope, so we did not lose it altogether and he just had to lead the section afresh while I waited there, shifting my weight from one set of crampon points to the other.

We all reached the ridge without further mishap and luckily the climbing was now easier, as far as that term applies at 8000 metres. One moves as if in a perpetual mist, one registers things in a hazy way, confusion reigns in one's head. I felt deadened, at the same time the sun was shining very brightly. If I were to take off my glasses I would be immediately blinded. It was a world, bright to the point of pain, yet threatening, like an over-exposed picture.

It was now six or seven steps then a sit-down rest, then the next six or seven steps. Impossible to do anything more quickly, impossible to do ten steps rather than seven without black patches appearing in front of my eyes. Those last metres of the route were completely dominated by counting. Seven steps, rest. Seven steps, rest. I knew that should I try twelve or thirteen steps I would lose consciousness. One is balancing all the time on the brink of endurance, knowing seven is the limit, that beyond that lies total darkness. The end.

If the going became more difficult the number of steps had to be reduced. But at least I could see the summit, the worst was all behind me. It was now just a question of patience. Despite my total exhaustion and mental dullness I was aware that the end of all that I had been striving for so doggedly was near.

Reaching the summit of Nanga I decided on a little demonstration of joy. At the moment of reaching the summit I would jump up and shout: Hurrah! I'm not sure how this jump appeared, how the shout sounded. But one thing I am sure of is that it cost me so much that I had to sit down immediately, and for a long time I was unable to regain my breath. I solemnly promised myself never again to get drawn into such a show of emotion.

The summit of Nanga Parbat is a cupola, a few metres across, of very hard ice, penetrated just by the tips of one's crampons. When Sławek, Zyga and then Carlos joined me, it suddenly felt great, we thumped each other on our backs like exhausted boxers, unable to pull apart despite the bell. I looked at Carlos, only twenty-three years old and the first Mexican to climb a mountain of over 8000 metres. I still find it unreal to associate this boy's great Himalayan success with the land of his birth. We congratulated each other, then contacted base, talking to Paweł Mularz and the others. Through the mental dullness of exhaustion, I detected joy in their voices. Despite the tragedy, maybe deepened by the tragedy, success was important for this expedition. Now it had become fact. All this took time, but we could afford it, it was only one p.m. on 13th July. As we told base how we planned to descend to Camp 5 and complete the descent next day, we did not realise just how much more animation we had than actual strength.

So we set off down and in the first few metres the old Himalayan truth came home to me that human estimates of distance can be extremely distorted. Everything seemed so close. We would pick up the rope, and surely be back in Camp 5 in three hours. But we had not reckoned with being even more exhausted than during the ascent. Now it was five steps, sit, five steps, sit, and we only reached our cave bivouac at five p.m. There was no way we would get down to Camp 5 before dark, so we faced up to a repeat bivvy which was not going to be just a little snooze in the fresh air, but a night spent shivering and massaging one's legs in an endless fight against frostbite, with no more gas and no more food. A clear sign of how poorly rested we were was the fact that it took us all of the next day to get down to Camp 5, when under normal conditions this should not have taken more than two hours.

During this ghastly victors' descent I saw I was not the only one who was exhausted. I had to shout at Carlos now and again to stop him falling asleep as he stood on an almost vertical slope, supported by his ice axe. An accident was so close, one had to be alert all the time, and Carlos was no longer capable of concentration. That fantastically ambitious colt was collapsing on his feet. So I shouted things like, 'Carlos! Wake up! Go! Now take your ice axe. Now grab the rope. Now slide down slowly.' The same thing was happening to Sławek Łobodziński. Both of them were swimming, and had to be led as if on a lead. Zyga would go first, waiting to receive them.

And so the day passed. Then a mist came down and we did not know which way to go. Zyga said right, I said left. We reached a point where I was sure we were going the wrong way. I could see the slope steepening downwards and I could not remember that.

'Zyga, this is wrong.'

'No, this is definitely right,' puffed Zyga impatiently.

I made the others sit down while I went back up because I felt we were descending into the wrong couloir. After climbing back up the slope for about fifty metres, I was in luck. By pure accident I saw a flash of red in the snow and discovered my old badly torn mitten which I had attached to the fixed rope. I had found the correct route! Like it or not, they came back up and we all followed the saving rope slowly down again to reach Camp 5 after dark.

In Camp 5 there was only one gas cylinder which was just enough to melt snow for four pots of water. We are absolutely parched dry, thirsty to the point of pain, for two days we had had nothing to drink. Neither did we have anything to eat. The following day we reached Camp 4 which was also bare, and continued on down to the level of Camp 3 that same day. As we approached I could only think of the waiting tents full of gas and food. In front of my eyes I saw a mess tin steaming with soup. I was the first to reach the campsite and discover Camp 3 had vanished. The sérac which used to be above us and had acted as a shield against the avalanches had collapsed and completely buried the camp. Just here and there remnants were visible under great blocks of ice which by now had frozen together.

Fortunately, help was on the way in the shape of Michał Kochańczyk and Mirek Gardzilewski who brought us up some food and we managed to chip two tents out of the wreckage.

Ahead of us lay the most serious section, between Camps 3 and 2, which we must get down before the sun rose. We woke at two in the morning, and set off as three pairs one behind the other which added to the danger, for every few seconds a lump of ice or rock was accidentally dislodged, so it was necessary for us to organise our already shattered selves in such a way that one team was never directly beneath another. Even so Sławek suffered a direct hit to his camera lens and Zyga got one on the shoulder, while another rock scored a hit on my rucksack, detaching an ice axe. It was like moving through a battle zone.

Just before Camp 2 there was an eighty-metre traverse where the snow had become quite mushy. I slid across on the slack rope, sometimes higher, sometimes lower. Suddenly my foot broke through into a crevasse and I fell over onto my back, my rucksack dragging me down the slope, one leg jammed in the crevasse. I ended hanging head downwards by this one leg. I grasped the rope with both hands to try and drag myself back upright, but the rope was so slack that it just kept paying out. I could feel a growing pain in my knee, and the rucksack was pulling me down so hard that I was beginning to choke, with my head well below the level of my trapped feet. I could not get the rucksack off, nor count on immediate help because I had been rushing ahead like a madman. Soon, I knew, I would lose consciousness. Things were going dark before my eyes.,

In one last desperate effort, I dragged myself up on the rope as far as I could into a horizontal position then, with my last ounce of energy, threw myself downward. Something creaked in my leg, but it came free! I changed into a great living pendulum, but now I was hanging upright, head up, happy as a young child kicking around in the air with my freed feet. It had worked! My feet came to rest against the wall. It would have been the silliest way to go and it had been a really close call. Zyga also had a close shave, slipping as he was clipping himself into a fixed rope but, managing to grab the rope to slow his fall, he got away with a sprained ankle.

We all managed to reach base camp in one piece. Behind us was the conquered South-East Pillar of Nanga Parbat.

Behind us was also a descent on which we had wandered along the brink of human endurance, and not far from the base camp there was a grave. In it is buried forever our friend Piotr Kalmus.

10

A Rucksack on the Slope

Lhotse, South Face attempt, 1985

When I returned from the Nanga Parbat expedition at the end of July, 1985, I had never felt so tired. In the course of six months I had been on three great mountains with little time to rest between expeditions. Now it was taking its toll. I would not feel mountain hunger again for some time. But my home club in Katowice was in the final stages of organising an expedition to the South Face of Lhotse, one of the biggest unclimbed Himalayan challenges, a wall that has defeated the most daring climbers. How could I back out? Though I said nothing aloud, I was not convinced about this attempt on that legendary wall. But I had a score to settle. Lhotse was the only 8000-metre peak that I had climbed by the normal route, not in winter. The South Face would be really something. If only I were not so tired. The thought that I had barely come back and now I had to pack and go, put me off the whole idea. So it was agreed I should leave a month after the others, but I was still dragging an unaccustomed load of exhaustion up to base camp with me and nothing I saw there changed my mind. I was simply not being attracted by the mountain. Only once before had I felt like this, when I stood with Wojtek beneath that shining East Face of Gasherbrum IV.

At base camp the lads had hardly been hanging around. They were already quite high and about to set up Camp 4. Not wasting any time, I set off onto the face the following day. Things were happening, I found myself somewhat left behind, and was aware of the rather silly situation. The front pair were going along like clocks and they had smelt the summit. They had been going for a while now, so wanted to get to the summit as quickly as possible. It was hardly appropriate for me to barge

Lhotse, South Face, showing the highpoint on the 1985 attempt

in at this stage. I joined the supporting group, carrying supplies to higher camps.

The first summit attack took place a week after my arrival. Krzysiek Wielicki, Jasiu Nowak, Artur Hajzer and Mirek Dasal set up a camp at 8000 metres and climbed on up to a ridge which looked promising. The whole problem of Lhotse's South Face revolves around the section above 8000 metres where all the difficulties are concentrated. Their first attempt was repulsed at 8100 metres, and they agreed to make the next effort closer to the centre of the face. Now it was my turn to go to the front, with Rysiek Pawłowski and Rafał Hołda. We spent the night at Camp 5 at 8000 metres, and planned to fix ropes the next day as far as we could, 200 metres, maybe even 300 metres up this very steep rock wall, probably the hardest section of the whole climb. The following day we would push on up, or retreat.

In the morning Rysiek was feeling unwell, so stayed behind and I set off with Rafał Hołda, travelling light. The rock wall turned out to be so continuously difficult, about Grade V, that we spent all day struggling up eighty metres of it. By two we had fixed the eighty metres of line we had with us. I placed a peg and abseiled down to Rafał, then we began to descend to the tent. Next time I looked around, Rafał had vanished. He had been about fifteen metres behind me. I had heard nothing, no shout. Then I noticed, some hundred metres lower, a rucksack rolling down towards a precipice. I looked all around me very carefully. Maybe Rafał was standing somewhere blending into the surroundings, maybe he had only fallen a short distance. But there was not a trace of him. The snowy cauldron was covered in hard packed snow. Going up in crampons, the points would dig into the surface as if it were bread, but one slip and it would be like sliding down from the top of a giant ski-jump slope over a 300-metre vertical drop which was clearly visible from base camp. I radioed down in desperation, telling them to have a look through their binoculars. Only gradually it sank in that a tragedy had taken place. Rafał must be dead. He was one of the youngest members of our expedition.

All this time the weather was perfect, with blue sky and sunshine. I sat in Camp 5 wondering what to do next. But I was losing faith. I had reached 8100 metres and I could see the difficulties were hardly receding at all. We had to find another variation, or battle away with our present line, nibbling away at least at several metres of rock a day, until we had established 300 metres of fixed ropes, almost up to the summit. It had taken, so far, from September to the end of October, and over five kilometres of line had been fixed. Soon it would be November. It was getting late. The days were getting short, it was becoming colder.

All this was going through my mind as I talked to the lower camps on the radio. Eventually I asked, 'What now? I don't think we will manage this route.'

As I said those words I realised that it was the very first time I had been the one to suggest retreat. Below, the others had gone up to the base of the face and searched everywhere for some sign of Rafał, but all in vain. I was overcome with depression. I'd had enough of this wall. I wanted to know what I was to do. If I was to stop the assault then I had to pack up Camp 5 and start coming down with all the equipment. If there were others wanting to come up for another attempt I would leave everything where it was and go down for a rest. But I knew I could not rush them then, when a tragedy had only just taken place.

Eventually I put the question. We had another possibility to contemplate, for there were also on the South Face three young Frenchmen from Vincent Fai's expedition. They were very ambitious, but they had no Himalayan experience, and they wanted to do the face alpine-style! From the start I had taken their ambitions with a pinch of salt, and did not expect them to have a cat-in-hell's chance. But they made an impression on us, especially on Artur Hajzer who, observing these magnificently equipped colts, began to believe that the wall could be climbed. What is more he had established a liaison with them.

'I feel, Jurek,' he told me over the radio, 'that we should give it one more go. And the French lads would like to join in on the action to make one final effort for the top. Over.'

So I left all the equipment behind and went down for a rest. Base camp was subdued.

They had not managed to find Rafał's body which had probably fallen into the bergschrund at the base of the wall.

Planning the new attempt, we decided that one team would not be enough, there must be at least two, the first to push the fixed line up another 80–200 metres to surmount the rock barrier, the second team to go for the summit travelling light. Of course nobody wanted to be in the team doing all the hard work and then, just below the target, turn back and go down. So we decided that each team should push out the route as far as it could. By now only Vincent Fai himself of the three Frenchmen was willing to give the joint plan a go. Artur went up with him to Camp 5. We left a day later and waited at Camp 4. Things above seemed to be moving more slowly than they should. En route from 4 to 5 I got in touch with Artur on the radio and he explained that Vincent was not too well and wanted to rest for one night and then start work.

I voiced my opposition to this as strongly as possible. At 8000 metres you cannot rest. You may think you can, but after a night at 8000 metres you can only feel weaker. So now I was not only brutal but also unyielding.

'Either you go now to fix line or we take down the camp and pack up. I do not see the slightest chance that you can succeed as a pair. Over.'

I heard Artur trying to convince Vincent. As we talked we could see each other at a great distance, which made our contact more real. Then he was trying again to persuade me to agree to their waiting to have one more go. But I still insisted on going down.

Why did I do that? I have always been the one who, even in the most desperate situations, has said we must go up. Here, all of a sudden, I was no longer so sure. Mirek Dasal, who was beside me, hardly took part in the whole discussion. Artur, however, could barely hide his surprise. He later admitted that because it was me saying that I saw no chance, he simply accepted my decision to turn back. But he never did completely agree with it. That was the end of the expedition to the South Face of Lhotse.

The next day we were back down at base camp. Often at the end of an expedition there is time to rest in a relaxed atmosphere as one waits for the descent with the porters. But this time everyone was feeling rather down as a result of Rafał's death, and all I could think of was home, and about getting there as soon as possible. This was my over-powering weariness with mountains talking. The action had come to an end and nothing else interested me any more. I suppose I was running away from the Himalaya. During the course of one day I covered a distance which is normally done in a week by a major expedition. Arriving in Lukla, I was incredibly lucky, because with the help of some baksheesh I managed to get onto an airplane and I was back in Kathmandu. In a day and a half I had descended from 8000 metres to 1800. Another record for me.

In the capital I met the advance party of a winter expedition to Kangchenjunga for which I was listed as a member. So was Krzysiek Wielicki. I could not cope with all this, everything was taking on a crazy pace. Here was my next commitment and all I wanted to do was go back home to rest. The expedition leader, Andrzej Machnik, bore me no grudge, but at the same time it was difficult to detect any sign of his approval. They had a vast amount of work to do, as the vehicle loaded with their equipment was still floating out there on the ocean somewhere, aboard a ship with a changed schedule. But I had just had enough and in two more days I was back home in Poland.

To this day I wonder why I let pass that opportunity of climbing the South Face of Lhotse. Maybe it was that something which at a certain moment stops one from making another step further. I do not want to use that rather grandiose word destiny or even instinct. No doubt Rafał's death contributed to things. Also, there was not enough linking me with that wall, three-quarters of which had been climbed without me. I was not there when they were pitching the camps and setting up the fixed ropes. I was only involved in finishing the route off between Camps 4 and 5. I had now developed that feeling which told me that I had put so much into that face that it was a shame to turn back now. Maybe it was first and foremost just exhaustion? This was my fourth demanding expedition of the year. First I had climbed two unfamiliar-to-me summits in winter, then there was Nanga Parbat.

The telephone stayed quiet, a characteristic sign of failure, which I was gradually getting over. On top of everything I had the feeling of wasted time. But if I had followed the whispering voice inside me and not gone to the Himalaya then, the outcome would have been the same. So I rested, got involved with my family and the house, or would drive over to our hut at Istebna. For the first time in a long while I did not have to worry about setting up another expedition. Most important, I tried to recover psychologically. My two young boys helped me to do this.

Only now and again a vision returns, from which I will be unable to free myself probably to the end of my life: a slope of hard snow, sparkling in the Himalayan sun, down which a rucksack is tumbling . . .

11

Eternal Rest

Kangchenjunga, winter 1986

Even the most wonderful rest cannot last for ever. On 12th December I left Poland, with Krzysiek Wielicki, flying via Moscow and Delhi to Kathmandu, then overnight by bus to the east of Nepal where we started marching into the mountains. After two days we caught up with the tail end of the Kangchenjunga expedition. Artur Hajzer who had stayed on in Nepal, had been put in charge of getting the delayed truck with the bulk of the expedition equipment out of Bombay Docks and bringing it along behind the expedition vanguard who had already set off for the mountain. Krzysiek and I hurried on past the slow-moving porter column carrying just our own equipment. Kangchenjunga is the most easterly of the fourteen 8000-metre peaks and the route to its base goes through much wilder country than is met with on the way to Everest or Lhotse. The walk starts at an altitude of only 500 metres, among a paradise of palm trees, ripening oranges and bananas. But every day we noticed the changes in the landscape. At 4000 metres we left behind the last meadows, or rather pasture, and reached the Kangchenjunga base camp on the lateral moraine of the glacier at about 5200 metres, four days before Christmas Eve. Andrzej Czok, Przemek Piasecki and several climbers from Zakopane were already there, having set up camp on 10th December, and in those first ten days they had already managed to establish two camps on the mountain.

Physically I was feeling great. Even my frostbitten feet, which I had felt a bit on Lhotse, had stopped hurting altogether. But the most important thing in the mountains is to feel well within oneself, and I judged my psychological state to be much better than it had been at the start

123

Kangchenjunga, first winter ascent of the South-West Face,
11th January, 1986

of my previous expedition. First of all I was one hundred per cent convinced by the project itself. We would be following the normal South-West Face route with the objective of making the first winter ascent of Kangchenjunga. I was now only two peaks behind Reinhold Messner. This also raised the stakes as far as Kangchenjunga was concerned. I did however realise that, even if I conquered this mountain, I would still be one behind Messner, and I would be going back home when he would be setting off to complete his fourteenth eight-thousander. Reinhold was two peaks ahead and in full control of the situation. Counting mountains like goals in a football match only leads to delusion.

For December and the winter conditions prevailing in the Himalaya, the weather was beautiful. It was very cold, even at base camp it was −25°C, but there was no wind. Krzysiek and I loaded ourselves up with everything we might need higher up and set off at a very leisurely pace for Camp 1, then on to Camp 2. From there we pushed on to get the load up as high as possible. At about 7000 metres we dropped our loads and went back down again. It was 23rd December, tomorrow was Christmas Eve which we wanted to spend all together. Over the radio we heard that Artur had just arrived at base camp with the tail end of the expedition. The expedition had been divided into two groups, the first had brought up the most essential equipment and food for a dozen days or so, the second group brought up all that had come by sea and which had been delayed because of the ship's re-routing. Base camp was swarming with activity. At last all our equipment had arrived – thirty or forty drums. We could live it up and enjoy the festivities in style.

But, unfortunately, we did not all end up spending Christmas Eve together. Some of us sat around in advance base camp, while most of the others were down below. This was all the result of our ruthless calculations. To go back down would have taken one day, to come back up another, and we would have had to spend one day down there. In total we would have lost at least three days. So there we were, condemned by our own decisions to some of the traditional Christmas Eve abstinences. Though that did not worry us too much.

Krzysiek Pankiewicz prepared the food with me. He even managed to make a respectable cake on the lid of one of the equipment drums, with real jelly and blackberries from a tin. It looked tasty. We improvised a table with two drums, elegantly covered over, another two drums served as our seats. Following tradition, we would await the appearance of the first stars in the sky. It began to blow a bit by the afternoon, a strong wind tugging at the parachute sheet which covered our tent. The weather was changing. But that evening we did not worry about the wind, as we searched the sky for the first star. Easier to spot here than in smoky Katowice. In the mountains the times of day are far more pronounced.

There it was! Full of emotion, we sat down at the table and, in that moment, the whole festive atmosphere evaporated. Krzysiek had sat down on the cake. We had certainly never before eaten a cake served like this, as each helping was scraped off Krzysiek's backside.

We tried to make this Christmas Eve a bit like the ones back home. We started by saying a prayer, we sang a few carols, then came a time for reminiscing. All that was missing was just the tiniest drop of alcohol, since the spirits had only got as far as base camp. But there were no real regrets. If we had wanted to we could have been sitting by the big Christmas Eve table down in the base camp, drinking fortified Góral tea from the Tatra and eating more than just that squashed cake. What did turn out to be a shame was that our self-sacrifice gained us nothing at all. The wind had been rising all the time. In the early morning of Christmas Day there was such a wild storm blowing, it was not even possible to go outside the tent, between the tents great snowdrifts appeared. We sat there, inactive, till New Year's Eve.

Up to now, whenever I had been on an expedition with Andrzej Czok, I had always climbed with him. But Andrzej had already started climbing with Przemek Piasecki, and I arrived with Krzysztof Wielicki, both of us acclimatising to a similar degree, so quite naturally we teamed up. It would have been pointless to rearrange the teams. So when the wind abated slightly on New Year's Eve we left as a foursome: Andrzej and Przemek, Krzysiek and myself. We worked well together and decided to carry on working in this grouping to the end of the expedition.

Kangchenjunga is the world's third highest mountain. It is 8598 metres high, and in reality it is more of a massif, composed of four 8000-metre peaks: Kangchenjunga South (8476 metres), Kangchenjunga Central (8496 metres), Kangchenjunga main peak, and Yalung Kang, the West Summit (8420 metres). The normal South-West Face route is by no means difficult when climbed in normal summer conditions. Winter is different. Kangchenjunga is to some extent a Polish mountain. The first ascent of the South Summit was made by a Polish team, as was that of the Central Summit; Poles were also responsible for a new route on Yalung Kang. A successful winter ascent by us would complete this relationship. We really would be able to call it a Polish massif.

We spent New Year's Eve at Camp 1, frequently having to clear snow away from the tents, where, in the evening, men's talk prevailed: 'So here we are, gentlemen, dug into the snow, and our dear ladies are just now putting on their evening dresses . . .' But even the most interesting reminiscences and the most imaginative speculations do not last for ever. The eyes got heavy, by eight silence descended on the tents. We slept.

The following day we reached Camp 2 and repaired those wind-battered tents that were still usable. At least no fresh snow was lying around, as it had all been blown away from this side of the mountain. We could move on old, hard snow and reached the proposed site for Camp 3 at 7200 metres with no problem. Here we slept and continued on up as a foursome to set up Camp 4. At this altitude Krzysiek and I were performing very clumsily, despite the acclimatisation left over from our Lhotse expedition one month ago. Four weeks lounging around at lower levels had taken their toll. Neither Andrzej nor Przemek had acclimatised fully yet either. At 7800 metres we only put up one tent, and Andrzej and Przemek turned round and went back down to Camp 3.

Krzysiek and I nursed a secret hope that, after a night at 7800 metres, we would be able to go on towards the summit. But on the next day the weather broke and snow began falling. We left the camp set up and descended all the way down to base camp. At the same time another team set off from base camp to resupply the higher camps. This team should have a well trodden and marked route to follow, after which they could go on to the summit. Their only handicap would be their lack of adequate acclimatisation. So the idea was that they should go up as far as they could.

The bottleneck of the operation was now Camp 4 which had only one tent standing, but everything there ready for the use of two people. When it was our turn to go up again we had to decide whether to make a four-man attack on the summit or a two-man attack. We decided to set off as a four and wait higher up until the other teams had had their go out in front. We could take an extra tent to add to the existing one at Camp 4 which would enable us to attack the summit all together. We met the others descending halfway between Camps 2 and 3 after turning back at Camp 3. When we reached there I could see that Andrzej Czok was still not acclimatising well, and far from his usual self out in front. Instead he dragged along behind, coughing. But everyone coughs in these mountains, especially in winter when the air is very dry.

The following day I discussed openly with Krzysiek the idea that we should go up to Camp 4 first and the others should follow on on the next day not carrying so much. There was no need to pretend, they were not going as strongly as we were. But in the end the decision was reached that we should all go up together and so we shared out the loads equally between us.

On the way up our foursome spread out badly. Przemek reached Camp 4 half an hour behind Krzysiek and me, and Andrzej another hour later, clearly very exhausted. He was not the Andrzej I knew, always in excellent condition and the best, the most reliable ox as far as mountain work was concerned. Now he was only making progress by sheer willpower and he never stopped coughing, despite the medicine he had been advised to take by radio contact with the base camp doctor.

At Camp 4 we first of all had to dig out our buried tent. As Przemek and Andrzej were putting up theirs, Krzysiek and I were already cooking something up and we soon had a drink ready for them. All this fiddling around always takes up about two hours before one can finally settle into one's sleeping bag and relax. But it was hard for me to fall asleep. Through those two thin tent walls that separated us I kept hearing Andrzej's incessant coughing. Once again we contacted base. The doctor recommended that Andrzej tried a steam inhalation from above a boiling mess tin of tea, and then took some more of the recommended medicines.

'Just in case, take some Furosemid as well,' he added.

Furosemid is a diuretic. At altitude the body sometimes starts to retain excess water and bloat out. On the face or hands this poses little problem, but it is much worse if the water accumulates in the lungs or in the brain, pulmonary or cerebral oedema respectively, which are both killers.

After this last advice from the doctor we talked a little longer, then lost our enthusiasm for chatting. Everything seemed to have settled down, we had gone back to our tents and got into our sleeping bags, but I could not dismiss Andrzej's condition.

'So what do we do tomorrow?' I asked.

'I'm really feeling rough. I think I'll be going down,' Andrzej said.

'Fine,' said Przemek. 'In that case we'll go down together.'

Krzysiek and I felt fine, so I said, 'Okay, so we'll try and go for the summit.'

Silence descended on the camp, broken only by Andrzej's occasional cough. The night passed with a short doze and then preparations. We first of all had to thaw out our boots, then dry out our socks, then boil up a drink and force ourselves to eat something. At 5.45 a.m. we were ready to start. It was 11th January. I was the first to leave the tent, it was still dark.

'Right, we're off now!' I called to the other two.

From the other tent we heard Przemek's voice. 'We'll have a bit of a lie in. We've only got a descent ahead of us.'

We set off. After a few hundred metres I lost all feeling in my legs, and Krzysiek experienced the same problem. But, slowly, rhythmically, we carried on. At ten a.m. the sun finally reached us, warming and raising our spirits. Krzysiek cut out a small platform, sat down on it, took off his boots and rubbed the soles of his feet. Then we were off again. We had a long way ahead of us, 800 metres of height to gain. In winter. A very long way.

I remember little of it. First of all an overpowering wish, with every step, that it could be all over. That ghastly, almost senseless trudging, step after step. We were on the normal route, so every now and again we saw a piece of rope sticking out of the snow. We did not belay each other, nor were we tied together. We moved along at our own pace. Krzysiek overtook me, I was unable to keep up with him, and he reached the summit before me. He did not wait for me there but turned about and started to come down. We passed each other in silence just a few metres below the top. Then I reached the summit and left on it two little plastic teddies I had taken from my boys at home. I also took a few photos.

All this must appear strange. After all, if one goes up into the mountains with other people, one wants to share the joy with others. Krzysiek actually broached the subject himself later.

'I'm not really sure how it came about. I waited on the summit for you for about half an hour. Just when I saw you approaching, I got up and started down. As if I could not have waited those extra few minutes.'

But a person's mind works differently up there, thinking is very definitely dulled. For example, I kept thinking on the summit that I had a radio with me. So that the battery would work better I had placed it in a warm pocket. But then it got in the way as I was climbing, so I had transferred it carefully to a pocket in the flap of my rucksack, so that there would be the minimum amount of effort involved in taking it out and fixing it into the radio on the summit. When I got there the first thing I did was reach for the battery and realised it was not there. It had gone. I rummaged around in the flap pocket, cursing quietly. I simply could not work out what could have happened to it. At last I gave up. Communicating with base camp is, after all, not the most important thing. But I was annoyed, for I had lugged this radio which I could not now use all the way up the mountain and it had represented an extra kilo. I caught up with Krzysiek and we reached Camp 4. It was desperately cold, so before doing anything I crawled into my sleeping bag to warm up, then I cooked something and finally I picked up the radio, reached for my rucksack and discovered that the battery had been there all the time in the flap pocket. High up in the mountains people often pose questions to themselves, but they rarely manage to answer them.

So we were able to establish contact with base camp after all and report that we had reached the summit. The answering congratulations were, however, muted, and from the exchange of conversation between base camp and Camp 3, we realised that the situation with Andrzej was becoming serious. We were very surprised about this. Going down one always regains one's lost strength. But now it was different. Andrzej and Przemek had started off down, but Andrzej had only managed to get down half of the way by himself. Eventually he became so weak that he simply could not carry on. Przemek had carried on down to Camp 3 on his own where he met up with Artur Hajzer, Krzysiek Pankiewicz and Ludwik Wilczyński among others, who went back up with him to carry Andrzej down. They were now in continuous contact with the doctor at base camp, who was recommending a very strong dose of Furosemid. He was worried about Andrzej developing pulmonary oedema.

A team including the doctor was leaving base camp with oxygen for

Andrzej, planning to climb through the night, and a pair from Camp 3 had set off down to meet them and rush the oxygen cylinder and breathing apparatus back up. The situation was deteriorating by the hour. It was simply horrifying. Nobody could accept the fact that it was Andrzej who had collapsed like that, and was so gravely ill.

Krzysiek and I were told to stay up in Camp 4 as there was too much coming and going at Camp 3. We were both a bit overcome by exhaustion anyway, but more so by the drama taking place several hundred metres below. It was agreed we should come down in the morning to help carry Andrzej down to base.

It was another very cold night, we got up and got ourselves ready with no regrets. Before leaving at eight we made the prearranged contact and heard the stark news that Andrzej had died in the night.

He was in one tent with Przemek and, thanks to that, he was more comfortable than the other four in the neighbouring tent. Przemek had kept making him drinks, and fed him. At nine p.m. Andrzej had felt a bit better. Przemek was relieved, he settled down to making another brew. At ten he had turned round to pass over the next mug of tea, and Andrzej had showed no sign of life.

That was the abbreviated story we were told over the radio by Ludwig Wilczyński. We sat motionless and in silence, then we contacted base. Andrzej Machnik, the expedition leader, answered us. 'The expedition is over, over. We are stopping all further action. Take down whatever you can from 4 to 3. We'll talk again when you are there, over.'

At Camp 3 we found Krzysiek Pankiewicz and Artur Hajzer with Andrzej's body. Przemek, drained psychologically and physically, had already been helped down in a bad state. The oxygen had only made it up to the start of the fixed ropes, but we later realised it would not have made it in time anyway.

Andrzej was lying there in a sleeping bag, as if he was simply sleeping. We began to discuss the situation. Either we carry down his body, or we bury him there, at 7400 metres. I wanted to bring him down but when somebody asked how we would manage this, it dawned on us how powerless we were. Krzysiek and I were both very tired after our summit push, and Artur had helped carry Andrzej down to Camp 3 which had cost him a lot of effort. But there were people below, who could help, among them three members of a Tatra mountain rescue team. Their opinions were now important.

'I'm in favour of carrying Andrzej down,' I told them, 'but I will not insist. You are the experts. Tell us if you think we have any chance of making it.'

I knew it was easy to talk, but that the journey would be desperately hard. The body would have to be lifted across crevasses, lowered down drops, and carried for long distances over terrain where it is often difficult to move around with free hands. It was a question of taking on a major evacuation job which could easily take a week.

After a discussion involving many voices an opinion emerged that in theory it was possible to carry down the body, but practically we lacked the required strength to do this. The retrieval would take a very long time. And all that would be achieved would be that Andrzej's body would be brought down to base camp where there are only glaciers, so he would end up being buried in a crevasse, just as he would at Camp 3. To carry him down further where he could be buried in the ground would take at least another week. So we should bury him right there, at 3, where he died, following the simplest Himalayan tradition. Why should he, after death, be pulled about further?

The burial ceremony fell entirely on us four. We found a suitable crevasse fifty metres from the tents. It had the shape of a very deep, gradually narrowing wedge. It was still before midday as we pulled Andrzej over to the edge of the crevasse in his sleeping bag and bivouac sheet. He looked wonderfully at peace. It was quiet and the sun shone, as if the mountains which he had grown to love so much did not want to disturb him now.

'Our Father, who art in heaven . . .'

It was hard to accept that Andrzej would never get out of that sleeping bag to set off into the mountains again. Andrzej Czok was not just one of us, he was the soul of the community in Silesia, he really was somebody. It was with him that I first started going to the Himalaya. Much linked us, not just in the mountains but also in the valleys.

'Hail Mary, full of grace . . .'

Until now I had always held that in the mountains there is no place for great feelings, neither for euphoria nor grief, that man is just not able to have them. Now I knew I had got this wrong.

'Rest eternal give unto him, Lord . . .'

We bent and lowered Andrzej's body down gently on ropes till it settled. On him lay his ice axe with his name on it. As we covered him with snow and ice I knew that I must say something. I straightened myself.

'For the last time we say goodbye to Andrzej,' I began but at that moment I knew I was unable to say another word, because something had grasped at my throat, those mountains around us, glistening in the sun, had become hazy, and I was crying.

We marked the place with a simple cross made from bamboo route-markers. A month later, as I was developing the expedition photographs, I came to one taken a day before Andrzej's death, between Camps 2 and 3. Standing are Krzysiek Wielicki, Przemek Piasecki and Andrzej Czok, beside whom is a bamboo marker with a section of rope cutting across it. It forms a cross very similar to the one we placed over his Himalayan grave two days later. Whenever I look at that picture I wonder: destiny, a sign?

The next day, after a rather unnecessary base-camp argument with Andrzej Machnik, I set off down with Krzysiek Wielicki and Artur Hajzer. It was the third expedition in a row which had ended in tragedy.

At the airport in Warsaw a TV sports commentator bombarded us with questions. We told him what had happened and no more. The programme was mainly designed to be sensational. Some liked it, others did not. Of course the tragedy was a key part of it. Some reporters can keep their lust for blood in check, others can't. In this respect I do feel that Polish reporters are still fairly acceptable.

I went to Istebna, where my wife and children were waiting for me. At last I was home. But here a reporter from the *Katowice Workers' Tribune* turned up to write a story about the trip. I told him everything, giving him material for a four-part article to appear on four Saturdays in a row. Three weeks later the rest of the expedition returned, among them Machnik, who complained to the *Tribune* that they should have waited to talk to him as leader of the expedition. So a fifth article appeared in which he managed to find some fault in what Krzysiek Wielicki and I had done. I ignored this, but I felt an unpleasant taste had been left behind after this expedition.

I had one more duty to attend to, which I would pass on to no one else. I had to go to see Andrzej's wife. She already knew all the details, as many days had passed from the moment I telephoned through the tragic news from Kathmandu to Bilczewski, and the story had been repeated on the radio, in the papers and on television. But this did not change anything. I had to go and see this family I knew so well, bearing the guilt of being still alive when he was dead. Waiting for me were Andrzej's wife, his very young daughter, his mother and brother. Only one brother because his other brother had also died. In the mountains.

12

Do As You Please

'So you are this Kukuczka? You don't look like a mountaineer.'
        The Swiss guide was not so much looking into my eyes, as rather lower, to just below the belt where I display a rather unsportsmanlike girth, having gained a bit of weight during the last inactive months. But that was no reason for this guy to make remarks about it, himself as thin as a racehound, who all his life does nothing but run about in the Alps. There were others like him around, Germans, Austrians and Swiss, mainly guides. We all met up at Dasso, the last village on the way to K2 which can be reached by vehicle. All was noise and activity. Soon the expedition would start moving. There were more important things to attend to than personal comments made by Swiss guides, so I walked away. We can have a chat at 8000 metres, I murmured to myself.

How did I find myself in this international group? I will try to explain this concisely. After my sad experience with the leader of the Kangchenjunga expedition, I decided that would be the end of my tagging on to large expeditions, that I must make every effort to go to the Himalaya under my own steam in the smallest group possible, alpine-style. About the effectiveness of this I had convinced myself and many others as well. Indeed, now my hair stood on end at the thought of working in a much bigger group with all its potential for conflict. Fine, so now what?

Sitting quietly at home one day, there was a telephone call from Szczecin.

'Hello, Jurek! It's Tadek Piotrowski. Herrligkoffer has invited me on a K2 expedition. I can bring someone else along with me. Are you interested?'

All my carefully made pronouncements went by the board in an instant as I replied that of course I was.

Doctor Karl Herrligkoffer from Munich was a famous Himalayan expedition organiser; this K2 expedition would be his twenty-fourth and he was to celebrate his seventieth birthday on it. He had always been an organiser, never a climber, which breaks the normal pattern that people are first climbers and then, when they are no longer so physically able, become more involved in organising and leading expeditions. Karl was long in the tooth, so he upheld the canons of traditional mountain-eering. With him everything started from the signing of a contract that all films made in the mountains would be handed over to him, that 550 kilos will be carried up to Camp 3 and 120 to Camp 4. His very Ger-manic, carefully calculated approach to the whole business does not suit everybody. Nor me. Nobody had to this date ever forced me to sign any contract beyond the pledge I sign before my departure that my family would not, in the event of my death, insist on the cost of the repatriation of my body being covered by my insurance. But that is another story. Herrligkoffer, I had heard, was not favourably inclined towards young mountaineers and in particular to exponents of the alpine-style of ascent which goes against the ideology of the great expedition to which he himself adheres. But the prize was the South Face of K2. For such stakes one can fall into line over anything. I had dreamt about it for years. I would have been most unhappy if anyone else had done it before me.

Tadeusz Piotrowski himself was the other factor in my saying yes to Herrligkoffer. At the end of the 'sixties and in the early 'seventies he had been the most outstanding Polish climber in the Tatra, a real specialist in winter ascents, with numerous firsts to his credit in the Tatra, the Alps and Norway. Together with Andrzej Zawada he made the first winter ascent of Noshaq, a very important breakthrough because nobody to that date had made the ascent of a seven-thousander in winter. In 1974 he had taken part in an expedition to Lhotse on which Latallo had died. That was at a time when somebody had to be to blame if any accident occurred, and on this occasion a lot of this fell on Tadek, as a result of which he left the club and for several years simply vanished from climb-ing circles. But he was active and well known for his authorship of several mountaineering books written during this period. He did not climb, but it was impossible to take the pen out of his hand.

After four years things had blown over and he joined us on an expedition to Tirich Mir. Then he took part in other expeditions, but he did not seem to be having much luck with getting to summits. He never made it to the top of any eight-thousander. Luck is a necessary ingredient in the mountains. How often has a member of an expedition with time running out felt fit and keen to have a go at the summit, but not been able to because others nearer the summit were the ones picked to go up instead. So Tadek, who from his earliest days was known as a human tank of great endurance who never developed any problems, always carried around a totally unjustified reputation for not being successful at altitude. On Tirich Mir at 7700 metres I had seen how relaxed he was mentally and physically, clearly not doing anything at his absolute limits. I knew he had great reserves.

So now when he telephoned me I felt a great satisfaction. He could have asked any one of his many friends to take up Herrligkoffer's proposition. That is what teaming up for an expedition is all about. Nowhere is it written that if someone has a list of achievements behind him, that he is the one everybody will rush to. No, one chooses who one would like to climb with.

My only duty towards the organisation was to furnish the expedition with twenty down jackets and twenty sleeping bags. All that was needed was to raise one million złotys and order the down. Our home climbing clubs and the Polish Alpine Association helped us cover our flight costs to Islamabad. The rest was not much of a problem.

In Pakistan Tadek and I went to Karachi to collect the expedition equipment, 300 loads each of thirty kilos, which had arrived by sea, and saw it onto a lorry to Islamabad, staying behind ourselves for several days to complete some visa formalities and a lot of other tedious paperwork.

So it was only in Dasso that we met everybody properly. This was the first time I had taken part in an expedition organised by western mountaineers. The differences were immediately noticeable. While we were in Karachi getting the equipment out of the customs hall, Tadek and I were already becoming nervous. At every stage we were being asked to pay extra charges, reaching into our pockets for fifty rupees here or a hundred rupees there, our Polish souls rebelling. We were so upset that we telephoned Herrligkoffer, who was waiting for us in Islamabad. And instead of hearing some sort of advice or encouragement we heard, 'I cannot understand what you are talking about. Pay whatever they ask, pay even five times more than they ask and do not worry your head about it.'

How could we talk to him, we who had learnt from our very first trip abroad about the need to count every 'hard' cent and to think carefully before spending a single rupee? Sometimes I would wander about for two days just to fix something up for ten rupees less. And now Karl was clearly disgusted by the trivial nature of the problem we had faced him with.

'If you have to pay five thousand, pay five thousand. What is the problem?'

I just could not understand this. Any time that I had been involved in hiring a truck for a Polish expedition I'd been involved in long and nerve-wracking negotiations over the price, wasting a lot of time. Now I was operating in a world of people for whom a sum of one hundred, two hundred, one thousand or even two thousand dollars made very little difference to the expedition budget. Once we were all together we could simply go to the restaurant and order whatever we wanted, rather than what we could afford. I no longer had to cook for myself in the very cheapest hotel so as not to spend too much money.

Government regulations require the issuing of shoes and socks to porters. Polish expeditions equip their porters with socks available in Polish shops, and very basic plimsolls. The porters carrying Herrligkoffer's luggage received a brand new pair of Adidas trainers which they rushed off to sell immediately, ending up walking, be it on snow or on grass, in their own faithful sandals with soles made of rubber shaped to their feet. Herrligkoffer's 300 porters were each also given a pair of beautiful Swiss wool socks. I had dreamt of such socks for a long time and, as I watched the porters accepting their socks, I knew full well that none of them would ever wear them. They are simply not accustomed to wearing socks. They would run down to the nearest shop in town and sell them for next to nothing. I was not jealous. I would not try and relieve one of the porters of his socks. But I became very much aware that my material situation resembled more the situation of those porters than that of my fellow expedition members.

Western profligacy continued to be apparent during the walk-in. There was a sirdar, his deputy, and several assistants who fixed everything. It really choked me watching them ripping Herrligkoffer off at every turn. They were simply fleecing him. I knew all their tricks by heart, and Karl just paid and said Thank you! It did not even cross his mind that someone looking him straight in the eye could be cheating him. And this was his twenty-fourth expedition to the Himalaya. Very simply, these minor matters had never really interested the professor. But I became so worked up about it, I said to Tadek, 'I don't think I can stand this any more. Just look how they are treating him.'

'Look the other way. Why should it concern you? Calm down,' he advised me with stoical calmness.

I gritted my teeth and told myself it was really no concern of mine. All the same, I have learnt that it is possible to close one's eyes to the occasional minor swindle, but the sirdar should never be allowed to forget who is boss.

Karl Herrligkoffer clearly had no control over what was going on. The sirdar was a man he had trusted from his many expeditions to Pakistan, always polite, always charming towards Karl. Karl had first-class non-stop personal service. The cook was at his side to answer to his every beck and call, a cup of tea, tent always pitched, bed made up, in other words total comfort. Having all that, even this very experienced leader did not realise that at every step the exceptionally helpful sirdar was squeezing a bit more out.

This was the first expedition for which the leader had ordered several helicopter flights in advance. That did allow one to relax psychologically at base camp, knowing that, should need arise, one was in excellent contact with the civilised world.

There were no problems with the food either. It all came ready-to-cook, just throw it into a pot and after ten minutes out comes a steak, potatoes and cabbage. And what wonderful kitchen equipment, everything that could possibly make life pleasant at base camp was provided. There was plenty of hot water and it was not rationed like on Polish expeditions where one knows that heating water means using paraffin and that cannot be squandered on washing.

I don't want to criticise the organisation and provisioning of Polish expeditions out of hand. They are often much better supplied than an amateurishly organised small expedition from the West which is desperate to save on everything. But here I was under no pressure, I did not have to deny myself a decent wash. If I felt hungry, I just went along to the mess tent and ate. I did not have to wait for the meal to be served. Karl Herrligkoffer's expedition was a major international undertaking, and I could really appreciate the total freedom it allowed one to concentrate entirely on climbing.

However, after only a few conversations on the walk-in I discovered that these young people did not have any great mountaineering ambitions. It was Tadek and I who were the ones pushing for a new route and for trying the South Face alpine-style. I was walking along beside some of the top young Swiss guides, but my words could have been spoken into an empty room. They think differently. To reach the summit anyhow will be enough, then back home as fast as possible. I tried to understand them, but our temperaments were simply incompatible. They are directed by cold calculation. An alpine guide has his clients, and it is enough for him to write down against his name that he has climbed K2. That will impress his clients. None of them will worry too much about which route he climbed it by. What is more, many will be quite satisfied if he can only claim to have taken part in a K2 expedition. Certainly it is possible that he might have a tough time, as long as it is not too tough. He might even be involved in some sort of an incident that he can talk about for years after. But first and foremost he must not risk too much. An adventure, yes. Risk, no.

To be able better to compare western and Polish mountaineers it is necessary to have a look at a western car. It is excellent on perfect roads. A Polish car is poor, heavy, uneconomical, but it survives much better on rough tracks where it could sometimes replace a tank. The westerners are also first-class performers in perfect weather, when they can see the route, when they are relaxed and there is no risk. Then they out-perform others. But they have to have the conditions just right, they have to have a beautifully finished motorway with no pot-holes. If the road is not too good they rapidly pack up.

All this was quite astonishing, bearing in mind that Herrligkoffer had selected his team from the specific point of view of a major sporting achievement. To him this was a prestige expedition. He said this quite openly. It would be one of his last, maybe his actual last, to the Karakoram, and he wanted it to be crowned with a memorable success. The aim of the expedition spoke for itself. It was on our permit: the South Face of K2 and a new route on Broad Peak. He had set the bar high, and he wanted to achieve success.

But these aces he had chosen clearly had a different concept to mine of what was involved in the serious business of climbing this mountain. There were also differences of opinion all the time between the Swiss and the Germans, the Germans and the Austrians and the Swiss and the Austrians. We two Poles they left carefully alone, a bit like two rotten eggs that should not be touched because they did not know what it could lead to. We did not complain. Socially they were a pleasant enough bunch, but one question worried me. How much were they really worth in the mountains? And could they be talked into doing a new route?

Between me and Tadek there were no misunderstandings. We had discussed the matter for two weeks while we were waiting for the delayed container of equipment in Karachi. Every day we would go down to the port, every evening we would return to the hotel, so we had plenty of time to think and discuss. Tadek initially approached the project with some reservation.

'If that new route doesn't work out we can always get up K2 by the normal route,' he would say.

I kept luring him with photographs of the South Face, like those of a beautiful girl, and I watched them having an effect. One day he said, not just simply to get me out of his hair, 'Well, yes. We have to try it.'

I put away the pictures, knowing I had done my job. Tadek had been caught. He now spoke as one who was completely convinced that it was an excellent project, and worth the effort.

But the most important discussions were still awaiting us. I was very interested to see what position would be taken up by Karl Herrligkoffer. Already in Dasso he had asked us a few questions as if to test the ground.

'How do you rate our chances of climbing the South Face of K2? I think this variant appears interesting.'

He suggested a possibility which did not really attract me. I saw here the seeds of a situation where he might not shift from his idea. So I decided to be very open about it.

'I have been on that face before and I'm sure it can be climbed. But I did notice the possibility of another variation which, in my opinion, would allow us to get around this very difficult and dangerous sérac.'

He did not argue. In fact he said, 'I value the opinion of others very much.' I noted these words carefully in my memory. They were the sign of a wise expedition leader. Then in one of the subsequent conversations during the walk-in he said something which we simply did not expect.

'You two will be playing the first violin here. You really convinced me about your variant, we will plan everything from now on according to your suggestions. Whatever you need you will get.'

We were in business. He had completely accepted our idea with no provisos. After that he had to look after himself, dealing with his own health problems. His acclimatisation was slower than ours. He stayed behind and arrived at base camp a long time after us.

He had not arrived by the time we started unpacking the loads and taking the equipment we would need for the South Face. But already a group had stated that it was going for Broad Peak by the normal route and were not interested in anything else. Tadek and I observed this in silence. Only three Swiss and one German, all guides, seemed to accept my reasoning and our suggested route. There was no question of boredom at base camp which was as busy as a great international hotel, for several other expeditions had decided to have a go at K2: Italians, English, French (with Wanda Rutkiewicz), Americans, more Poles led by Janusz Majer, South Koreans, Austrians and a solitary Italian mountaineer, Renato Casarotto, who was roaming around the great mountains.

After a few days the six of us left this beehive for the South Face. Conditions were rather poor, with a cover of soft snow, a total curse to wade knee deep in, and so several days passed before the opportunity of starting the real mountain work arrived. As we were walking up to the proposed site of Camp 1 I already noticed that the Swiss were

K2, a new route on the South Face, 8th July, 1986

beginning to drop behind. Every time I looked round the gap had widened. I sensed their mood deteriorating, and all their convictions about this more ambitious route rapidly melting away. When they had dropped back about a hundred metres they yelled that they were turning back.

When I had had time to catch my breath from the hard work of carving a trail through this deep snow I shouted back, 'Shame. But come up at least as far as Camp 1. You have a lot of equipment which needs to be carried up there. We cannot really repack our rucksacks here in the middle of a snowfield . . . Come on up, we'll pitch our tent and then we can have a chat more comfortably.'

I heard no reply but after a moment they all set off again, slowly, step by step, but upwards.

We reached the campsite at 6000 metres and I waited for them to take up the conversation. It was the Swiss who admitted very frankly that the place was far more dangerous than they had expected and that, though they had barely started, already their strength was ebbing away.

'It is only a matter of acclimatisation,' I tried to reassure them. 'You are just rather "finished" by the altitude. The normal route is equally dangerous. There is no motorway there either, it is also quite difficult. Maybe a little easier than here, but only a little . . .'

But Beda and Rolf shook their heads, tomorrow they would go down. There was nothing more either Tadek or I could say. We got into our sleeping bags. The following morning the two Swiss started down. Four of us remained. Our aim that day was to go up just a short way and then come back. We were following a snow-ice arête. The snow was still very tedious, and the terrain dangerous with the threat of avalanche. The only solution was to go as fast as possible, keeping to the edge of the most dangerous snowfield, staying well away from its centre. I looked around and saw that Diego, our remaining Swiss, had fallen far behind and was sitting hanging his head, saying nothing. I did not give this much thought as I had other things to occupy me at that moment. I was on a sharp section of the arête which was heavily corniced. One of these cornices suddenly gave way under me, causing a sizeable avalanche which luckily went down the other side of the ridge. The cornice broke off just beside my feet but I was still on firm ground and joined to Tadek by a rope so, even if I had fallen with the cornice, I would have been held.

But it was enough for Diego. Without a word, he off-loaded all that he had been carrying up, leaving it on a snow platform, repacked his sack with lightning speed and rushed off down.

There were now three of us left to fix line a bit higher before going back to sleep in Camp 1, then descend to base camp. Here conditions were suitable for a calm discussion with the others. I belong to those who believe that one cannot force anybody to do anything in the mountains. Especially when it comes to climbing. So I began in a very conciliatory manner.

'The decision still belongs to you. If you are not going with us then that's hard luck. We just have to reorganise the equipment into what's required for the South Face and what you will need on the normal route. That will be an advantage to us anyway, as we will be descending by the normal route.'

Everything would have been fine if Herrligkoffer had not overheard this conversation.

'What do you mean? I am the leader of this expedition which has as its aim the South Face of K2. I do not want to hear about anything else!' And as if that was not enough he added, 'Either you go with the Poles to the South Face or you pack your bags and go home!'

My fears had been confirmed about the noticeable differences of opinion in this German-Swiss-Austrian-Polish expedition. The situation was not turning against us, we were still being handled very carefully, positively courteously, but the Swiss, Germans and Austrians were always having an argument about something, fuelled by the fact that the expedition was not designed to be run on three different fronts. Trying to divide the equipment up for three separate expeditions didn't work.

I tried to defuse things by assuring Karl that it did not really interfere with us if the others wanted to do the normal route. Indeed, I was privately quite happy that the route was not going to be cluttered up by a lot of ambitious people. But that wouldn't do for Herrligkoffer. I was running out of arguments. Forced labour did not really appeal to me, and I was strongly inclined to attempt the face alpine-style. But this would have demolished the concept of a great team working together, and would not have made our leader very happy. So I kept quiet about this, which was probably a good thing as Karl appeared to be exceptionally adamant.

'I simply do not agree to an ascent by any other route,' he pronounced. 'I have, incidentally, spoken to our liaison officer who also does not agree with another route being climbed. I repeat: either you help the Poles, or you go home.'

This offended the Swiss, nobody was going to tell them which way they had to go. But further argument was cut short by a new development. Herrligkoffer still did not feel well, so he decided to go back down. Just before his departure by helicopter he called a final expedition meeting at which he repeated that Tadek and I were the spearhead, then, to everybody's amazement, he nominated his sirdar as the new expedition leader. The following day he flew out. From that moment the Swiss decided to do their own thing on the normal route, even though they did not have a permit for it, and the expedition broke up into small groups.

In our next attempt Tadek, the German Toni Freudig and I wanted to get to 6400 metres, to the place where I had bivouacked with Wojtek two years ago, beneath the dangerous sérac. When I reached the spot I felt very tense. We were about to discover if my supposition about this whole South Face route variant was correct or not. We made a comfortable platform, pitched our tent, slept, and the following morning only Toni stayed behind in the tent. Tadek and I went on up to have a look beyond that bend, to confront my theory with the icy reality. As I approached the sérac I quickened my pace. Was there a way through or not?

When I stopped and took in the hitherto hidden scene I could see that the configuration was ideal. Certainly a short distance had to be covered beneath the sérac, but infinitely less than on the right-hand variant. Then there was a clear way up a rounded arête which would protect us from the nasties that kept falling off that sérac.

I felt like bellowing with joy, instead I just turned round to Tadek.
'Well? What do you think?'

'Shit! All right! We could do that right now. This really is the key to the whole route, like an open gate in a wall,' he answered with satisfaction.

We calmly examined everything, then went back to the tent, where Toni was cooking, to discuss our discovery. Next morning, very early, we would set off and fix ropes up that safe arête. Toni listened to our still rather excited conversation but he himself did not show too much enthusiasm. His stomach was upset and he would spend another day in the tent.

At four a.m. Tadek and I left in the dark, to cross beneath the sérac before sunrise. We almost ran beneath the sérac. It still took about fifteen minutes but we were safely across. We started up our arête, which was actually quite hard. First of all we decided to fix rope all the way up to make it easier next time. We managed to fix all 400 metres of it that day and left the rest of the equipment at our high point before going back down. At the camp Toni stated that he was still feeling bad and that he would return to base the following day. There were now the two of us left.

The next day we packed the tent, in fact everything, and followed the fixed lines right up to about 7000 metres, then we crossed a snowfield and at 7200 metres set up another camp. Clouds began rolling up as we cut out a platform for the tent, the weather was changing. The following morning we knew for sure. It was snowing. We must get down as quickly as possible. We left the whole bivouac set up and attached to the rock face by a piton. That same day we reached base camp, knowing that on our next attempt we could safely be tempted to try out a summit push. We prepared all our equipment very carefully, the right amount of food and fuel, repacking, and working out new ways of saving weight, but the rucksacks were still heavy. And we waited for a change in the weather. So one week passed, then ten days.

At the end of June the sun finally reappeared. We waited for another two days to allow those great masses of fallen snow to settle down and avalanche away. Then we set off with the decision to go for the summit. The first day we got to 6400 metres, the next to 7200 metres. So far everything was straightforward, as we were just following our prepared route. On the third day we broke new ground when we approached the base of a gully called the Hockey Stick, overcame a step and found our way into the depths of the gully where, at about 7800 metres, we set up our next bivouac.

The next day we climbed to 8200 metres. We were now very high. But I could see that this gully, which from a distance so accurately resembles a hockey stick, led up to a rock barrier barring our way to the final summit ridge. We searched for any possibility of cheating our way past this obstacle, but could see none. So we should have to overcome this barrier directly. We chose the line we felt offered us our best chance of finding our way over this formidable obstacle and set up a bivouac beneath it.

The next day we left the tent and sleeping bags and set off towards the rock wall with only our rope and climbing gear. In the first few metres I saw that it was going to be damned hard, and that we would never manage it in just one day. No chance. Today we would go as far as we could towards breaking the back of this barrier. We would fix the ropes and go back down to the tent for the night. Only on the next day would we push for the summit.

The barrier was about a hundred metres high and almost vertical. The hardest section was about thirty metres long and about Grade V+ in difficulty. It was the key to the wall. I gained height one centimetre after another. We did not have too much equipment, altogether three pitons, one ice screw and two thirty-metre ropes, one thin, one thick. That had to suffice for the fight with the rock which was murderously hard at this altitude. I fought for every step. I won't hide the fact that this was the hardest bit of climbing I have ever managed to do at this altitude in the Himalaya. I find it impossible to describe this now, because it is hard to explain how one managed to spend a whole day on a thirty-metre section of rock: that continuous shifting around searching for the appropriate holds; that endless studying; ah, there's a crack, maybe it would serve as a suitable hold, maybe that could be used as a foothold. Then I try out the foothold and reach up for the crack, no, it is no good, I must find another one nearby. Where? Yes, there. I move up ... ten centimetres. One tiny step. Now I have to protect myself, I must find a crack, hammer in a piton, clip a karabiner into it, then the rope into the karabiner. Before I manage all that another hour passes. Another step up. No good. I have to go back down. And so on. All the time I led and Tadek belayed me.

The worst was that every time my eyes wandered away from the rock, I could see on the horizon the build-up of great anvils of cloud, thunder clouds, heralds of a deterioration in the weather. Maybe it would last another day, just one more day? The only safe way now led up by this wall. We had at all costs to reach the summit ridge by this route and then descend by the normal route.

We did not spend much time discussing this. A look and a gesture sufficed. In the afternoon snow began drifting down, the flakes gathered in the cracks in the rock wall. We must go to the summit. We simply had no alternative.

We returned to our bivouac for the night, where I began to cook, but one false move and our last spare gas cylinder fell, I did not even hear it, far away into the snowy depths. We were unable to finish cooking our supper and, more important, making the drinks which our bodies were craving so insistently. One is effectively dehydrated all the time up there. Now we knew that any dreams we had about a big drink would not be fulfilled for a long time. But it is precisely here that one must drink a lot. Even when you no longer feel thirsty, even when you feel the need to sleep more than anything else, when you say to hell with this I just want to sleep, you have to force yourself, in order to supply your body with those extra few litres of water. That night we did not have enough to drink.

In the morning I found a small candle stub over which I melted a cup of snow. That was our last breakfast. It had to be enough. We left behind all our bivouac equipment. Climbing those near vertical walls wearing a heavy rucksack would be totally impossible. Then we set off. We quickly re-ascended the section we had fixed ropes up yesterday, then another sixty-metre section, not as difficult as the last, but equally harrowing. Somewhere between two or three o'clock we had the barrier behind us. Above us, just beyond a cornice, I could now see the summit ridge. I pushed through the cornice, made a few more steps and, for the first time in a long time, I was back on easy terrain. By the time Tadeusz reached me it was already three, a bit too late to be thinking of the summit really but, although it was snowing and misty, every now and again I could see something through it all. I could see what was the summit, and it was not far away.

'We'll come back here to bivouac,' I said to Tadek. 'Now let's go up.' He agreed and, after dumping some gear, we set off upwards.

Along the way we saw relatively fresh footprints. In the past few days of beautiful weather, while we were stuck on that desperately difficult rock barrier, fighting centimetre after centimetre upwards, several summit ascents had been achieved by the normal route. Among these were our Swiss pair Beda Furster and Rolf Zemp who had preferred this to the fight for the face. But now the weather was foul, the visibility poor, so the sight of footprints raised our spirits. They had helped us, if unwittingly, after all, by breaking trail on this last section.

After half an hour the footsteps, unfortunately, vanished in the thickening snow fall. With every step it was more difficult for us to orientate ourselves. I knew a bit about this section of the route from descriptions I had read. The last few metres to the summit Wanda had told me about herself. She had got there a few weeks ago on 23rd June. But all of this was of no use when the visibility was almost nil. All I knew was that you have to go up. It had gone six, it was getting dark. By seven it would be completely dark. I reached a sérac and found some pieces of soup packet wrappers beneath it. I was frightened . . . In all the descriptions I had read two séracs were mentioned, one at about 8300 metres, beneath which Wanda had bivouacked before her ascent of the summit, the other just before the summit. Holding these papers, remnants of French instant soups, in my hand I thought in horror, if these are the traces of Wanda's bivouac it means that I've made a mistake. Could we have only reached the first sérac?

As I stood there looking down at the coloured papers in the snow, Tadek arrived. I told him my fear, but he was unable to gather his thoughts.

'God knows,' he replied. 'It's so misty, it's impossible to tell. At worst we kip here and carry on up tomorrow morning.'

'No, if we do that, we'll not be able to make another step upwards, we will be only capable of descent.' I rejected the idea forcefully. I knew that a bivouac in that situation at that altitude was a recipe for disaster.

'So what will you do? Where shall we go?' In Tadek's voice I detected a very audible note of helplessness.

'Up. We are probably nearer than we imagine. We must get up. That is why we came and did so much hard climbing.' I gathered up my last remnants of strength and determination to convince Tadek about something of which I was myself uncertain. 'I don't care what happens,' I added. 'I'm going up just to see what happens after that sérac. Maybe I can recognise something.'

With great effort I got going again and worked my way round the sérac. Above it I could see that the angle eased considerably beyond. I felt that the summit was near. I turned around and shouted triumphantly to Tadek: 'The summit is just here, just a tiny bit further!'

I did not wait for a reply, but carried on, knowing, or rather sensing, that it was just a matter of a few steps. After a short while I was on the summit. I sat down, wracked by the effort, to rest my lungs, heart and muscles. I reached for the camera and took some photographs. It then dawned on me that Tadeusz had not arrived. But there he was, coming up, panting from fatigue. We exchanged a few words of congratulations.

'This is your first . . .' I gasped and clapped him on his back with congratulations.

'And your eleventh,' he answered, his voice broken by his own joy and total exhaustion.

So far Tadek had never set foot on the summit of an eight-thousander. But for his first he had picked off the second highest mountain in the world, reached by the hardest route so far climbed on it.

We took more photographs for another fifteen minutes, then set off down. We would have to bivouac, but we could help ourselves by getting down as far as we possibly could. So we began the race against the gathering gloom. By the time we got down to where we had left the rest of our equipment, it was already night. As I changed the battery of my torch, my stiff and tired hands refused to work properly. I dropped the battery, condemning us to total darkness. It was snowing so heavily that there was no question about any further descent, so we decided to stay put. We dug out a shallow cave and hid ourselves in it, shivering from cold and tiredness, cowering close to each other to await dawn.

There was no wind to disperse the morning mist and the snow falls. How could we find the way now? I tried to mobilise all those details I had memorised from all those photographs and set off. But after ten metres it became dangerously steep. I turned the other way, even steeper. The most frightening moment in the mountains is when one does not know which way to go. But one cannot just stand there. Slowly, following our instincts rather than our misted up vision, we worked our way down. Then we came across an old rope and regained our confidence. But the descent took a long time, the ground was by no means easy. We had ropes with us and we had to use them to abseil down. I abseiled too low on one occasion and found myself in much too steep an area. I was worried that we had started dropping down the South Face and I reclimbed ten steps, which turned out to be a horrific unexpected physical effort. But nobody could make it for me. The reward was to get back up there onto the correct route.

Descending this steep section took us all day. As dusk approached, the mists thinned a bit and I could see that we only had about a hundred metres to go before these steep slopes came to an end and the ground became more amenable. All the time we had to use the rope. First I would use it to help Tadeusz down, then he would belay and I'd come down myself, and so on. It was night before we were no longer surrounded by those great drops which had taken so much out of us.

We were now on snow and had to bivvy again. This was our fourth night at very high altitude. I could feel and see that we were at our physical limits. We no longer had the urge to dig out a suitable cave, making do with just a depression which could at best shelter us from the wind, only our legs wrapped in the remnants of our emergency sheet. And so we survived another night.

Dawn came, the clouds dropped and it stopped snowing. At last I could see where we were. We had to continue down a shoulder, below which we should come across the camp of the Austrian expedition. After a night like our last it took us a long time to get ourselves organised. Just putting on our crampons seemed to go on for eternity.

I could see that Tadeusz was even slower, so as soon as I was ready I said, 'The route is clear. I'm going on down to see what it is like ahead. In another hour that blasted mist could return and we'll be going down like blind men again.'

'Go on,' agreed Tadek.

'But don't forget the rope you're sitting on, it may be useful still.'

I set off down. I must have gone down less than 300 metres, with every step the view improved. There below me I saw tents. I sighed with relief. I was now certain that we were on the correct route, and that we did not have far to go. But Tadek was not hurrying. I sat and waited. Waiting means dozing, which one falls into against one's will. Exhaustion was taking its toll. As I came round after another doze, I saw that Tadeusz was very near me.

'Look down there. Tents. We are almost home.'

'Great.' He cheered up. 'Let's just rest a moment and we'll carry on.'

'Take out the rope, there's a bit of a step ahead. After that it is easy.'

'The rope won't be necessary. Anyway I left it up there,' answered Tadek.

Well that was that. I began to descend and realised that it was getting steep. Worse, the hard snow beneath me was changing to ice, which meant a tedious descent, facing the slope, ice axe in, crampons in, then the ice axe, then the other foot.

Tadeusz was coming down behind me. Halfway down I looked up, he was following my footsteps. I looked up again exactly in time to see a crampon fall off Tadek's foot!

I shouted something, but what happened in the next second I just could not have foreseen. The other crampon was falling down as well! Tadeusz was left clinging onto his ice axe. I shouted 'Look out!' But it was too late, no warning could be of any use. Tadeusz only seemed to struggle to hold on for a second, but he was in the position of someone who has just had a ladder removed from under him. He tried desperately to improve his grip on the ice axe which was firmly placed into the ice, but he failed. The ice axe stayed in place. Tadek fell.

I was directly below him. He just shouted 'Jureeeek!'

I could do nothing. In the first moment I thought of catching him, before it dawned on me that I was only supported by the tips of my crampons stuck into a tiny bulge of ice. All I had time to do was to drive both my axes into the ice as hard as possible. I felt a great blow, Tadeusz literally slid over me and carried on falling.

Before I recovered and realised that I was still conscious and standing on my feet a second or two had gone by. When I turned round all I could see were little lumps of ice rolling down the steep slope and the long mark of the slide carved out of the shallow snow covering the ice beneath it. After a hundred metres or so, where the slope steepens to a precipice, the last trace of Tadek vanished for ever.

I tried to shout, then I realised that there was no sense in that. Instead I decided to follow his slide marks. About twenty metres further down I found both his crampons. I was not too dazed to note that the buckles of both of them were done up. I took them with me in the belief that they would still be useful to Tadek. I carried on down, but I was very tired. Every so often I stopped and immediately started to doze. Hours passed. As if through a mist it dawned on me that this search was not achieving very much. I gave up and turned towards the tents. In the first, just by the entrance I found some canned fruit. I found a stove and used it to melt the contents. After I had made another drink I crawled into a sleeping bag. Then I started to look around for a radio.

As I fiddled with the unfamiliar controls of the Austrian radio with one hand, I organised another brew with the other. I had to drink as much as I could after going for almost three days now without a drop of liquid passing my lips. I was dried out like a prune.

At last I thought I had made contact and began passing the infor-mation that Tadeusz had fallen, that people should be sent to search the base of the mountain. I arranged to make contact again the following morning. Pressing my ear to the radio, I thought I could hear some murmuring echoes of voices in the distance, then it all faded away and I fell asleep.

When I woke, the first thing I did was grab the radio, only to see that it was two in the afternoon. I had slept non-stop for over twenty hours. I had slept through the arranged radio contact time. I tried to make contact with base again, but to no effect. Getting out of the tent, I saw that someone was coming up from below. I was impressed by the speed of the rescue operation.

But the two arrivals turned out to be a couple of Sherpas from the South Korean expedition bringing up a load. I found it hard to com-municate with them. I threw at them all the English words I knew – 'Yesterday. Accident. Help' – and gesticulated frantically. But they only looked at me faithfully and repeated in broken English: 'I do not understand.'

Slowly it began to dawn on me that nobody had heard the desperate calls for help that I had made, in a total state of exhaustion, the previous evening. (Only much later did I find out that the radio which I was using so determinedly to give the information about Tadek had no batteries.)

So I went on down with my head lowered. The way was easy, I held onto fixed ropes. That evening I was well looked after by a South Korean. I started the conversation with Tadek's accident, but the Korean shook his head. He knew nothing about it. So I asked him to get in touch with the base camp, where the Korean tent was not too far from the Polish expedition camp, and I reported everything that had happened to Janusz Majer. The next day I thanked the Koreans heartily for their hospitality and set off down, reaching base camp in the evening.

Janusz and his team searched the base of the mountain as best they could, but they found no sign of Tadeusz. The Swiss also went up to the foot of the face and a bit above, but not a trace. In this situation it only slowly hit me that 'my', in other words Herrligkoffer's, expedition was greeting me warmly, congratulating me. But all the time I also heard those terribly tragic questions. What happened? How did it happen? Why did the crampons come off? And I was still deadly tired.

I did not know at the time that this was to be the most tragic season in the history of that mountain. Tadeusz was its fifth victim. First there were two Americans, Smolich and Pennington, who died in an avalanche, then a French married couple, Maurice and Liliane Barrard, had disappeared on the descent of the normal route. Now Tadek. In all that summer there were to be thirteen deaths on K2 between that June and August of 1986, among them another two Poles, Dobrosława (Mrufka) Wolf and Wojtek Wróż.

I had frostbitten hands and toes, and the Italian doctor recommended I get down as fast as possible. So I accepted gratefully the suggestion that I go back to Skardu by helicopter. A ten-day march-out on frostbitten feet could be quite macabre. The last few minutes before my departure from base camp I spent with the charming solo Italian climber, Renato Casarotto. He was just setting off for the mountain for the third time, but stopped by my tent and we had a cup of tea together. He had been trying the South-South-West Ridge and had already got as high as 8200 metres. This was going to be his final attempt, he confided. He also wanted to come to Poland to give a series of lectures. So we would meet again soon. He clasped my hand for a long time before going on his way.

When I was in Skardu I heard a report over the radio about a lone Italian who reached 8300 metres on K2, who then turned back and, on the descent, not far from the base camp, fell into a concealed crevasse, and was so badly battered that, though they got him out, he died on the surface. A week after my return home I got a train to Szczecin to see Danka, Tadek's wife. I knew that she was well advanced in her pregnancy, expecting her second child after a fourteen-year break. I did not know her at all well, having only met her once at a Tatra beauty spot. Now I stood in front of her door and a long time passed before I pressed the bell. I had with me all the films Tadeusz had taken during the expedition, except of course those which he had taken on the summit of K2 and which he had had with him when he fell. I also had a few bits and pieces belonging to him, and I would give Danka the photos I took myself on the summit. There were a lot of Tadeusz, and from these, although they were taken in the gathering gloom, one could see the sheer joy shining through that totally exhausted exterior. On one of them, where he is about to step onto the summit, he has his hands raised high, flying.

I stood at the door, then someone answered. Danka could see I was nervous. She said something, as if joking, right at the doorstep defusing the atmosphere. She turned out to be the bravest of women, and one could not imagine a more tragic situation. She helped me so much. I spent a whole day at her home. Friends and neighbours who were nothing to do with mountaineering came round as well. I knew they were all looking at me, thinking perhaps how things might have turned out differently, and I could not escape a feeling of guilt.

But they said sincerely, 'Jurek, we have lost Tadeusz, but now we will have our eyes on you. We'll keep our fingers crossed for you now.'

I'm not sure if anyone can fully appreciate how much those words meant to me then.

13

That's It . . .

'Taking things logically, I shouldn't be going with you. All around you people seem to die . . .'

Artur Hajzer said it half-jokingly, but behind those words lay an echo of what many people were saying behind my back. I shrugged my shoulders, and said nothing. The story of my last four expeditions spoke for itself: four trips, four fatal accidents. Nobody remembered that all my previous expeditions had ended successfully for me and my partners.

Before the K2 invitation I had begun mounting an expedition to Manaslu and Annapurna. Artur Hajzer had the same background as I did, he had taken his first steps in the Scout Tatra Club. I had been with him on Kangui and on the South Face of Lhotse, and knew him for a realist, ambitious, hard-working and an excellent organiser. That was why I suggested that he join the Manaslu trip, and while I was on K2 get on with the organisation with Rysiek Warecki, who was going to film the expedition for the Katowice Club. Everything was shaping up nicely, together with 5000 dollars hard currency which had been arranged over the telephone with the president of the GKKFiS.

When I returned on 18th July I was met by Artur Hajzer with a rather sheepish expression.

'I have bad news. We have no money.'

Everything for the expedition was ready, except for the złotys, which were to be obtained by the president of the Ministry of Mining. Somehow we solved this problem. We obtained a big discount on the air freight, and a fifty per cent discount on our tickets, greatly helped by the official stamp from the office of the President on the letter sent to

LOT. But what really saved us was a far-from-trivial loan from the Polish Alpine Association, which amounted to 1,800,000 złotys.

Wojtek Kurtyka was waiting for us in Kathmandu. As I was setting off for K2, he had been going with a Japanese expedition to the Trango Towers, only about 6200 metres, but difficult. We met up on the walk to the Baltoro Glacier. He had said he wasn't sure what to do in the autumn, and would quite like to go to the Himalaya again. I had said come with me to Manaslu and Annapurna. So he was there waiting, as were Carlos Carsolio and Elsa Avila, the Mexicans I climbed with on Nanga Parbat, together with an Austrian, Edek Westerlund. Edek had been very useful, making contact with various western equipment manu-facturers, as a result of which for the first time we had the high quality equipment I used to envy so much among those climbers who had hard currencies at their disposal. We were very proud of it, especially Artur, the youngest among us and the least accustomed to such trips.

We had two permits, one for Annapurna and the other for Manaslu. Manaslu is considered a slightly easier mountain technically, so I decided to tackle it first. A very long, but beautiful, wild valley leads to base camp, with waterfalls along the way and faint trails leading through virgin bush country. The delightfulness of this walk-in could not be marred by the monsoon rains, or the endless leeches attacking us from every bush, or the now traditional episodes with the sirdar, or rather his assistant, who of course tried to fiddle us. But we managed to overcome this thanks to video technology and a knowledge of numerals in Nepal-ese. We had a camera with us and shot film all the time. Filming the porter wage-paying ceremony provided irrefutable evidence that the assistant sirdar was paying the porters 40 rupees a head when he pre-sented us a bill for 45 rupees a head. On the last day of the walk-in we followed everything he did with the video-camera! It got the assistant sirdar dismissal and brought the sirdar to heel, but we used up a lot of nervous energy over this business that would never be replaced, and in the culminating moments of the great row I thought of Herrligkoffer who repeated so stubbornly that we should not get involved in arguments over money and pay what was demanded. Freedom from stress is worth something. Why trouble oneself about minor things such as money in the presence of such beautiful mountains? Unfortunately, this approach is only possible for those who can afford it.

The Manaslu base camp is quite low at 4400 metres. To reach the glaciers and snow line takes another two hours or so, but this is the last place flat enough to pitch tents on. After two days we started off into the mountain to carry out a reconnaissance. Our aim was the first ascent of the East Ridge of Manaslu, which culminates in the beautiful

Manaslu, a new route on the North-East Face, 10th November, 1986

unclimbed East Summit, at 7895 metres just 260 metres lower than the main summit. In other words, a nice tit-bit, a very high, unclimbed summit, a short descent, then not far away, the main summit.

We started looking for a safe way to gain the ridge, while waiting for the monsoon rain to come to an end. But a week passed with no change. It continued raining. Edek Westerlund and his wife Renata came to the end of their holiday, and had to go home, taking with them our camera-man Rysiek Warecki who according to Renata, a medical student, had contracted pneumonia. A helicopter was summoned to take him back to Kathmandu.

While we were still at base camp I was also half-waiting to hear news of Messner. I knew he was on Makalu and that he also had a permit for Lhotse. To get from one to the other would present no problem, so there was every likelihood that he would complete his eight-thousander 'collection'. He goes up the eight-thousanders by the normal route as a rule, and is an excellent alpinist, so he would have to be extremely unlucky not to achieve his aim, an aim which had a great prestige, not just in sporting terms.

So I was waiting for news of his success on Makalu, and when it came I could not help feeling a bit sad. He was, after all, going to be the first. At the same time I felt a hint of relief. At last the excitement surrounding our 'race' had subsided. Now I could continue towards my own target more calmly. I still needed Manaslu, Annapurna and Shisha Pangma. I left the mess tent to be completely alone, just for a moment. Looking up at the mountain, through the snow and the mists, I could catch glimpses of the East Face of Manaslu, and I said to myself, That's it. Tomorrow we go up there, Mr Kukuczka.

In the gully leading up to the ridge, there was a great mass of snow that could simply break away from beneath our feet. With unjustifiable optimism I said, 'Just wait, when the weather improves and all this snow settles, we will be able to go up this like it's a motorway.'

But it got worse not better. The snow just built up, and we took each step with our hearts in our mouths. At some stage these great masses just had to come crashing down. The avalanche danger increased to the point where everything seemed to hang by a thread. One moved doubled up from peg to peg, from niche to niche, just to keep out of the open. It was safest to go up by the ridge itself, but to stick to it was practically impossible and the ridge finally ended in an icefield on which the snow was building up and lying in wait for us.

On the third attempt, swimming up through these great masses of white fluff, four of us, Carlos, Artur, Wojtek and I, reached a really dangerous section. We were at 6000 metres, the weather was beautiful, but Wojtek suddenly came to a halt.

'Stop, gentlemen! Blow this, I'm not going on. It's too dangerous here. The game is over, I'm going back.'

I did not hide my disappointment, and a debate developed.

'Wojtek, we have accepted the risk from the word go. We knew it would be like this. There're only 200 metres of this blasted snowfield left, after that we will be back to the safe ridge! Surely we have to win through this in the end?' I knew I was urging him into a very dangerous battle. But we had to reach a communal decision. The time for this section of the expedition was rapidly running out. We only had food for a month and were already scrupulously rationing it. 'If we go down to base now the food situation by itself will preclude another attempt. If we turn back now then that's it, the expedition is over. So everyone should now vote: up or down.'

'I'm going down, this is senseless,' Wojtek said.

'I'm the youngest here. I'll accept that, but I would prefer to go up,' admitted Artur.

With the whole slope primed to avalanche at any instant, it all now depended on Carlos. We did not for a moment expect he would be the one to defuse the situation. He began in an unusually serious tone.

'As Mexico's economy is deteriorating rapidly, it is my firm belief that this is going to be my last expedition to the Himalaya. For that reason I'm going on and I'll do everything in my power to get to that summit.'

We burst out laughing on hearing this most unexpected argument, and I was very grateful to him, not just because he had managed to take away the unpleasant atmosphere that had been created by this voting, but also because his vote had tipped the scales on the yes side. A different mental approach had been created.

Maybe we *could* afford to mount another attempt on the summit if we cut down a bit more on eating? But we must think carefully about this. Another attempt would extend our period on the mountain by ten days.

So we descended to base camp, and I sent a runner to the nearest village to buy potatoes and anything else he could find. He returned eyes gleaming with triumph, carrying not only potatoes, but some eggs and illegally smuggled in Chinese vodka. We were beginning to feel very angry about the thief who had stolen two drums at the start of the trip in which, among other things, had been thirty kilos of flour and rice. Now gathering up our energy for this final attack, we were committed to a typically Nepalese menu: rice-potatoes, potatoes-rice, to which, like the greatest luxury, was added half a can of meat between five people, from which we made a sauce. To go with this we had chapatis made from just flour and water.

But monotony of this expedition was beginning to wear Wojtek down. All the waiting, first the rain, then the desperate floundering in deep snow finally decided him to leave. The rest of us took up our last chance. It turned out that Carlos had slightly frostbitten hands and he returned to base. But he did not waste his time. On the other side of Manaslu a Colombian and Yugoslavian expedition were just packing up and Carlos went round to them in the hope of buying some left-over food. He brought back practically a whole sack full of custard, but nothing more solid.

Now everything hung on the weather. But it poured. A week passed, then another. Then the rain changed to snow. It covered everything. Only a month ago there had been a green meadow here. Four times we set off for the summit. On the second of these attempts we reached 6400 metres and set up Camp 2. We had effectively climbed most of the long East Ridge now, because at this point it merged into the slopes leading up to the unclimbed East Summit. The route was ready, in places there was fixed rope. On the way down we set up Camp 1 and from that moment we just watched the sky for the settled weather which would allow us to make our summit attack.

One morning at breakfast, we heard over the radio: 'Yesterday, the outstanding mountaineer Reinhold Messner reached the summit of

Lhotse. In so doing he has become the first person to reach the top of the fourteen highest mountains in the world . . .'

A silence descended on the mess tent, nobody listened to any further information coming from the radio. Eventually Artur could not stand the suspense.

'So?' he burst out. 'There's no need for us to hurry any more! We can take this mountain gently!'

On our next foray above Camp 2 Artur and I established a precarious bivvy site at 7000 metres, but even travelling light, we realised we could not make it to the summit and back in daylight from there. We had now been tackling the mountain for over fifty days and I proposed to Artur that we forget completing a new route and just settle for the normal one. At least we'd have a chance of getting to the summit.

We reached the normal route at 7400 metres and a desperate struggle ensued as we tried to pitch our tent in the dark and the tearing wind. Artur wanted to try to go down there and then, but I persuaded him we had no option but to stick it out and we huddled together for the night with the tent not so much erected as wrapped around us. In the morning we were so cold we gathered up all the gear and descended, acknowledging defeat.

Carlos, who had no idea of what we had been going through up there, rushed out to congratulate us, thinking we had made it to the summit. His genuine happiness at our imagined success broke me up. So little remained to the summit and here we were, returning with our heads down. By now the other expeditions in the area would all be back in Kathmandu celebrating their achievements. There was nothing to stop us packing up camp and joining them.

And yet I kept looking up at the mountain which had defeated us, and then, like a damaged record that just repeats the same phrase, I said, 'Maybe we should have one more go?'

Carlos jumped at these words.

'I'm coming! My hands are not so bad really, I'll have a go.'

Artur said nothing but he had not yet lost hope.

'Let's tackle it alpine-style by a different route,' I suggested, 'leaving out the whole of that long and tiring East Ridge. We'll go straight up that icy face.' I pointed to the unclimbed North-East Face of the mountain.

So on 5th November, when all other Himalayan expeditions had long left the area, we set off for our last attempt, as a three, carrying the tent and all our equipment with us. Our first bivouac was quite low; the second we only reached by nightfall, at the junction with our previously attempted route; the third where we had spent that uncomfortable night on a tiny ledge for half a tent. We were still on the new route. We scrapped the idea of giving up and doing the normal route. We were going for broke. When we approached the East Summit Carlos was dropping back a bit in the sapping cold. It was, after all, November, and we were almost at 8000 metres. The wind had eased only to the extent that it did not keep knocking us over, but it penetrated to the very marrow.

We made a bivouac at 7800 metres just before the col which leads to both summits. Then I climbed a very difficult wall for eighty metres, the full length of the rope, which took several hours before I could bring up the others. Another eighty metres and I reached the col. The wind which had been kind to us in those last few hours, buffeted us again ever more strongly here and clouds were gathering as I hammered in a piton, fixed the rope to it, and waited for the lads to come on up. Looking around, I could see I was at the most fifty metres from the virgin East Summit, and after half an hour all three of us were standing on it. But the snow had already started to fall. We left a sling and karabiner on the summit and began to abseil down into thickly falling snow, as the summit vanished behind us in an impenetrable mist, and we were fast losing all sense of direction.

Carlos, who had climbed that hard East Summit so bravely, was now beginning to lose his upward drive. After a long struggle we managed to pitch the tent on the col, which gave us a chance of survival, even though soaked sleeping bags had become blocks of ice and the tent was no longer weather-proof. Beside me Artur tried to start the butane stove, sheltering it between his legs as the flame slowly melted the lump of ice in the pan. Every so often he would fall asleep, swaying over the pot, his nose dripping into it. But all that concerned me was that the pot filled with anything liquid to drink as fast as possible. Carlos fell asleep in the corner, I was also keeling over. Artur fed the stove, then we changed over. Morning arrived. I was filled with pessimism and convinced we should have to find the normal route and descend by it. Carlos's now seriously frostbitten hands needed attending to. I gave him the first tablet to dilate the blood vessels. Then came the dreaded moment when we would have to stick our noses out of the tent.

I leant out and saw the summit right beside us. I felt I could have just reached out and touched it, sunlit, beautiful and close. It was only here, on the col, that the wind was howling so mercilessly.

'Leave everything, we're going for the summit!'

The astounded Artur put his head out of the tent, then said, 'But it's terribly far to that summit. It'll take us all day.'

To this very day I find it hard to believe that a summit seen by two people from the same spot could result in two such opposing views of the intervening distance.

'It'll take us at most two hours,' I insisted. 'Let's go. We can't afford to waste time.'

Artur was not arguing. 'Fine, we'll have a go.'

We gathered up our boots and crampons and I roused Carlos who was still curled up in his corner, but he shook his head sorrowfully and said he would wait for us. I told him to pack everything up while he waited, ready for a quick descent.

Going outside, Artur and I put on every possible layer of that wonderful clothing provided by our western sponsors, and we still felt that hellish wind penetrate everything, as we started off creaking step by step over that frozen snow, all the time in the shadow, which increased our awareness of the cold psychologically. But every step brought us closer to the edge of that purple-cold zone, and when we reached the sun everything changed immediately. We found new strength, which a moment ago we hadn't known we'd possessed. Our self-confidence returned, everything suddenly became possible. My calculation turned out to be close to the truth; after an hour and forty-five minutes we were standing on the summit.

The world looked so different from there, so bright and clean, as if storms and exhaustion did not exist. I only managed one photograph before the camera froze up, and we had to start back down to the tent where we dragged out the still sleeping Carlos, packed everything and began the descent by the normal route.

We did not bear Carlos a grudge for not managing to pack up the bivouac as requested. He was not well. In spite of the medicine, his fingers were swollen like bunches of bananas, and he had to be forced along by us. Even though we were going very slowly, he was dropping back. But with every step we were warming up. After descending 200 metres we felt as if we were in another world. The wind fell and in the sunshine it was actually warm at last. By nightfall we were just below 7000 metres. Only 7000, or already 7000? It did not matter, the most important thing was getting a bit more oxygen in our lungs. We pitched our tent, and spent the night there.

Next morning we helped Carlos organise himself and gave him another pill before carrying on down. Strange things were now happening to Carlos. I was not too surprised, having experienced similar myself on Mount McKinley. Ronikol, the dilatory medicine I was giving him, acts equally on all blood vessels, those in the brain as well. So Carlos was now beginning to totter down in a zig-zag and talk nonsense. Helping him as best I could, I discovered he had a desperately heavy rucksack, so we decided to share his load a bit.

'Carlos, what *have* you got in there?'

He just looked at us with a comatose expression. So we dug around in his rucksack and discovered several big rocks which he had taken from the Eastern Summit as a souvenir. Everybody takes a stone as a trophy from an important summit. I have several at home, and I had started getting confused as to which one came from which great mountain. But these boulders? I was so furious at his having wasted so much of his last shreds of energy carrying them down, that I picked up one of these great lumps of detritus, and was about to hurl it away as far as possible, when Carlos suddenly sobered up.

'Stop! No!' he shouted in anguish. 'I must take them down. In my university in Mexico they are waiting for these. I cannot go back without them . . .'

We took them down. I'm not sure what use the Mexican university made of them, but at that moment they turned out to be very useful in bringing Carlos round a bit. Things now went rather more easily.

The normal route is not one to fulfil one's sporting ambitions, but it certainly has attributes which we appreciated highly now. A Colombian team had been on it just a few weeks back. They had not made the summit, but they had got to where we were and, though fresh snow covered most of their tracks, there were still the tips of their marker sticks poking out of the snow which helped us tremendously in finding our way down this unknown and dangerously crevassed glacier.

Up above the wind had blown the fresh snow away; here, with every step, there was more of it. Every now and then it would collapse beneath us, causing a small avalanche, while séracs hung menacingly above our heads. That last day turned out to be one long exhausting mental nightmare, and when we thought it was coming to an end with the glacier we stopped, transfixed by a crevasse.

It was maybe four metres across and on the far side we could see footprints, left by the Colombians, who must have stepped over it quite easily. But since then it had had time to widen. The other side was now quite simply inaccessible. The footsteps just added to our feeling of helplessness. I explored for 200 metres to the left, but could see that in that direction the crevasse only widened. In the other direction was a jumble of séracs. What should we do?

'Artur, you are the tallest, try to jump it.'

Even a child can jump four metres. But we were dressed in down, wearing heavy boots and crampons, and at our very limits of exhaustion.

Artur took off his rucksack, and everything else which could hinder his jump. I stamped out a run-up for him, set up a belay and tied him on to the rope. This was an exceptionally ugly crevasse, not one which narrows as it gets deeper. At worst one could have abseiled into one of those and climbed up the other side. No, this one widened with depth, bell-shaped, and getting out of it would be extremely difficult.

Artur breathed in as much air as his oxygen-starved lungs could manage and started his run up, but as he reached the launch point he stopped. He tried again. The same. He just couldn't screw himself up for the final launch over to the other side of that icy mouth and sat down resignedly in the snow.

I had a go. But every time I reached the take-off point, I too realised this jump was not really on. Artur went off to look for another way round, with no more success than me. Beyond, mocking our feebleness, was an easy slope leading back to camp, to our tents, food and drink. I couldn't bear it any longer.

'This is the jump of a lifetime,' I declared, pretending to make a bit of a joke of it. On my third run up I had stopped caring. I was off, reaching as far forward as I could with the axe and landing on my stomach, my feet dangling in space. I pulled up on the hard-dug-in ice axe. I was on the other side. Artur, seeing now that it was possible, also jumped, and even Carlos, with the greatest effort, managed to make it across. The following day we reached base camp.

This was the first time that Carlos had taken off his boots in our presence and we saw what he had not said a word about to this moment. His frostbitten hands were nothing in comparison to his feet which were like pumpkins, completely purple. Immediately I sent the runner off for a helicopter, but the helicopter could not reach where we were, so we had to bring Carlos down a good thousand metres more. Three porters carried him, and I went with them, leaving Artur to pack up the rest of base camp. The following day the porters would be up there to carry everything down.

When the procession with the frostbitten Carlos reached the nearest Tibetan village, Soma, a breathless runner arrived with a letter from Rysiek Warecki in Kathmandu. While we were waiting for the rain and snow to clear I had already written for our permit for Annapurna to be extended, and now Rysiek sent word there was a chance to extend the permit till 25th November.

I stood there and read the letter again. I did not know what to do. To be honest I had written off Annapurna. Now there appeared to be the glimmer of a chance. I sat down and scribbled Artur a note telling him to leave everything else, just bring the climbing kit and rush to

Kathmandu, there was a chance to do Annapurna and I'd gone ahead to fix it.

I boarded the helicopter with Carlos and flew straight to Kathmandu where we landed at the hospital. Thanks to his rapid hospitalisation Carlos survived the frostbite with only minimal losses. A Yugoslavian doctor tended him with great care, thus saving him any amputations. I meanwhile rushed to the Ministry of Tourism to extend our permit for Annapurna.

The officials looked surprised. 'If you are already here, what do you want to extend?'

'What? Annapurna of course!'

'Annapurna is all over. Sorry.'

Now I understood. If I had been at the foot of the mountain and sent a request from there that I just wanted a few more days, that would have been acceptable. But now that I had returned to Kathmandu, my request was no longer realistic. My presence allowed them to say no.

Poor Artur, when he received my letter he had dropped everything and run to reach me as fast as his legs would carry him, covering a ten-day journey in three. He arrived in Kathmandu as if he'd just completed a marathon run, only to find Annapurna off and me flown back to Poland – to start raising expedition steam all over again. He was shattered.

A few days after his return we met up again in Katowice. Artur no longer bore me a grudge. That had been replaced by the knowledge of having achieved a great success. He had an eight-thousander behind him, climbed by a new route.

When I looked at this ambitious climber, young by Himalayan standards, I could see in him strengths which complement my weaknesses. How could I reconcile what I wanted to suggest to him next with his hope of completing his studies at the University of Silesia? They had been dragging on for so long already. Too bad.

'Artur,' I said. 'Leave these studies of yours, you will still have plenty of time to complete them. Come with me to Annapurna.'

'Fine,' he answered without hesitation.

14

Cold Hell

Annapurna, winter 1987

The organisational hell of getting an Annapurna expedition off the ground now awaited me. I could count on Artur Hajzer, Rysiek Warecki and Krzysiek Wielicki. From the Warsaw group I would take the doctor, Michał Tokarzewski, a fine lad. Who else? I decided on Wanda Rutkiewicz because she had a commission to make a film for Austrian television, and the money for this would be useful. The others were not too enthusiastic about this. I've already expressed my opinion of women's mountaineering, but Wanda is a very pleasant person and she had convinced us, that is mainly me. The others simply said, You thought up this woman, you can have her.

There was still a lot of money to raise in a hurry. The situation was far from rosy. As I was sitting at home, pondering our poor start, the telephone rang. It was a reporter from an Italian sports paper wanting to interview me, which he did in good Polish. His name was Jacek Pałkiewicz. We covered Manaslu and came on to future plans. I explained I was thinking about a winter ascent of Annapurna, leaving in three weeks' time, but so far didn't have enough money to go. He asked a few questions about this and then rang off. A couple of days later he was on the phone again. Would I take him for 4000 dollars? He assured me he had walked across Borneo and sailed the Atlantic; he did not have any mountain experience, yet here he was trying to insist his 4000 dollars would entitle him to have a go at the summit of Annapurna in winter. I said I would talk it over with the others. Meanwhile there was another call from Italy – this time from his wife, urging us to talk him out of it! In the end we decided the winter walk-in would sort him out early enough, and we did need his money. So Jacek Pałkiewicz came too.

In Kathmandu on New Year's Day we suffered another setback. Due to a bureaucratic confusion in Warsaw we found our expedition wasn't formally registered, so didn't exist. This time Wanda came to the rescue, remembering a diplomatic contact she had. We were eventually allowed to put in another application and, at last, the permit came through. We were on the way. But which way?

The question to decide now was which side of the mountain to attempt. Should it be my original plan of an ambitious new route on the South Face, or should we approach from the north by the route of the French first ascent in 1950? That is a much easier route, but on the north side in winter we would not be able to count on even one hour of sunshine during the day. This route would be a cold hell. I knew from the records that there had been six winter attempts on the mountain, only one of which had reached the summit ridge, but they never made the summit. They were climbing in appalling weather and must have lost their way. On the way down four Sherpas and climbers died. Just reaching the north side of Annapurna is a problem. One has to cross a very high col where one could easily be brought to a halt. The Japanese winter attempt was forced to stop at this col, the porters simply refusing to carry on, and the expedition came to an end before the chosen base camp was reached.

Access from the south is quite easy, following one of the most popular trekking and tourist routes. So the question was do we start off with a difficult walk-in but then have a much easier climb, albeit in cold frosty gloom? Or the easier walk-in, then hard climbing, but in sunshine? I studied the reports from previous expeditions and found all the expeditions trying the south side reported deep snow. That rather surprised me, there should be less at this time of year. It should be blown clean by the wind. Eventually I decided. We would approach from the north, by the French route. I think that this was the right decision, but we did have serious problems on the walk-in. Enough to say that from our original sixty porters only nineteen reached base camp.

Jacek Pałkiewicz made it too, though it could be seen at every step that he just did not feel confident in the mountains. That he managed to get to base at all I consider was his major achievement and here he experienced something which made a strong impression even on the old hands. It was an earthquake, after which all the cliffs and hanging glaciers started collapsing around us, creating a great white cloud which reached the very camp. This must have been quite a shock for him. He was also having some kidney problems and, in the end, he simply had

Annapurna, first winter ascent of the North Face, 3rd February, 1987

to give up the expedition. But he had been good company, and he had helped us immensely, not just financially, but also by establishing sponsorship contacts for me with firms that I have maintained to this day.

Base camp lies quite low at 4200 metres, in a beautiful meadow. Here and there through the snow we could see grass. But to get there we had had to cross the col at 4400 metres. In summer cattle were grazed there, but in winter nobody from the village would go up that high. We had to pay five times the going rate to get us into that northern sanctuary.

Our first group arrived on 18th January, and we decided to start climbing straight away as time was running out. So the attack was launched on the 20th by three of us, before base camp was even set up. We managed to find a way to Camp 1, which required us to get round a very threatening icefall. The following day we got higher and after three days we set up Camp 3. Everything was being done back to front. We did not yet have a base camp, but already we had Camp 3 at 6050 metres, thanks to the acclimatisation left from our Manaslu expedition.

The cold troubled us most of all. We were climbing a mountain in perpetual shadow. The sun had one pleasant surprise for us, its rays did warm up our base camp for just a few hours every day. But this blessing was not extended to the northern slopes of the mountain. Only mountaineers can appreciate what that endless cold shade means, where it is impossible for a moment to get away from that bitter, penetrating frost, that takes away one's will and hope. In the tent it is cold, you go out and it is cold, you walk and it is cold.

On our return to base, Rysiek Warecki and Krzysiek Wielicki set off carrying more supplies up to Camp 2 at 5600 metres to continue our rather topsy-turvy approach to establishing the camps. The rest of the equipment was only now arriving at the base of the mountain. Among it there was a large quantity of rope, tents and sleeping bags, without which we could not attack the higher sections.

The next day we set off as a four, Krzysiek and Artur, Wanda and myself. Only now did I realise that, whether I liked it or not, I was tied to Wanda. After all I was the one who had asked her along. We intended to set up Camp 4 or maybe even Camp 5, then go down to base to gather ourselves for the next ascent which would be the summit assault. We were moving in a semi-alpine style, though pedants could no doubt point out some differences. We took tents with us, and we took the equipment up as high as possible on the assumption that we would be setting up camps only during the descent. The frost continued to bother us, and the ice. In winter the mountain seemed to put on a glassy coat. We climbed on ice so hard that even the tips of our crampons could barely penetrate it. With every step one had to kick several times for the crampon's spikes to grip. This glass begins at 6000 metres. Our progress was becoming very slow.

Above Camp 3 we were forced to cut ice ledges to bivouac. To save energy we just cut out one ledge for one of our two-man tents, and the four of us squashed into it. Every so often we heard the drumming of tiny ice fragments, sometimes like a handful of dried peas being thrown against the tent, sometimes like gravel. It did not escape any of us that the tent could be hit at any instant by something substantially bigger. But there had been no alternative place to pitch it. In the morning our flysheet was covered in tiny holes. It looked like a sieve and did not add to our spirits. We did not regret having to leave that godforsaken gully, and made another bivouac on safer ground.

We were now at 6800 metres. After the night here, we planned to leave our tents behind and go down for a rest to base camp, before returning for the summit push.

But that evening I realised I was feeling in very good shape and I suspected Artur would be similarly acclimatised thanks to the Manaslu expedition. Maybe we could avoid going down? As I sat in the tent and drank tea with Wanda, I suddenly threw down my challenge.

'I'm going up tomorrow! Who'll come with me?'

Silence, I saw manifest surprise written on Wanda's face, and a good few seconds passed before someone answered from the other tent. It was Artur.

'Me!' he said.

The situation seemed to have sorted itself out very simply. Wanda was not yet acclimatised. Nor was Krzysiek Wielicki yet a hundred per cent run in. Krzysiek had recently amazed everyone with his twenty-four hour ascent of Broad Peak. He is clearly a first-rate speed climber and, had he wanted, could surely have made the summit, despite being under-acclimatised, as long as it was all done fast. But he was still a bit influenced by the outcome of a tragic Makalu expedition with the famous Swiss climber Marcel Rüedi, who already had nine eight-thousanders to his name. They had gone up from base in a similar lightning push, without acclimatisation. On the way down, Ruedi, on his own request, stayed behind in a tent. Up till that point he had shown no sign of being unwell, but died suddenly, probably from pulmonary oedema. After that tragedy Krzysiek was unfairly accused of having left his companion on the mountain. I know the effect of such words after Kangchenjunga and K2, and I only mention this now to explain how it can weigh one down psychologically. Krzysiek may well have wished to go for the summit with us, but been afraid that Wanda would then try to go down on her own. So he said, 'Fine. Then I will go down with Wanda. We will make a summit attempt next time.'

When silence descended over us all again, I began to feel guilty. Had I dumped Krzysiek? But I consoled myself with the assurance that he really was not yet adequately acclimatised, and in the morning, I set off up with Artur. We reached 7500 metres and noticed the weather beginning to change. It had been fine up till then, in other words it had been sunny if rather windy. Now it stopped blowing, instead clouds were rolling up. This could be a sign of better weather. In cloud it is never so bitingly cold. But clouds herald fresh snow, which could make route-finding difficult.

We set up the tent and now I was beginning to feel that this push was not doing me much good. I was beginning to move like a fly stuck in tar. But I was optimistic. We would have a sleep. In the morning we would feel up to it.

During the night it began snowing. An impenetrable mist enveloped us, the weather was simply bad. I started getting dressed, but I felt very weak and could tell the same was true of Artur. Against all sense of logic and sound tactics, I proposed a rest day where we were. Artur grunted something and with obvious joy burrowed himself back into his sleeping bag.

That rest helped me a lot. Every so often we had to go outside to dig out our tent. And so a whole day passed. We slept another night and the following morning got ready to set off. At first the wind blew and snow billowed up around us, but it was not the same wind as before. From base camp. whenever it was windy we could see the summit shrouded in a great plume. Now the visibility was bad. The summit appeared only now and again, at which moments I tried to memorise the lie of the land. We could see that we still had two final couloirs to negotiate which turned out to be very difficult hard ice. Just 200 metres from the summit we encountered great technical problems, and left all the rope behind at this point to help us during our descent.

We reached the summit at four p.m., late in the day for that time of year, as we had only one hour of daylight left. Whenever I recount stories of my ascents I am always showered with questions such as: 'And then? What did you experience up there?' I let people down. What is there to say? Often one just feels nothing. One just concentrates on breathing. So I say: 'When I am on the summit, just the fact that I have conquered the mountain stops being of any relevance. What is important is to get down fast, and get back to the tent. That is our main aim.'

That is how it was now. The summit had been ticked off, it belonged to history. What was important was life itself, and getting down to our tent before dark. But by nightfall we only just managed to get out of that couloir full of glassy hard ice. We were now moving by torchlight. The route I had tried to memorise on the way up was useless. By nine it was pitch black and we were still trying to find the tent. It should be somewhere nearby. Maybe it was a bit lower. Our legs were buckling under us from exhaustion, but our search was futile. At ten, ploughing through the snow, and losing confidence in the point of this search, I suddenly stepped on something soft. Our tent!

It was completely covered in snow and I had found it by pure luck. We dug it out and got inside, purring joyfully.

During those two days in which we had first given ourselves a rest day at 7500 metres, and then climbed to the summit, the weather below had completely broken down. Half a metre of fresh snow had fallen at base camp. It had also dumped in those couloirs we had to descend. Every few steps a great slab of snow would break away from under us causing an avalanche. We descended with our hearts in our mouths. Luckily the route was marked to a certain extent and the most dangerous sections had fixed rope on them, though admittedly covered by half a metre of fresh snow.

As we returned to base camp Wanda and Krzysiek were just getting ready for their attempt. The weather improved again, but in the sun, which we had missed so much, we could now see great plumes billowing from the summit again. It was blowing up there very hard.

Wanda and Krzysiek got as far as Camp 4 before Wanda admitted she had been getting weaker all the time and they decided to come back down. She had developed quinsy early on and never got really fit.

The doctor went out to meet them and help her down. As for Krzysiek, if he had felt really determined, he could have started all over again for the summit alone. He could have made it. But he chose to descend with Wanda instead. So by 12th February the trip had effectively come to an end. It had, so far as winter expeditions go, taken no time at all. On the sixteenth day after reaching base camp Artur and I were on the summit.

It had turned out to be a very atypical expedition in several senses. Everything had been done back to front, nevertheless everything had taken place very efficiently. On the walk-out there was an atmosphere among us of a job well done. A lot of credit must go to Krzysiek, who sacrificed his own ambitions. Walking down bent double under a heavy sack, I turned round and looked him straight in the eye where I saw no regret or grudge that I had gone to the top with Artur not him.

I thought also of Jacek Pałkiewicz, who had had his very first experience of these great mountains and their dangerous reality. I don't think he had considered his retreat as a personal defeat.

We left behind us Annapurna which had succumbed to its first winter ascent. True, by only two climbers. But we had not added any names either to the long toll of those who have contributed to the tragic reputation of the mountain.

15

Fourteen Times Eight

W e reached the hotel in Nialam late at night. We were booked in and they were expecting us. After a full day of travel we were very hungry.

'Is there a restaurant here?'

'Of course . . .'

'Wonderful, we would like to eat something.'

'No. It is not possible. It is closed now.'

'Maybe something could be made? Anything? You knew we would be coming after a long journey.'

'We understand. We will try to find the cook.'

After a moment they returned.

'Unfortunately, the cook has gone to the cinema. You will have to forget dinner.'

It felt a bit like being back in Poland. But what made things worse here was our inability to communicate with anybody. We were hungry, angry, and our luggage had been carefully packed away into the truck, so it was not really possible to unpack it all just to arrange a bivvy in a hotel bedroom. In desperation we went on the town where, at one in the morning, in a hut serving as a restaurant we woke the manager, who got up to cook us some rice with vegetables.

At last we could think about sleeping. As we were going off to our rooms we were asked when we wanted to get up. We replied we would appreciate a lie-in and would get up at eight in order to leave at nine.

'At eight?' Our questioner grimaced. He was clearly surprised and even rather annoyed. Maybe it was too late for him? The devil only knew. We were so tired, we were not interested in thinking about anything any more. We went to sleep. And that was how our first day in China came to an end.

How did we get ourselves here? We left for Shisha Pangma at the end of July, 1987. My Katowice club was organising the trip. There were few participants and they knew each other well: Janusz Majer, Artur Hajzer, Rysiek Warecki who was filming, Wanda Rutkiewicz and the doctor, Lech Korniszewski. Then there were the Mexicans, Elsa Avila and Carlos Carsolio, Ramiro Navarrete from Ecuador, the Englishman, Alan Hinkes, the American, Steve Untch, and two French women climbers, Christine de Colombel, who had been on K2 with Wanda, and Malgosia Fromenty-Bilczewska.

In Tibet we discovered that the road from Kathmandu to Kodari had been destroyed by flooding. Normally it takes six to eight hours by bus, but as the road was cut in about eight places, we had to start carrying the loads in normal expedition style. So at the very start we had extra associated costs and delays. But we managed to get to the border and crossed the beautiful bridge of Sino-Nepalese friendship. Now we had to part with our Nepalese porters, our Chinese liaison officer was waiting for us, and from now on he would take full responsibility for organising our travel and our stay in China. We were entering another world, not in a geographical sense, but as regards attitudes and customs.

Our first encounter I have already told you about. The following morning I woke up, looked at my watch, it was eight. Everywhere silence reigned. Not even a lame dog to be seen. It appears that in China, Peking time is used – five and a half hours' difference. That means that when people get up as dictated by the rising sun the clock already shows midday. Whenever times were mentioned we had to define if we meant Peking, Nepalese or European time. We still ended up making mistakes.

Shisha Pangma has one of the few base camps that can be reached direct by jeep. The Tibetan plateau is a flat steppe, with occasional clumps of grass. Vehicles can drive around on this as if on a table top and climb from 2400 to 5000 metres. Compared to other expedition walk-ins this was total comfort. Then at the most unlikely place the liaison officer said firmly, 'Stop! This is it. This is base camp.'

We stumbled out of the vehicles rather disoriented, but it did not take us too long as we looked around to realise that we were still a very long way from the mountains which were barely shimmering above the horizon.

'To the best of my knowledge a base camp is at the base of a mountain.' I tried to influence this rather surprising decision.

'No. We will not drive any further. It gets too high there, hard and difficult. We have to think about our health as well.' The liaison officer was not to be moved. 'This is where we set up the base camp and that is it.'

And so we arrived at our first clash, in which we made it clear to him that we had not come here for a walk on the steppes, but for mountain climbing. The mountains were still about two and a half days' journey away and it was perfectly obvious that the vehicles could still go a long way further. But our arguments had no effect.

We had no choice but to leave our liaison officer and translator there, also the cook for whom we had paid a lot of money in order to be relieved of the task of cooking. The liaison officer was quick to step in over him anyway, informing us the cook was at his disposal.

And so we the advance party set off, but this was by no means the end of our problems. First, we had more loads than could be taken by the yaks that had been ordered. The next thing was the paraffin. In order to simplify our progress and not carry it with us from Nepal we had ordered a hundred litres to be delivered here. The trucks were meant to have brought it for us. They did bring it, but it turned out that the Nepalese stoves were not going to work using Chinese fuel at any price. We tried once, then again, they hissed, belched smoke, but would not burn.

The situation was serious. Dark thoughts haunted me. Without fuel we could not cook, without that the expedition would fall apart.

Should we send off a jeep in search of new stoves? It was 500 kilometres to the nearest town, but I could see no alternative.

'It's no good, you have to send a jeep for some stoves,' I told the liaison officer.

'No, it is not included in the expedition pricing.'

'We will pay what is required, of course. It is simply a necessity.'

'No. I can only do what I have been told to.' The liaison officer was clearly indignant. The situation appeared hopeless.

In the morning the situation was further complicated. I should have known better. Coming up so fast by vehicle across the steppes we had gained 2000 metres in one day and now everybody was hit, some more than others. Some had turned a pale blue and were vomiting non-stop. And all the time everyone was engaged in the repair of those stoves. Climbers, the cook, the drivers, we all had our own theory. Some said there was too much air reaching them, others said not enough; some that the pressure build-up was too low; others had started adding petrol to the paraffin. The results of these experiments were varied. At last one of the drivers found the best solution to this unhappy marriage between Nepalese stoves and Chinese fuel. He reached the conclusion that petrol and paraffin were of too high a calorific value and that it was necessary to control the air intake. So we started building thin metal-foil shields. Now things began to work at last and we could cook ourselves a hot meal. Our mood improved. The yaks arrived, together with their so-called yak-drivers. Each of them must be fully equipped from the boots up, or one could pay the equivalent amount to their association, only a fraction of which, we were sure, would actually reach the yak-drivers. We had to play our cards carefully, because we needed to request more yaks.

The local Tibetans live in conditions which probably have not changed much for the last thousand years. They are people who do not like to wash. Under a thick layer of dirt, they go around dressed in rags, which gives an impression of great poverty until you see them take from under those same rags a huge wad of money. They live almost entirely from their yaks, plus some sheep and goats, and no doubt smuggling is involved in there somewhere. Already by the second day we had lost two loads, including poor Carlos's boots. From that moment we started watching our equipment very closely.

We finally managed to come to an agreement over more yaks and were able to set off from the godforsaken place we called the Chinese base camp.

The walk-in took three days, and the going was difficult. It started to rain, then snow. The route followed slopes which kept subsiding, and the local yaks turned out to be quite wild, constantly dislodging their loads. At 5600 metres, just before base camp, the snow was so deep that it covered the scree slopes. The yaks were not used to walking along untrodden paths. They simply scampered off, not knowing in which direction they were meant to go. So we had to go first to make a good trail, then they would follow along happily. But when one gashed its leg on a boulder the yak-men called a halt and would go no further.

And so, some two hours short of our proposed base camp we had to bribe the yak-drivers themselves to help us carry all our loads on their backs. To set an example we started carrying some ourselves. They agreed, though it did cost us a lot.

We could now set up a proper base camp, and everything was going according to plan, except for the fact that Janusz Majer was beginning to feel increasingly unwell. On reaching base camp he laid down flat and was unable to get up again. The next morning he was beginning to hallucinate. We unpacked the loads, took out the oxygen cylinder, made a stretcher and started carrying him down to meet the doctor halfway. He diagnosed a serious circulatory deficiency, coupled with an inflammation of the veins, but managed to get Janusz back on his feet again after a week, though he would be unable to take part in the climbing.

Shisha Pangma, a new route by the West Ridge, 18th September, 1987

However, we were just happy that he was back sitting with us at base.

We were not alone there. An Italian expedition was coming to its end without achieving very much. They complained about the snow. It had been snowing non-stop from the day that we arrived, with all the characteristics of monsoon weather, mist and poor visibility preventing us seeing the mountain we wanted to climb.

The base camp was located at 5600 metres, in other words it was very high. From here the mountain at 8013 metres did not appear to be much higher. It is hardly an awe-inspiring mountain in comparison to the other eight-thousanders, especially since climbing only really starts at 7000 metres. Below that there is a plateau called the corridor, as smooth as a table, which has to be followed for twelve kilometres. The climbing starts at its end. Because Shisha Pangma belongs to the easier eight-thousanders I had decided to take my skis to the Himalaya for the first time. I wanted to try to ski down this rather more easy angled mountain. I hoped to do two new routes on Shisha Pangma. Wanda hoped to achieve the first woman's ascent. I also wanted to climb two virgin tops in the area.

On 28th August we attempted an acclimatisational ascent, bivouacking at a point where we hoped later to set up Camp 1. Here we experienced something which served as a warning that there are no such things as easy mountains. I was sharing a tent with Artur. As we started to get ourselves ready next morning a dreadfully familiar loud crack reached our ears. We froze. When the mounting roar came, Artur was the first to stick his head out of the tent. He could see there was no mistake.

'Avalanche!' he bellowed.

We both threw ourselves at the small exit and somehow fought our way out of the entrapping material wearing only our socks, and tried to put as much distance as possible between ourselves and the great cloud that finally came to a halt some fifty metres short of our tent.

Alan and Steve had not realised anything serious was happening. On hearing the shout 'Avalanche', they did not even have time to get out of their tent. Now they stuck their heads out and surveyed this snowy battlefield, shaking their heads at what could have happened. We needed to recover after that and it was only on the next day that we set off for the mountain.

The plateau was not only long but it was also about a kilometre wide. Bounded on one side by Shisha Pangma and on the other by a virgin summit, it really did resemble a corridor. We skied to its end on our special lightweight skis equipped with skins and modern dual-purpose safety bindings.

At the end of the corridor we set up camp and next day set off to climb that virgin summit of Yebo Kangari, which is a sort of partner to Shisha Pangma.

On its 7200-metre summit the weather was beautiful, Tibet stretched out before us as if on the palms of our hands. It was one of those wonderful moments, unmarred by exhaustion, or icy wind, or choking snow storm.

Now came our skiing experiment. I had to admit as I locked those fancy bindings, I hardly felt confident. To save weight we had chosen very short, 160-centimetre skis. But we managed to get down. Now for Shisha Pangma.

Artur and I had set ourselves the aim of climbing Shisha Pangma by the virgin West Ridge, and the hitherto unclimbed West Summit. This is the most eye-catching and hardest ridge on the mountain. We also had another target, the couloir in the centre of the North Face, but Steve and Alan had got their eye on this as well. There were twelve of us preparing to climb the mountain and I explained that I did not want people to consider this to be an expedition in the traditional sense, with a leader directing operations to one end. We should all do what took our fancy. If some of them wanted to do the normal route, that was fine. If others wanted to establish an extra camp somewhere, they should feel free. If someone wanted to climb the couloir in the face, like Steve and

Alan, then please go ahead, there was nothing to stop them. The only thing I asked was that everybody declare where and with whom they were going, simply so that we did not get in each other's way.

'We are here on holiday,' I said. 'Let us treat this like a climbing camp in the Alps, where everybody chooses exactly what he wants to do.'

And that is what happened. We all had the same Camp 1, through which all of our routes would pass, so it was important to coordinate our movements quite carefully to avoid all getting there at the same time for a bivouac. But that was the only factor which people had to take into consideration when making their plans.

Artur and I prepared ourselves for our alpine-style ascent of the West Ridge, and worked out a deal with Rysiek Warecki who wanted to do the normal route: we would take the skis across the corridor and there we would leave them for Rysiek who would be able to use them to help him up the lower sections of the normal route where the snow is very deep. Then he would leave them for us to pick up on our descent.

All we now needed was for the snow to stop, but ten days passed and the weather was still completely paralysing everything. The Italians had left at the beginning of September, having achieved nothing. They had got as far as the corridor and had then retreated. Carlos benefited from this as he was able to buy some articles that had been stolen from him at the beginning of the trip. Luckily a pair of spare boots which we had taken with us fitted him, so now he was ready to join in the fray. But when the twelfth day of waiting passed, it seemed as if Carlos would at best get back to Mexico in his luckily acquired new outfit. The only change in the daily routine was the kitchen duty, since our official cook was of course down at the Chinese base camp waiting on our liaison officer. So every day the food was different: French, English, Mexican, American and Polish, and we came to the conclusion that the worst cuisine was French. For neither of our French ladies seemed able to live up to the national traditions embodied in the works of Brillat-Savarin under the title of *The Physiology of Taste*. They were quite simply not good at cooking.

After twelve days of inactivity, I sat down to write a letter requesting that the expedition be extended. It was directed to our liaison officer who was lying, belly up, somewhere far below. I established a new date on which the jeeps should come up, sealed it carefully and handed it to the mail runner, and from that day on the weather began to smile at us.

We climbed the West Ridge almost exactly according to plan. There were some difficult sections, others were easy, all in all it did not present us with any major problem. It was a bit like our own Eagle's Ridge overlooking Zakopane, but set at 7000–8000 metres. At the same time another group was approaching the summit by the normal route. This included Wanda, Elsa, Carlos, Ramiro and Rysiek Warecki. Also in the area were four members of an international commercial party of Swiss, Germans and Austrians, organised by Stefan Werner.

Although we were setting off at different times, we all ended up in the area of the subsidiary summit at the same time. Shisha Pangma has two summits. Arguments as to which is higher go on to this day, though topographers have established that the second summit is a couple of metres higher. But there are still those who claim that the first summit is of greater importance.

Once I saw the situation for myself I could understand why. It simply saves a three-hour march over a rather varied ridge. The Austrians reached the first summit, stood on top of it, and snapped away with their cameras, stating that was the highest summit as far as they were concerned.

We decided we would carry on to the real summit, knowing that three hours of any sort of walk above 8000 metres would not be easy.

It was however four in the afternoon. Artur and I had full bivouac equipment with us, as we had been climbing the mountain alpine-style. So we did not have to worry too much about where we would sleep. But Rysiek, Carlos, Elsa, Ramiro and Wanda were travelling light, their camp was some 700 metres lower down. Although we had established that everybody would do their own thing on this mountain, I felt I needed to remind them they might get benighted, but they had torches and were confident they'd manage. It was hard to press the issue because Rysiek and Carlos had each carried one ski for me right up to this point. The last section had been too steep for the skis to be of any use to them. It was an act of pure friendship. But now there was no holding them. First Carlos set off, then Rysiek and Ramiro, Elsa and Wanda. Artur and I let them go ahead. We had no inclination to have a race, for we not only had heavy sacks on our backs but also plenty of time.

When we reached the col between the two peaks, just before the main summit itself, we dumped our loads and debated whether to bivouac where we were and go on to the summit in good light for photography in the morning. But the summit was so close, it seemed ridiculous to be planning to set up camp.

'Let's go for it!' I said.

And that is what we did. I decided to go up this last section on skis. Before I managed to get them on Artur had set off with his camera and was now ahead of me. By the time I caught him up he was already on the summit which is how there is a first-rate film of me on the summit.

On our return the verdict was unanimous: 'You made a good job of that "summit film". It looks just as if you were really up there!' The film was taken on an ancient French Bolie camera, very simple, with a handle, and still the most reliable in the really high mountains. The best ones are those that were being used during the second world war.

By the time we were winding the film, the summit had become deserted, the gang had been and gone, and as the sun sank down to the horizon, in its last rays the exceptionally wide views took on the most breathtaking colours. Never in my most daring dreams did I imagine that this is what it would be like. I was standing on the summit of my last eight-thousander, the last bead of my Himalayan rosary. It had happened.

It all dawned on me slowly. As usual at this altitude, thoughts had to fight their way through exhaustion, the thumping heart, the gasping fight for air. I just could not fully express my joy at this significant moment. I was simply overcome by it all. A person is not designed to be able to express his joy in every imaginable circumstance. Only once, on Nanga Parbat, had I had the urge to express my feelings by jumping up and throwing my arms in the air, and a miserable jump it had been. Never again.

But why was I unable to be spontaneously, simply and genuinely happy at this moment? That this was my fourteenth summit no longer seemed important. It could quite well have been the third or the seventh.

We walked back along the ridge to set up our dome tent in the dark. Things did not go well by feel and we lost one of the tent poles, so suffered such an uncomfortable makeshift night that when I got up in the morning the first thought that crossed my mind was, Christ! If we had to go to the summit now, I doubt I would be able to take a single step. Slowly we packed our things. One more adventure awaited me – the skis.

I could say that I am a reasonable skier. But I had made most of my descents on well beaten routes. My experience of alpine skiing was extremely small. Skiing in virgin, mainly very soft snow, is another art. Added to that there was the twenty-three-kilo rucksack and the 8000 metres. I started making a very long traverse skirting round the first summit. The snow was deep and soft. I could not see my ski tips, at times I moved so slowly that I hardly felt I was moving at all. Artur was walking down behind me, and the distance between us was not increasing. I was unable to ski more than ten metres at a time. After that I was so puffed that I had to sit down in the snow to regain my breath and rest.

For the first time it dawned on me that skiing can involve a tremendous effort. In a twinkling, all my visions of an effortless, elegant and quick escape from this mountain evaporated. They had been dreams born from fragments of film of top skiers flying across virgin slopes. I was not about to fly like a bird. It all became desperately hard work. By the time I reached the edge of the plateau, the total saving I had derived from this white madness was that of being one hour ahead of Artur who was trudging on down, meekly, on his two legs, as God had destined him to.

At base we loaded up all the equipment into rucksacks and set off down. There was no time to reminisce about that great mountain, although we had plenty to reminisce about. Wanda had now climbed four eight-thousanders and she is the only woman to have achieved such an impressive record. Elsa was the first woman from a Latin-American country to have set foot on a high mountain, and at twenty-three the youngest woman to have reached the top of an eight-thousander. Carlos now had two eight-thousanders behind him. This meant a lot to him. Alan and Steve had climbed a very elegant new route up the centre of the North Face. Rysiek Warecki reached the summit, and pointed out at every opportunity that he was the first Pole to reach the summit of Shisha Pangma, because in the last few metres of the ascent he had pushed ahead in front of the others.

Artur and I had our new route on the West Ridge and two very high virgin tops to our credit.

I walked down, other people's and my own reasons for joy thumping around in my head, like a badly packed rucksack. Then this changed to a litany of names, of the fourteen highest summits in the Himalaya, they helped me walk down, they gave me rhythm, in the same way as when one is going up and one has to count.

Fourteen . . .

Fourteen times eight . . .

Has something really come to an end? No, the vertical world never comes to an end. It is there. Waiting. I'll come back.

But wait, I have thought like this once before. When? Of course! That first time, when I had been defeated by Nanga! That was a long time ago, a whole fourteen highest mountains ago. What else did I think of after that first encounter? Oh yes, that the Himalaya are for people after all.

I was right.

Postscript by Krzysztof Wielicki

(translated by Ingeborga Doubrawa-Cochlin)

I t is 12th January 1986, a frosty, windy but pleasant day at an altitude
of 7400 metres. We are on the plateau under the south bastion of
the Kangchenjunga massif. Yesterday Jerzy and I conquered the
summit for the first time in winter, but today . . . we are saying farewell
to Andrzej Czok who had been Jerzy's climbing partner of long-standing
and a brilliant Polish mountaineer who died yesterday in Camp 3. We
kneel down by the crevasse, Andrzej's last resting-place, place a cross
of sticks and say a prayer. Jerzy stands by the grave for a long time
saying his own personal farewell and asking aloud, 'Why, why has God
taken away such a good person?' For the first time I see tears in his
eyes, then anger and frustration that he had been unable to help Andrzej.
'Perhaps we had a chance to help? Perhaps we made a mistake?'

It is now February 1987 but not such a pleasant day, although it is
warm and we are lower down. It is base camp under the North Face of
Annapurna I. We can see Jerzy and Artur on the moraine, fortunately
coming back from the summit safely. We go out to meet them. Jerzy is
waving his hands high in the air, and singing at the top of his voice a
song that was popular in Poland at that time, 'I love you life'.

Sorrow and happiness, tragedy and victory were very much a part of
his life. This was the sort of world he inhabited and he loved it and
enriched it with his experiences, often taken to the extreme and full of
emotion. The reader will have learnt from this book that Jerzy Kukuczka
was one of the leading Himalayan climbers of our time. He accom-
plished several outstanding climbs in the modern style. In my country
he became a symbol of bravery and courage and a model for the younger
generation of climbers looking for adventure in the mountains. During

the 'eighties, the golden years for Polish Himalayan climbing, Jerzy Kukuczka was simply the best.

But who was Jerzy Kukuczka or 'Jurek', or 'Kukus', as he was known affectionately by our group? At first meeting, there was nothing special to distinguish him from the other climbers in his circle. He was quiet, a man of few words, a private sort of person. He would only become really animated when the conversation turned to mountain climbing. Otherwise he would rarely open up and, even when he did, it was never completely, even to those who were closest to him in good or bad times. He had an air of mystery about him which gave him a certain psychological superiority over both his partners and his rivals. He would always have something in reserve, whether it was an unexpected decision or simply a piece of bacon or a clove of garlic kept for the right moment.

He was not a man of conflict. By that I mean he would never start or get involved in any argument. Once he had made up his mind on his course of action, he would be inflexible and would never give way. From that moment on everything would be subordinated to the achievement of his goal, although never at the cost of other climbers. He owed most of his outstanding success only to himself and in this he was greatly helped by his decisiveness and, in the positive sense of the word, his obstinacy.

He was very popular with other climbers, not only for his modesty but also for the great respect he showed for the mountains and the achievements of his fellow climbers. He was not in the least interested in creating an image in the media, in fact he did not really care about it. His whole life was directed towards the realisation of his climbing dreams and ambitions, not towards becoming a media personality or hero. Having been blessed by nature with very good health, a remarkable talent and robust psychological stamina, he obtained from the mountains all he wanted. He was certainly a very successful climber, in fact he got us so accustomed to seeing him returning from the mountains with another triumph that we took his success for granted; and being part of one of his expeditions gave us an astonishing sense of security.

It is now 1981 and we are in the New Zealand Alps. Here, for the first time, I am roped together with Jurek. Before this, our paths had crossed, from time to time, and we both had Everest behind us. But now, after reaching the difficult summit of Mount Hicks and doing a long traverse, we begin to abseil the 600-metre wall. Jurek establishes the second abseil on a large outcrop of rock. I go down first, followed by Rysiek and we both wait for Jurek. Suddenly there is a loud cracking noise! We both stop breathing as we see Jurek fall with the rock following! We think this is the end . . . By some miracle or other Jurek's fall is halted on a ledge about six metres above us. His rucksack, packed with all the sleeping-bags, cushions his landing. Below us there is a sheer drop of about 500 metres! Certainly on that occasion he was very lucky (and so were we). But I think he was born with extraordinary luck and it followed him wherever he went, although I also feel he had to work very hard to achieve that luck.

In the everyday routine of life, Jurek had different habits which were well known by his climbing partners and which he never tried to hide. When not actually climbing, he would sleep in his tent for hours and hours and so he often had to prepare his own meals which were always better than ours. If you asked him if he wanted something sweet he would reply, 'Yes please, a herring!' His favourite 'vegetable' was *golonka* – a special Polish ham. He loved to eat and drink well and would never refuse a glass of vodka or 'fortified tea' as Polish climbers call it; and you could always find a spare bottle amongst his belongings! He had no special diet but generally ate what he liked and he would run a mile at even the slightest hint of the latest food fad or fashion or any suggestion of a special diet.

It is July 1984, at base camp on the glacier at Broad Peak. It is raining very heavily and we are waiting rather nervously for the return of Jurek and Wojtek Kurtyka who went to climb the traverse of Broad Peak. Finally they arrive back after being away for eight days and, we presume, totally exhausted. But no, Jurek, who is very hungry, goes straight to the kitchen and prepares a large meal of spaghetti for us all. Then in the evening he joins us for a game of cards which finishes in the early hours of the morning. Physically he was unbreakable. He would recover his strength in a very short time and, apart from aspirin, he never took any medicine. Against frostbite he had the practice of using very loose boots, one size larger. I tried this idea myself and it certainly worked, although it took some time getting used to wearing them with crampons.

I do not know if he was superstitious or not. He always left a little toy or a mascot on the summit and all his personal equipment was marked with the number nine. And why? Because on his first expedition in Alaska, he was placed at number nine in the hierarchy of importance; quite low down the list! Of course, he quickly became a leading climber in our mountaineering world, but he always stuck faithfully to his number nine. Symbols were important to Jurek, even his car had the number-plates '8000'!

Although he always set himself the highest targets, he would never reveal his plans before leaving on an expedition. He had no formulised philosophy or theories about what he was doing or how it should be done. He accepted all styles and methods for reaching the summit which was the most important element in his climbing. When using the classic style, he would attack the mountain with a large team and when using alpine-style, he would sometimes use a small team or go totally alone in summer and winter, by day and by night.

When in 1987, one year after Messner, Jurek completed all fourteen 8000-metre summits, the so-called 'crown of the Himalayas', many people were convinced that he would be satisfied with his achievements and set his sights lower. But he remained faithful to his ambitions and did not change his goals or aim lower. On the contrary, he dreamt now about the traverse of Kangchenjunga and, once again, the South Face of Lhotse.

In June 1989, Jurek announced at the Katowice Club that he was going to the South Face of Lhotse in the autumn. Unfortunately, Artur Hajzer and I were unable to go with him since we had only just got back from our third attempt on the South Face of Lhotse ourselves; 1985, 1987, and then 1989. Before leaving base camp, we decided that we would not return there for at least two years and we would leave the Wall to others, although we felt we had a moral right to it ourselves.

Perhaps Jurek should postpone his departure and wait a little longer? Perhaps it was a mistake to go so soon? But Jurek would not budge from his decision. Besides he felt he had a score to settle with the Lhotse Face, particularly after 1985. Furthermore, an international expedition led by Messner had come back in the spring after an unsuccessful attempt on the South Face of Lhotse. So Jurek felt an additional challenge to undertake his expedition as quickly as possible. It was the fourth Polish expedition to Lhotse to end in tragedy. Three times we had been close to the summit, once, in fact, only about 200 metres away. But it was for others to achieve success not for us. That is life! Jurek was about five metres from the small col where Artur Hajzer and I had spent one night in a snow hole in 1987. It is still a hard climb from there to the summit but it is very near.

The thread of his life was brutally cut short on 24th October 1989. He died a mountaineer's death in classic circumstances: a very steep wall, a fall, a severed rope and the final drop down the precipice.

On All Souls' Day in the Cathedral at Katowice, there was a Mass with several hundred mourners from close family to complete strangers; people who had admired his life, his talent and his achievements. The Requiem Mass was a deeply moving experience and the trumpeters from Jurek's mountain village of Istebna sounded a last farewell. We all filed out of the church very quietly and very humbly.

Krzysztof Wielicki, Tychy, 20.3.92.

INDEX